FOREWORD BY **PAUL DUNN**

THE ACCOUNTING PROFIT BLUEPRINT 2026

Double your accounting practice profits within 12 months

ISBN: 978-1-923601-38-3

Published by Vivid Publishing
A division of Fontaine Publishing Group
P.O. Box 948, Fremantle
Western Australia 6959
www.vividpublishing.com.au

NATIONAL LIBRARY OF AUSTRALIA

A catalogue record for this book is available from the National Library of Australia

Acknowledgements

This book was not written in isolation.

First and foremost, my thanks go to the contributors who agreed to be part of *The Accounting Profit Blueprint 2026*. Each chapter reflects real-world experience, hard-earned insight, and a genuine commitment to improving the profitability and sustainability of accounting practices. You gave your time, thinking, and your intellectual capital, and the book is stronger because of it.

A special thank you to Tracy James for managing the compilation of the writers' contributions.

Thank you to the many accountants, practice owners, and advisers who have influenced this work over the years — through questions, challenges, case studies, and real conversations. This book is ultimately for you. If it helps even a small number of practices build stronger profits, better systems, and more sustainable careers, it will have done its job.

— Darren Gleeson

Table of Contents

SECTION 3
TURN ADVISORY INTO YOUR PROFIT ENGINE

SECTION 4
BUILD A FIRM THAT SCALES

SECTION 5
PREPARE YOUR FIRM FOR THE FUTURE

Foreword

By Paul Dunn

Over the past several decades, I've had the privilege of working closely with accounting professionals all around the world.

That's taken place through conferences, on-going advisory work, the Accountants' Boot Camp programs, and through collaborations with my great friend Ron Baker, including books such as *Firm of the Future* and *Time's Up!*.

During that time, I've seen extraordinary technical progress in the profession. But I've also seen something else. Something even more significant.

The firms that really thrive and create great value for everyone involved are rarely the busiest firms. They are the most intentional.

They're intentional about the clients they serve. Intentional about the services they deliver. Intentional about the systems they build.

And they're intentional about the kind of firm they're creating.

Many (perhaps it's more accurate to say 'most') accounting firms grow in ways that feel almost accidental. New clients arrive. Team members (please don't ever refer to them as 'staff') are added.

Work expands. Revenue increases. Yet despite that growth, the owners often find themselves with less freedom, more pressure, and a business that seems to demand constant attention.

It's what I sometimes describe as the 'growth paradox.' Success becomes heavier.

The reason is rarely a lack of technical expertise. Accountants are among the most highly trained professionals in business. And they now have the most stunning tools we could ever imagine to do extraordinary things exponentially faster.

The real constraint is usually something far simpler and far more powerful.

It is design.

I'm very clear on it. Design determines whether growth creates opportunity or stress.

Design determines whether technology produces leverage or simply complexity.

Design determines whether Advisory Services become a meaningful part of the firm's future or remain an aspiration discussed at Conferences.

Here's the critical point: design determines whether the firm becomes a valuable business or simply a demanding job.

For many years, accountants were primarily producers of work. The profession revolved around compliance tasks, deadlines and reporting requirements. Hours were measured, utilisation was monitored, and the economics of firms were largely driven by the mechanics of production.

Today, the most successful practitioners are evolving into something far more powerful. They are becoming what I call 'architects of their practices'.

They are stepping back from the daily mechanics of work and asking deeper questions about structure, systems and strategy. They think differently about the clients they serve, the services they provide, the experience they create, and the economic model that supports the firm.

Instead of asking, "How do we get the work done?" they begin asking a far more powerful question:

"How should the firm be designed so that the right work gets done in the right way?"

That shift from production to architecture is one of the most important transitions taking place within the accounting profession today.

Now at first glance, the title of this superb book '*The Accounting Profit Blueprint*' might suggest a focus purely on financial performance.

But profitability in professional firms is rarely about margins alone.

Profitability is the outcome of alignment. Alignment between the value delivered to clients, the services offered, the capabilities of the team, the systems supporting the work, and (very significantly too) the pricing models used to capture that value.

When those elements are aligned, profit tends to follow naturally. When they are not, firms struggle. And that struggle will continue unless and until the design and alignment are in sync.

One of the strengths of this book is that it approaches these questions from a practical perspective.

The contributors represent people who have worked directly with firms, who understand the operational realities of modern accounting practices, and who have spent years helping practitioners think more deliberately about how their firms function.

Too often, conversations about the future of the profession remain theoretical. What you will find here instead are frameworks, ideas and experiences grounded in real practice.

That matters, because the economics of accounting firms are evolving. And evolving fast.

Historically, profit in professional firms was driven by three familiar concepts: utilisation, realisation and leverage. For decades these ideas shaped the management of accounting firms around the world.

Today, new drivers are taking their place.

Automation and digital systems are expanding capacity. Advisory relationships are increasing the value accountants create for clients. Pricing models are (thank Goodness) rapidly shifting away from time toward outcomes. And technology is transforming efficiency into strategic leverage.

All of this means the traditional structure of firms is being challenged.

Technology, of course, plays a powerful role in this transformation. Artificial intelligence and automation are dramatically increasing the speed at which accounting work can be completed.

Processes that once required significant manual effort can now be handled at what seems like breakneck speed through AI-based systems. And by the way, that shift will never be slower than it is today. Think about that.

For example, just today sitting here this weekend on a break in Tokyo (what a good time and place to write a foreword) a new AI App was announced that claims to do all of the work autonomously (yes, the reasoning as well) to produce a full-blown Partnership return.

AI systems are getting better at structured reasoning all the time. Clients expect faster turnaround and clearer value. And finding humans to do this work isn't easy. When those forces converge, business models change.

And consider this: when (not 'if') partnership returns become largely automated, what will your firm be known for? What will your firm be designed for becomes the crucial question?

Let's be clear though: technology alone does not create great firms.

Technology amplifies design. Good design becomes extraordinary. And poor design becomes painfully visible.

Here's the sad truth: poorly designed firms simply become faster versions of the same old problems.

The practices that are set to thrive in the coming decade will not simply be the ones that adopt the latest tools. They will be the ones that combine those tools with clear thinking about how firms should operate.

And that brings us to the purpose of this book.

A 'blueprint' does not prescribe a single outcome. Instead, it provides structure, perspective and guidance. It offers principles that allow something strong and enduring to be built.

Every accounting firm is different. Different clients, markets, ambitions and cultures will always shape the final design. But the firms that flourish share one common trait: they are built deliberately rather than accidentally.

They are designed. And this book is a fantastic 'how-to' for you.

Let me add two more critical things for you before you get into the magic of this book.

At the start of this Foreword, I mentioned my work with the Accountants' Boot Camp. 17,700 accountants came through that program. And I started every one of those events with this simple and hopefully profoundly important observation:

"Your job is not to report on history.

It is to help your *selected* clients create it."

And the italics in that last sentence are crucial to design.

You're not designing for everyone. You're designing for the clients you're privileged to serve.

This book is perfectly designed to help you do exactly that.

Enjoy.

And take action on it too, remembering this truth as you do: "the power of any idea is only ever in its implementation."

Go for it.

You, your family, your team AND your clients will all be very glad you did.

Paul Dunn is a four-time TEDx speaker, entrepreneur, and one of the most influential thinkers on purpose-driven business. He is the co-founder of B1G1, a global movement that enables businesses to embed giving directly into everyday commercial activity. Through B1G1, companies connect ordinary transactions to real-world impact, and by 2026 the B1G1 community had created more than **392 million giving impacts** across projects worldwide.

Earlier in his career, Paul founded Results Corporation and Results Accountants' Systems, where he created the widely respected **Accountants' Boot Camp** and built a global network supporting thousands of accounting firms to improve their marketing, client relationships, and business performance.

An international keynote speaker and bestselling author, Paul has spent decades helping entrepreneurs and professional firms rethink the role of business in society. His work focuses on aligning growth with meaning—showing how commercial success and measurable impact can be structurally built into the design of modern businesses.

Introduction

By Darren Gleeson

Most accounting firms don't have a revenue problem. They have a business design problem.

Across Australia, thousands of accounting practices are busy, growing and technically competent. The partners work hard, the staff work hard, and the phones ring. From the outside, many of these firms appear successful. Yet inside the firm, the story is often very different. Partners are working 50 or 60 hours a week; tax season feels like a war every year, and staff constantly escalate decisions because authority and systems are unclear. Revenue slowly increases, but profit rarely improves in the same way.

In other words, the firm grows, but life does not get easier.

The uncomfortable truth is that many accounting firms are not struggling because of competition or the economy. They are struggling because the business itself was never deliberately designed.

The objective of this book is simple: to help accounting practices double their profits within twelve months by redesigning how the firm operates.

The $1 Million Firm

Let me describe a firm I see all the time. It is a suburban accounting practice generating about $1 million in annual fees. The client base is loyal, the phone rings regularly with new enquiries, and the team consists of six or seven staff supporting one or two partners. On paper, it looks like a successful firm.

Inside the practice, the partners are exhausted. They work 55 to 60 hours a week, and staff constantly ask questions because the authority to make decisions is unclear. Jobs pile up around deadlines, and clients expect immediate responses because the partners have trained them to expect that level of access. Revenue creeps upward each year, but profit rarely follows.

One partner once said to me, "Darren, the business is bigger than it used to be, but it feels heavier every year."

That sentence perfectly describes thousands of accounting firms. The firm has grown, but it has never actually been designed.

The Pressures Facing the Profession

Accounting firms today face genuine pressure. Economic uncertainty affects clients; inflation has pushed up wages and overheads, and recruiting experienced accountants has become extremely difficult. Work-from-home expectations have also changed how firms operate. At the same time, regulatory oversight continues to increase, with the Tax Practitioners Board expanding compliance requirements and the ATO continuing to grow its audit and enforcement workforce.

All of this adds pressure to accounting practices. However, these forces are not the root problem. They expose a deeper issue.

Most accounting firms were never deliberately designed to operate in today's environment. They evolved organically, client by client and year by year. When external pressure increases, those structural weaknesses become visible. The typical response is to work harder. Partners extend their hours, take on more operational responsibility and personally solve more problems. Unfortunately, effort does not solve structural problems. It only delays confronting them.

The Compliance Trap

For decades, the accounting profession has been built around compliance production: more tax returns, more financial statements and more BAS lodgements. The traditional model says that if you want to grow the firm, you add more clients, hire more staff and keep the work moving.

Over time, that model has quietly created a trap.

Compliance work expands endlessly, deadlines multiply, and regulations become more complex each year. Clients expect faster responses while resisting higher fees. As a result, accountants become extremely busy, but that does not necessarily mean they are profitable.

Michael Gerber described this problem decades ago in *The E-Myth*. Many business owners start as technicians and become trapped in the business rather than working on it. Accounting firms are one of the clearest examples of this principle.

Partners spend most of their time preparing, reviewing, and answering questions about work. Very little time is spent stepping back and designing how the business itself should operate.

The data confirms this pattern. Through TaxFitness, we surveyed accounting practices across Australia and asked a simple question: Do you benchmark your firm's performance each year?

About ninety per cent said no.

In other words, nine out of ten accounting firms are running their businesses without systematically measuring or benchmarking their performance. No accountant would ever advise a client to run their business without analysing margins, comparing results or measuring operational efficiency. Yet that is exactly how most accounting firms operate.

The Profession's Strategic Blind Spot

Accountants are experts at helping other businesses improve performance. They analyse profitability, recommend systems and advise clients on strategy. However, those same disciplines are rarely applied inside accounting firms themselves.

Very few practices operate with structured strategic planning. In fact, fewer than five per cent of accounting firms maintain documented plans covering the next twelve months, a five-year direction and a longer-term vision for the firm. Instead, most firms operate reactively. Work arrives, problems appear, and partners respond.

Over time, the partner becomes the system. Clients call the partner, staff escalate decisions to the partner, and pricing or scope issues are handled by the partner. Eventually, almost everything flows through the partner. At that point, the firm is not scalable; it is fragile.

Growth Does Not Solve the Problem

When firms feel pressure, the instinctive response is growth. The thinking is simple: add more clients, hire more staff and increase revenue.

However, growth does not fix structural problems; it magnifies them.

If a firm has weak systems, growth creates chaos. If pricing discipline is poor, growth multiplies underpriced work. If the firm depends heavily on partner involvement, growth increases the number of issues requiring partner attention.

Over the past decade, many accounting firms have grown larger, but very few have become easier to run. Revenue increases while freedom decreases. The firm becomes bigger, yet the partners feel more trapped inside it.

Technology Will Not Save Poorly Designed Firms

The profession is currently experiencing a wave of excitement about technology. Artificial intelligence, automation, workflow systems and advisory platforms are transforming how accounting work is delivered.

Technology absolutely has the potential to improve accounting firms. However, technology cannot fix structural problems. If you automate a broken process, you create a faster broken process. Technology amplifies structure; it does not create it.

Over the next decade, compliance work will increasingly become automated as governments digitise tax systems and data flows directly from business software into regulatory platforms. This will not destroy the accounting profession, but it will expose weak business models.

Firms built purely on compliance production will face increasing pressure on fees and margins. Firms built around insight, strategy and advisory will become far more valuable. The difference will not be technical knowledge; it will be business design.

A Personal Lesson

My views on this subject come from experience rather than theory. I started my accounting practice thirty years ago with no capital and no safety net. The only thing I had was a credit card. Each month, I placed about $1,000 in marketing on that card and hoped the phone would ring enough to cover the bill.

In the first year, the practice generated about $50,000 in fees. In the second year, it grew to roughly $75,000. Slowly, client by client, the practice developed.

One lesson became clear very early. If a firm grows without structure, it eventually traps the owner inside the business.

Over time, that small practice evolved into Success Tax Professionals, which today has 75 franchise offices across Australia and serves more than 50,000 clients each year. Through that journey, I have seen hundreds of accounting firms from the inside. They differ in size, location, and personality, yet the same pattern reappears. Firms that grow without structure become heavier every year, while firms that are deliberately designed become easier to run.

That realisation eventually led to the creation of TaxFitness and the ideas that underpin this book.

Why This Book Exists

The purpose of this book is straightforward: to help accounting practices double their profits within twelve months.

This does not require working longer hours or dramatically increasing the number of clients. It requires designing a better firm.

The contributors to this book have spent decades working inside accounting practices and alongside them, providing advisory services, systems, training and software to help firms operate more effectively. Across hundreds of practices, we have seen the same pattern. When the right clients, services, pricing structures, systems and advisory opportunities are in place, profitability improves quickly and often dramatically.

In many cases, firms have doubled their profits within twelve months simply by redesigning how they operate.

A Final Thought

Many accountants entered the profession because they wanted freedom: the freedom to run their own business, control their time and build something valuable. Yet many partners eventually find themselves working harder than they ever expected inside firms that depend entirely on them.

That outcome is not inevitable. It is the result of design decisions, and design can be changed.

You do not need more clients, more staff, or more hours. You need a better blueprint.

Because struggling firms rarely lack effort. They suffer from a lack of design. Once a firm is properly designed, profit becomes the outcome of the system rather than the exhaustion of its people.

The 12-Month Profit Transformation Roadmap

Many accounting firms believe that improving profitability requires a major restructuring, new partners, expensive consultants, or several years of gradual change. Most firms already have the ingredients required to become far more profitable. They have clients, staff, and systems that support the practice's work. What many firms lack is not capability but deliberate focus on how the firm makes money.

Across the accounting profession, there is a strange contradiction. Accountants spend their days advising clients about pricing, profitability and business performance, yet many accounting firms rarely apply the same commercial thinking to their own practices. Instead, the firm grows. More clients are added, more staff are hired, and the workload becomes heavier each year. Revenue increases, but profitability often improves far more slowly.

This roadmap exists to challenge that pattern.

Across hundreds of accounting firms, the same lesson appears repeatedly. When practices deliberately improve a small number of key areas—firm design, compliance, profitability, advisory services, and operational systems—the firm's economics begin to change. Partners regain control of their time, clients receive more valuable advice, and profitability improves.

Often far quicker than partners expect.

The purpose of this roadmap is to show how the ideas in this book can be implemented over twelve months. The goal is not to change everything at once. Instead, the objective is to focus on a sequence of improvements that strengthen the firm's economics step by step.

Months 1–3: Clarify the Firm You Want to Build

Most accounting firms evolve rather than being deliberately designed. Clients accumulate gradually, services expand opportunistically, and systems develop informally as the firm grows. Over time, the firm becomes larger, but it does not necessarily become easier to run or more profitable.

The first stage, therefore, requires partners to step back and ask a simple but uncomfortable question: *What type of firm are we trying to build?* Which clients create the most value for the practice? Which services generate the strongest margins? Which work consumes enormous amounts of time but contributes very little profit?

When firms answer these questions honestly, they often discover that a relatively small group of clients and services generates most of their profitability. Once that becomes clear, decisions about pricing, positioning and growth become far easier.

Months 4–6: Improve the Economics of Compliance

Compliance work remains the foundation of most accounting firms. Tax returns, financial statements, and regulatory reporting create the regular touchpoints that bring clients back to the firm each year. However, many practices treat compliance purely as production work rather than as a commercial opportunity.

Every compliance engagement contains insight. The firms that improve profitability use those engagements to trigger planning conversations, review business performance and identify advisory opportunities. Compliance should not be the end of the conversation with the client. It should be the beginning.

Months 7–9: Systemise Advisory

Most accounting firms already provide advisory services. The problem is that it usually happens inconsistently. Advice is offered during meetings; questions are answered over the phone and planning ideas are discussed informally.

While these conversations are valuable, they are rarely structured and often not priced appropriately. As a result, the firm provides insight but fails to capture its true commercial value.

When advisory becomes systematic—through structured tax planning, benchmarking and business performance discussions—the economics of the firm change. Revenue per client increases, client relationships become stronger, and the accountant becomes actively involved in helping clients improve their businesses.

Months 10–12: Build Systems That Support Growth

As advisory services expand, many firms encounter the same problem. The partners become the bottleneck. Every important decision flows through them; staff rely heavily on their guidance, and the workload grows rather than diminishes.

The final stage focuses on strengthening the systems that support the firm. Clear processes, defined responsibilities, and effective delegation allow work to move efficiently through the practice and enable the firm to grow without increasing pressure on the partners.

The Result

When these improvements are implemented consistently, the accounting firm's economics begin to change. Clients receive more valuable advice, pricing becomes more disciplined, and staff operate with clearer systems and stronger direction.

Profitability improves, and the firm becomes easier to run.

Many firms are surprised by how quickly this can happen.

While every practice is different, it is not uncommon for accounting firms to materially improve profitability within 12 months by deliberately redesigning their operations.

The chapters in this book explain how to make that transformation happen.

The only real question is whether the reader chooses to implement them.

Profit Transformation Checklist

If you only implement the actions on this page, your firm will already be ahead of most accounting practices.

Use the following checklist as a practical starting point for implementing the ideas in this book.

- ☐ Define the type of accounting firm you want to build.
- ☐ Identify the clients that generate the highest value for the firm.
- ☐ Review pricing across your client base.
- ☐ Identify low-value or unprofitable client work.
- ☐ Use compliance meetings to identify advisory opportunities.
- ☐ Introduce structured tax planning for business clients.
- ☐ Introduce benchmarking or business performance reviews.
- ☐ Schedule advisory conversations with your most valuable clients.
- ☐ Establish clear pricing for advisory services.
- ☐ Document key firm processes and workflows.
- ☐ Strengthen delegation and define team responsibilities.
- ☐ Review firm profitability and performance quarterly.

Accounting firms that implement improvements like these often see meaningful increases in profitability within a relatively short period.

Firms that do not usually remain exactly where they are—busy, overworked and wondering why the numbers never seem to improve.

Accounting Firm Profit Scorecard

Accountants spend their careers measuring the performance of other businesses. We analyse financial statements, calculate ratios, benchmark industries and advise clients on how to improve profitability. Business owners are expected to understand their numbers and manage their businesses accordingly.

Yet many accounting firms rarely apply the same discipline to themselves.

That is one of the quiet contradictions within the profession.

Across Australia, there are thousands of accounting practices working extremely hard but producing far less profit than they should. Partners work long hours, staff operate under constant pressure during peak periods and the firm often grows in size without becoming significantly more profitable.

In many cases, the issue is not technical capability. It is not a shortage of clients. It is not even a shortage of effort.

The issue is that the firm has never deliberately measured its own performance as a business.

Many accounting practices operate for years without systematically reviewing client quality, pricing discipline, advisory services or operational efficiency. The firm becomes busy, but not necessarily profitable. Work increases, stress increases and partners begin to assume this is simply the nature of running an accounting practice.

It is not.

High-performing firms operate very differently. They measure performance, benchmark their results and make deliberate decisions about the type of firm they want to build.

This scorecard is designed to help you begin doing the same.

It provides a simple way to evaluate the commercial strength of your accounting firm. The objective is not to achieve a perfect score immediately, but to identify where improvement will have the greatest impact.

Rate your firm in each category using the following scale.

1 – Very Weak
2 – Needs Significant Improvement
3 – Acceptable / Average
4 – Strong
5 – Top Performing

Complete the scorecard honestly. The firms that benefit most from this exercise are those prepared to be brutally honest about where they stand today.

Accounting Firm Profit Scorecard

1. Firm Strategy and Positioning

Area - **Score (1–5)**

1. Clear vision for the type of accounting firm we want to build
2. Clearly defined ideal client profile
3. Well-defined services and positioning in the market
4. Strong differentiation from competing firms

Subtotal: ___ / 20

---

2. Client Quality and Profitability

Area - Score (1 – 5)

1. High proportion of profitable clients
2. Ability to disengage from poor clients
3. Strong relationships with business clients
4. Clients view the firm as trusted advisers

Subtotal: ___ / 20

---

3. Pricing Discipline

Area - Score (1–5)

1. Fees reflect the value delivered to clients
2. Fees reviewed regularly
3. Limited fee resistance from clients
4. Clear pricing structure across services

Subtotal: ___ / 20

---

4. Advisory Services

Area - Score (1–5)

1. Structured tax planning services offered
2. Business advisory conversations with clients
3. Benchmarking or performance analysis provided

4. Advisory services clearly priced and systemised

Subtotal: ___ / 20

---

5. Systems and Operations

Area - Score (1–5)

1. Clear workflows and documented processes
2. Staff understand roles and responsibilities
3. Compliance work delivered efficiently
4. Technology used effectively within the firm

Subtotal: ___ / 20

---

6. Leadership and Team

Area - Score (1–5)

1. Partners focus on leadership rather than production work
2. Staff capable of operating with limited supervision
3. Strong delegation within the firm
4. Clear accountability across the team

Subtotal: ___ / 20

Total Score

Maximum Score: **120**

Score	Interpretation
100 – 120	High-performing firm (Top 20%)
80 – 99	Strong firm with improvement opportunities
60 – 79	Average firm with several areas to improve
Below 60	Significant opportunity to improve profitability

Most accounting firms score between **60 and 85** when they complete this exercise honestly.

That should give the profession pause.

Accountants regularly advise clients to measure performance, set targets and continually improve their businesses. Yet many firms do not apply the same discipline to their own practices.

This book exists to change that.

Top 20% Accounting Firm Benchmarks

One of the most powerful ways to improve performance is to compare your firm against high-performing practices.

Top-performing accounting firms share several common financial characteristics. While every firm is different, the benchmarks below provide a useful reference point for evaluating the commercial performance of your practice.

Important: Net profit refers to profit **after paying partners a market salary for their work in the business.**

Performance Metric	Average Firm	Top 20% Firm
Net profit margin (after partner market salary)	0% – 15%	30% – 45%
Revenue per partner	$500k – $750k	$900k – $1.5m
Revenue per team member	$120k – $160k	$300k+
Advisory revenue	0% – 10%	25% – 50%
Average client fees	Low to moderate	Higher value clients
Partner time spent on advisory	Limited	Significant focus

These benchmarks highlight an important point.

High-performing firms are not necessarily working harder than other firms. They simply operate differently. They focus on higher-value clients, stronger pricing discipline and structured advisory services that increase the value delivered to their clients.

How to Improve Your Score

Your score highlights the areas where your firm will benefit most from improvement.

If your lowest scores relate to **firm strategy and positioning**, focus on the chapters in **Section 1 – Design a More Profitable Accounting Firm.**

If your lowest scores relate to **compliance profitability**, focus on **Section 2 – Turn Compliance Work into Profit.**

If your lowest scores relate to **advisory services**, the chapters in **Section 3 – Turn Advisory into Your Profit Engine** will be particularly valuable.

If your lowest scores relate to **systems, leadership or operational efficiency**, focus on *Section 4 – Build a Firm That Scales.*

Finally, **Section 5 – Prepare Your Firm for the Future** explores the broader forces shaping the accounting profession and how firms can position themselves for long-term success.

Used properly, this scorecard becomes more than a questionnaire. It becomes the starting point for improving the performance of your accounting firm.

Final Reflection

Before moving to the next chapter, pause for a moment.

If you could improve only **three areas** of your accounting firm in the next twelve months, what would they be?

Write them down.

Those three decisions will determine whether your firm continues operating the way it always has—or whether it becomes a significantly stronger and more profitable business.

SECTION 1

DESIGN A MORE PROFITABLE ACCOUNTING FIRM

Clarify the type of firm you want to build and structure the business model that supports stronger profitability.

"The best way to predict the future is to create it."
— Peter Drucker

Section introduction by Amy Holdsworth

From the outside, a firm may look successful. Revenue is solid. The team is capable. Clients are steady. But internally, pressure accumulates in predictable places: review bottlenecks, inconsistent delegation, unclear service boundaries, and an increasing reliance on the owner to hold quality together.

That is not a performance problem. It is a structural one.

Before we talk about workflow, systems, or operational efficiency, we need to examine the architecture of a firm itself. Operational refinement only works when the underlying design is sound. If the structure is unclear, no amount of process documentation or technology will remove the pressure. It may improve visibility, but it will not remove dependency.

This section focuses on that structural foundation.

Amanda Gascoigne begins by addressing alignment. Her Practice Sweet Spot framework challenges firm owners to define success deliberately rather than inheriting it from industry norms. Size, revenue, and headcount are often mistaken for progress. Amanda's work cuts through that assumption and forces a more commercial question: is a firm designed to support both profitability and sustainability, or is it drifting toward complexity without intention? Vision, client selection, service design, culture, and technology only work together when they are consciously aligned.

I (Amy Holdswoth) then examine structural readiness for growth. Growth without documented workflows, defined service scope, role ownership, and disciplined pricing does not create freedom. It increases review pressure, WIP lockup, and dependency. Many firms pursue expansion before stabilising their operating structure. The result is higher activity but not necessarily higher margin. Sustainable growth requires systems that can absorb complexity without pushing everything back to the owner.

Toni Eisenhut closes the section by exploring what happens when growth outpaces operating design. Her Growth Squeeze framework articulates a stage many partners recognise but struggle to name. A firm grows, yet execution remains partner-dependent. Decisions escalate. Meetings multiply. Leadership capacity shrinks. Toni addresses how to shift from partner-held execution to embedded accountability so the business can carry its own weight.

Together, these chapters focus on deliberate design. A firm should not rely on availability, personal intervention, or informal escalation to function. It should operate through clarity: clear vision, clear authority, clear structure, and clear standards.

If that foundation is in place, workflow improvements, advisory expansion, and technology investment become leverage. Without it, they become layers added onto instability.

CHAPTER 1

The Framework for Success – Finding Your Practice Sweet Spot

Amanda Gascoigne

Introduction

Why Practice Design Matters More Than Ever

Most accounting practice owners don't set out to build a business that consumes them.

They begin with clear intentions - flexibility, financial security, professional pride, time with family, and the freedom to work with clients they genuinely enjoy. Yet somewhere along the way, many practices drift. Revenue grows, workloads expand, expectations increase, but profit, capacity, and satisfaction fail to keep pace.

The result is familiar across the profession. Long hours. Constant pressure. Fee resistance. Team challenges. A quiet sense that the business is running the owner - not the other way around.

This isn't a motivation problem.

And it's rarely a capability issue.

It is a problem of design.

For decades, the accounting profession has rewarded effort, responsiveness, and technical excellence. While these qualities remain important, they are no longer enough. In today's environment - shaped by regulatory complexity, accelerating technology, rising client expectations, and workforce change - practices that rely on hard work alone eventually stall. Or worse, burn out.

Profit does not come from doing more - despite many practice owners pushing harder, only to find themselves stretched, exhausted, and no further ahead.

It comes from alignment.

Practices that consistently perform well financially share a common trait: they are intentionally designed. Their vision is clear. Their clients are chosen, not tolerated. Their services are defined, priced, and delivered with discipline. Their teams operate with clarity and accountability. Their technology supports capacity rather than creating complexity.

In other words, these practices operate within what I refer to as their **Practice Sweet Spot** - the point where commercial success, personal fulfilment, and sustainable delivery intersect **without relying on constant effort or personal sacrifice**.

When a practice sits outside this sweet spot, the symptoms are predictable. Owners feel stretched despite working harder than ever. Teams are busy but reactive. Margins are thin, even when fees appear healthy. Decisions are made out of urgency rather than intention. Over time, misalignment erodes both profit and enjoyment.

Many profitability challenges are self-reinforcing. Misaligned clients drive scope creep. Scope creep overwhelms teams. Overwhelmed teams rely on the owner. Owner dependency limits growth and creates exhaustion. Exhaustion then leads to short-term decisions that push the practice further away from its ideal design.

This chapter challenges the assumption that pressure is simply the cost of success.

It introduces a practical framework for stepping back, reassessing, and redesigning your practice so that profit becomes an outcome of clarity - not sacrifice. The Practice Sweet Spot framework focuses on five critical pillars that influence every decision inside a firm: **vision, clients, services, culture, and technology.**

When these pillars are aligned, practices don't just become more profitable - they become easier to run. Decisions are clearer. Boundaries are stronger. Capacity improves. Teams perform better. And importantly, the business begins to support the life of the owner, rather than compete with it.

This is not about creating a perfect practice. Nor is it about rapid growth for growth's sake.

It is about designing a practice that works - commercially, professionally, and personally - and recognising that sustainable profit is built by intention, not accident.

The Framework

Method – Finding Your Practice Sweet Spot

Sustainable profitability in an accounting practice is rarely the result of a single decision. It is the outcome of multiple, interconnected choices that reinforce one another over time.

When those choices are aligned, a practice feels focused, controlled, and commercially sound. When they are not, even high-revenue firms can feel chaotic, exhausting, and fragile.

The **Practice Sweet Spot framework** is a method for designing an accounting practice that delivers strong financial results without relying on excessive hours, constant firefighting, or personal sacrifice. It recognises that profit is not created in isolation. It is shaped by how a practice is designed across five critical pillars: vision, clients, services, culture, and technology.

The Practice Sweet Spot sits at the intersection of these five pillars. When they are aligned, profit becomes more predictable, delivery becomes more efficient, and the business begins to support the life of the owner rather than compete with it.

What Is the Practice Sweet Spot?

The Practice Sweet Spot is the point where:

- The practice is commercially viable and profitable
- The work aligns with the owner's definition of success
- The team can deliver consistently without burnout
- Systems and structure support, rather than hinder, performance

Importantly, the Practice Sweet Spot is not static.

Practices drift over time - often gradually and unintentionally - as new clients are accepted, services are added, staff change, or technology evolves. Without regular recalibration, even a well-designed firm can move away from its ideal operating position.

What is equally important - and far less talked about - is that **no two practice sweet spots are ever the same.**

There is no universal version of the "ideal" accounting practice. Yet many practice owners spend years chasing a model of success that is marketed to them - often loudly and repeatedly - as the benchmark to aspire to. Bigger teams. Higher turnover. Faster growth. A particular revenue number. A particular structure. A particular exit.

For some practices, that pathway is exactly right.

For many others, it is not.

The problem arises when practice owners assume that discomfort, dissatisfaction, or exhaustion means they are failing - rather than recognising they may be pursuing a version of success that is fundamentally misaligned with who they are, how they want to live, and what they value most.

This is where deflation sets in.

Deflation from constantly feeling "behind".

Deflation from believing they should want something they do not.

Deflation from building a practice that looks successful on paper but feels wrong in reality.

Over the years, I have seen this repeatedly - highly capable, commercially astute practice owners questioning themselves, not because they lack skill or ambition, but because they are measuring their success against someone else's definition of it.

Several years ago, I intentionally brought this conversation into the open by facilitating a panel discussion titled **"To Scale or Not to Scale."** The purpose was simple: to give practice owners permission to see themselves reflected in *different* success stories.

On that panel were practitioners who *could* have scaled further - and had consciously chosen not to. Some had grown and then deliberately scaled back. Others had always remained small and boutique by design. What they shared was not fear, failure, or lack of ambition - but clarity.

They were clear on their vision.

Clear on what success meant to them.

Clear on the trade-offs they were - and were not - willing to make.

Two of the panellists were only able to articulate that clarity after doing the deeper work of unpacking their personal and professional priorities. Once they did, the decision to remain small, focused, and intentionally designed was no longer something to defend - it was something to protect.

That conversation was about more than scaling decisions. It was about helping practice owners feel **seen, validated, and respected** in a profession that often promotes a single narrative of success.

The Practice Sweet Spot framework exists for exactly this reason.

In my work, I support practice owners across both categories - those who want to scale, and those who want to stay small and boutique by design. The common thread is not the size of the practice, but the clarity of the vision behind it. One of my strengths is helping owners extract and articulate that vision, so what we design or redesign is completely aligned - commercially, professionally, and personally.

It does not push practices towards growth or restraint. It does not prescribe size, structure, or strategy. Instead, it provides a way to design a practice that aligns with your definition of success - whether that involves scaling up, staying small, or evolving deliberately over time.

A practice that sits in its sweet spot is not accidental, and it is not imitative.

It is the result of conscious choices made in alignment with vision, values, and capacity.

And when that alignment exists, profit follows - not because the practice is chasing someone else's version of utopia, but because it is operating in its own.

The purpose of this framework is not perfection.

It is intentional design.

The Five Pillars of a Well-Designed Practice

Each pillar within the Practice Sweet Spot framework acts as a profit lever. Weakness or misalignment in one pillar inevitably places pressure on the others.

Pillar 1: Vision – Defining Success on Your Terms

Every accounting practice is shaped - consciously or not - by the owner's definition of success. When that definition is unclear, outdated, or inherited from external expectations, decision-making becomes reactive and inconsistent.

Vision is not a mission statement, a set of values on a website, or a growth target pulled from industry benchmarks.

Vision is a **practical filter**.

A clear vision guides daily decisions about clients, services, pricing, workload, and boundaries. It provides a reference point when opportunities arise and pressure increases. Without it, practices default to growth by accumulation - more clients, more services, more complexity - often without corresponding profit or satisfaction.

This idea is captured powerfully in a quote often attributed to Tony Hsieh, former CEO of Zappos:

> "*Chase the vision, not the money; the money will end up following you.*"

In accounting practices, the opposite approach is common. Profit becomes the primary focus, and everything else is expected to bend around it. Over time, this frequently leads to misalignment - longer hours, growing pressure, and diminishing enjoyment - without delivering the financial rewards owners anticipated.

When vision is clear and intentional, profit becomes an outcome rather than the driver. Decisions are made with greater discipline. Trade-offs are assessed more calmly. The practice grows in the *right* direction, not just a bigger one.

A well-defined vision answers practical questions such as:

- What does success look like for me at this stage of life and practice ownership?
- How much do I want to work - and how do I want that work to feel?
- What type of clients and work energise me rather than drain me?
- What am I ultimately building this practice for?

Importantly, vision is not static. It should be revisited as circumstances change - personally, professionally, and commercially. What felt right in the early years of practice ownership may no longer be appropriate later on. Failing to reassess vision is one of the most common reasons practices drift away from their sweet spot.

Profit impact:
Clear vision reduces distraction, sharpens priorities, and leads to more disciplined, profitable decision-making. Practices with a strong sense of direction say "no" more easily - and that restraint often protects margin, capacity, and energy.

Pillar 2: Clients – Working With the Right Clients at the Right Price

Not all clients contribute equally to profit, capacity, or enjoyment - yet many accounting practices carry long-standing client relationships that no longer align with their desired direction.

Client selection is rarely treated as a strategic decision. More often, it evolves gradually and emotionally: clients are accepted during busy periods, retained out of loyalty, or tolerated because "they've always been with us." Over time, this erodes clarity and places pressure on every other pillar of the practice.

Client misalignment shows up in predictable ways:

- Fee resistance and ongoing price sensitivity
- Scope creep and blurred boundaries
- Delays in providing information and adopting technology
- Disproportionate time, emotional labour, and follow-up
- Increased pressure on the owner to step in and resolve issues

Within the Practice Sweet Spot framework, clients are not judged - they are assessed.

The question is not whether clients are "good" or "bad," but whether they are aligned with the practice's vision, service model, pricing structure, and delivery standards. When client selection is left unchecked, practices often find themselves redesigning services, bending boundaries, or absorbing inefficiencies to accommodate misaligned relationships.

The goal is not to maximise client numbers.

It is to build a client base that:

- Values the advisory relationship
- Respects boundaries and agreed scope
- Engages constructively with systems and processes
- Is willing to pay appropriately for the work delivered

Aligned clients reduce friction across the practice. They make service delivery more consistent, support healthier team dynamics, and allow technology and systems to work as intended. Most importantly, they enable the owner to lead proactively rather than respond reactively.

Client mix is also one of the fastest levers for change. Repricing, redefining engagement terms, or transitioning a small number of misaligned clients can free capacity, improve margins, and immediately reduce pressure - without adding new work.

Profit impact:
A well-aligned client base increases average fees, reduces write-offs, stabilises workflow, and improves energy utilisation across the practice. When the right clients are in place, profit becomes easier to protect - and far less exhausting to earn.

Pillar 3: Services – Designing a Profitable Service Offering

Many practices offer a wide range of services without clearly defining what is included, how it is delivered, or how it is priced. Over time, this creates inconsistency, margin leakage, and frustration.

A well-designed service offering is:

- Clearly defined
- Intentionally priced
- Delivered consistently

This does not require abandoning compliance work. It requires structuring services, so scope is controlled, value is visible, and advisory conversations occur naturally.

Profit impact:

Clear service design improves margins, supports advisory readiness, and reduces delivery friction.

Pillar 4: Culture – Building a Team and Environment That Supports Profit

Within the Practice Sweet Spot framework, culture is viewed as a delivery system - not a perk.

A profitable practice requires clarity around expectations, roles, accountability, and standards. When culture is weak or undefined, owners step in to fill gaps. Owner dependency grows. Delivery becomes inconsistent.

Strong culture means clarity, not perfection.

In practice, culture determines how work gets done when the owner is not in the room.

Profit impact:

Clear culture improves productivity, retention, and consistency, reducing reliance on the owner.

Pillar 5: Technology – Using Systems to Create Capacity

Technology should support the way a practice operates - not dictate it.

In many practices, technology is introduced reactively. New tools are layered onto existing processes in the hope of creating efficiency, often without first addressing underlying complexity or inconsistency. When this happens, technology rarely delivers the intended benefits.

As the saying goes, "*If you automate a mess, you get an automated mess*." - Rod Michael, formerly of Rockwell Automation

Within the Practice Sweet Spot framework, technology is not implemented ad hoc. Processes are first clarified, streamlined, and running smoothly. Only then does technology provide leverage - amplifying what already works rather than attempting to fix what does not.

Well-designed practices treat technology as an enabler, not a solution in its own right. The goal is not to adopt the latest tools, but to support consistent service delivery, reduce friction, and create capacity across the practice.

When workflows are clear and expectations are defined, technology can genuinely "up the game" - improving turnaround times, reducing rework, and freeing the owner and team to focus on higher-value work.

Profit impact:

When technology is aligned to well-designed processes, it increases efficiency, stabilises delivery, and supports sustainable profit growth - without adding complexity or noise.

Case Study

Realigning the Practice Sweet Spot

The practice featured here was a well-established suburban accounting firm led by a sole principal with a small team. On paper, it appeared successful. Revenue had grown steadily, demand was strong, and the client base was loyal.

Behind the numbers, however, the practice was under strain.

The principal worked long hours, often logging on after dinner and most weekends. Despite incremental fee increases, profitability had plateaued. Staff were busy but reactive, turnaround times slipped, and the owner remained the bottleneck for most decisions.

The issue was not effort.

It was misalignment in design.

Identifying the Misaligned Pillars

Three pillars were clearly out of alignment.

Vision:

The owner had never revisited their definition of success. What began as a practice built for flexibility and autonomy had gradually evolved into a business driven by obligation and expectation.

Importantly, the owner could not clearly articulate what success now looked like - either for themselves or for the practice. Without a defined and communicated vision, there was nothing for the team to align to. Staff were doing their best, but they were operating without a clear sense of direction or purpose beyond getting the work done.

When vision lives only in the owner's head - or not at all - it cannot be shared, reinforced, or brought to life by others. As a result, decisions defaulted to urgency rather than intention, and the owner remained the primary source of direction, reassurance, and approval.

Clients:
The client base had grown organically over many years, without deliberate curation. Many clients were fee-sensitive, slow to respond, resistant to adopting technology, and demanding of immediate attention. These clients consumed a disproportionate amount of time and emotional energy, placing ongoing pressure on both the owner and the team.

Rather than supporting the practice's desired direction, the client mix reinforced reactivity and eroded boundaries.

Services:
Services lacked clear structure and definition. Scope creep was common, pricing rarely reflected the effort involved, and write-offs were frequent. Without clearly articulated service parameters, delivery varied from client to client, increasing complexity and frustration across the practice.

Culture and technology were functioning adequately, but they were compensating for deeper misalignment elsewhere - particularly in vision, clients, and services. The practice appeared to be coping, but only through sustained effort rather than intentional design.

Implementation Guide

Designing Your Practice Sweet Spot

Designing a profitable, sustainable practice does not require a complete overhaul. The most effective changes are incremental, intentional, and well sequenced. Progress comes from disciplined design choices, applied consistently over time.

Step 1: Identify Where Your Practice Is Misaligned

Observe where time, energy, and margin consistently leak. Repeating patterns - rather than isolated issues - reveal which pillars require attention.

Step 2: Clarify Your Non-Negotiables

Define clear boundaries around clients, services, availability, and standards. What is not explicitly defined will be negotiated - and accommodation inevitably leads to erosion.

Step 3: Prioritise One or Two High-Impact Changes

Focus on the changes most likely to create immediate relief or meaningful commercial impact. Attempting to fix everything at once often delays progress. Momentum matters.

Step 4: Align the Team and Systems

Communicate changes clearly, reinforce expectations consistently, and step back deliberately from owner-dependent decisions and tasks. Alignment reduces reliance on the owner and stabilises delivery.

Step 5: Review and Recalibrate Quarterly

Design is an ongoing leadership discipline, not a one-off exercise. Regular review prevents drift and allows the practice to adapt without losing its sweet spot.

Over a twelve-month period, practices applying this framework typically experience improved margins, clearer decision-making, and reduced pressure - without increasing hours.

Step 6: Build Annual Alignment Reviews Into the Practice

Just as compliance obligations, pricing, engagement terms, and procedures are reviewed annually, practice design also requires regular attention.

Practices evolve. Clients change. Team capability shifts. Services expand or contract. Technology improves - or becomes misaligned. When these changes are not reviewed deliberately, misalignment creeps in quietly and pressure builds over time.

An annual alignment review creates space to step back and ask:

- Are our clients still aligned with our vision and values?
- Do our services still deliver value, margin, and enjoyment?
- Is our technology supporting the way we work - or adding friction?
- Does our culture still reflect how we want the practice to operate?
- Most importantly, does this practice still support both commercial success and personal fulfilment?

From time to time, this review will surface the need to reprice or transition clients, refine or retire services, adjust team roles, or rethink systems.

These decisions are not signs of failure. They are evidence of an evolving, intentionally designed practice.

When alignment is reviewed regularly, nothing needs to be dramatic. Small, considered adjustments keep the practice within its sweet spot - commercially, professionally, and personally.

Over time, this discipline is what allows profit, capacity, and enjoyment to flow together, rather than compete with one another.

Action Checklist

Designing for Profit and Sustainability

1. **Clarify your definition of success for the next three years**
   What do you want your practice to look and feel like? What are your non-negotiables around hours, clients, income, and family time?
2. **Identify one misaligned client to reprice or transition**
   Which client consistently drains time or energy? If you were meeting them for the first time today, would you choose to work with them?

3. **Redefine the scope of one service that consistently creates pressure, frustration, or poor margins**
   Where does scope creep keep showing up? What needs to be clarified, standardised, or removed so delivery becomes consistent and profitable?
4. **Reset one eroded boundary**
   Which boundary has softened over time - response times, availability, turnaround, or "just one more thing"? What will you say "yes" to - and what will you deliberately say "no" to - going forward?
5. **Schedule quarterly design reviews**
   What will you review each quarter - client mix, pricing, workload, capacity, team pressure points, and tech friction? What one adjustment will you commit to each quarter?
6. **Build an annual practice alignment review into your calendar**
   Just as you update checklists, forms, procedures, pricing, and engagement terms each year, what else now needs reviewing - clients, services, culture, and technology - to stay aligned with your vision?
   Small, intentional actions compound quickly.

Closing Guide

Design First, Then Protect It

Profitability is rarely accidental. It is the outcome of deliberate choices that align how a practice operates with what the owner values most.

When a practice is designed with intention, it becomes easier to run and more resilient. Pressure reduces. Decisions improve. Profit follows.

But design alone is not enough.

Even well-designed practices can drift over time. Boundaries soften. Old habits return. Effort quietly replaces structure. Without deliberate protection, the very alignment that once created ease can begin to erode.

The next challenge is sustainability.

In a subsequent chapter, we explore how to protect energy, capacity, and clarity - so the practice you've intentionally designed continues to perform without relying on burnout as a business strategy.

For practice owners who want guidance applying these principles in real time - across vision, clients, services, culture, and technology - this work forms the foundation of my **Better Practice, Better Life** twelve-month program. It is designed to support intentional implementation, not just understanding, and to help practices embed sustainable change over time.

Design creates clarity.

Protection preserves it.

CHAPTER 2
Are You Structured to Grow?

Amy Holdsworth

Introduction

Growth. It's the word that gets tossed around in every strategy session, planning day, and industry event. "We want to grow." "We're preparing for growth." "This year is all about growth." It sounds positive, ambitious even, but in accounting, it can be dangerously misleading.

Growth doesn't automatically mean success. Often it brings stress, overextension, or even collapse. Growth can magnify inefficiency, expose weak systems, and drain profit faster than it creates it. It's the business equivalent of building a second storey on a house with cracked foundations. From the outside, it looks impressive. From the inside, it's a disaster waiting to happen.

Right now, Australian accounting practices face a unique set of pressures: rising client expectations, tighter compliance deadlines, and increased competition from both traditional firms and tech-enabled platforms. Growth isn't just a goal; it's a stress test. Firms that scale without structure often find that revenue rises while profit margins shrink.

But done right, structured growth can transform your firm. Within 12 months, firms that align their systems, culture, and pricing strategically see measurable profit improvements of 20–50% without necessarily adding more headcount. When every client engagement is profitable, every process is efficient, and every team member is clear on their role, growth becomes sustainable, predictable, and rewarding.

This chapter will help you answer a critical question: Are you ready to grow, or is your current structure just masking chaos? You'll learn why sustainable growth isn't about chasing more clients or expanding headcount. It's about building a foundation that can handle expansion without sacrificing margin, consistency, or team well-being. By the end of this chapter, you'll understand how to assess your readiness, implement systems that multiply profit, and avoid the traps that turn growth into burnout.

Core Framework / Method

Understand What Growth Really Means

Too often, firms equate growth with busyness. Adding clients, hiring more staff, or taking on larger projects can feel like progress, but on its own, it rarely moves the needle on profitability or sustainability. In fact, unstructured growth can have the opposite effect: it can stretch resources thin, increase stress, and erode margins faster than revenue increases.

True growth is not just about doing more; it's about doing better. It's about building a firm that can handle more without compromising quality, team wellbeing, or profit. To understand growth properly, it helps to think of it as three interconnected layers: operational, financial, and personal.

Operational growth is the backbone of any scalable firm. It's about creating efficient, repeatable systems that can handle additional clients or services without chaos. This includes everything from client onboarding to compliance workflows, document management, and review processes. When your operations are structured, every team member knows what to do, when to do it, and how to escalate issues. This reduces wasted effort, prevents errors, and ensures that adding new clients doesn't mean starting from scratch every time. Firms that neglect operational growth often find themselves firefighting, with every new engagement consuming more time than it should.

Financial growth is what most people immediately think of when they hear the word "growth," but it's more nuanced than simply increasing revenue. Real financial growth is about improving margins, optimising cash flow, and ensuring every dollar of revenue contributes meaningfully to profit. This requires understanding which clients and services are most profitable, pricing appropriately, and monitoring costs closely. A firm can have record revenue, but if WIP is ballooning, staff are constantly working overtime, and margins are shrinking, it hasn't truly grown; it's just busier.

Personal growth often gets overlooked, but is just as important. Leaders must develop the capacity to make clear, confident decisions without being overwhelmed. Personal growth means having the bandwidth to step back, identify inefficiencies, and guide the firm strategically rather than getting lost in day-to-day delivery. Without leadership clarity, operational improvements and financial gains can stall because there's no one driving consistent decision-making or holding teams accountable.

Growth only becomes sustainable when all three layers (operational, financial, and personal) are aligned. If one is lagging, weaknesses are magnified. A firm with excellent systems but poor financial oversight may still bleed profits. A firm with strong financial performance but chaotic operations will see stress and burnout spike as client numbers increase. And a firm with capable staff and systems but unclear leadership direction can stall growth before it even begins.

The firms that thrive don't chase vanity metrics like headcount or total revenue. They focus on improving the underlying structures that allow growth to happen naturally. They understand that adding clients or staff is only meaningful when their systems, margins, and leadership can absorb the change. Growth is not about doing more for the sake of it; it's about building strength and resilience that compound over time.

1. Measure Your Structural Readiness

Before a firm can truly scale, it must be honest about whether it's ready. Many firms assume that growth is a matter of ambition; if we want more clients, we'll hire more people, and the rest will follow. The reality is different. Structural readiness is about evidence, not aspiration. It's about looking objectively at your firm and asking the hard questions: can your current systems, people, and processes handle more without breaking down?

Lodgement deadlines: Consistently hitting lodgement deadlines is a simple but powerful indicator of readiness. If you're barely meeting obligations now, doubling client numbers will almost certainly create bottlenecks. Ask yourself: Are at least 95% of your deadlines met on time, even during peak periods? Firms that track and review deadlines weekly or monthly have a clear picture of capacity and risk, which makes planning growth far more reliable.

Service offerings and pricing clarity: Do clients and your team know exactly what you offer, what it costs, and what's included? Ambiguity here leads to scope creep, conflicts, and hidden costs that undermine profitability. Firms that document offerings, standardise pricing, and communicate scope clearly can onboard new clients without reinventing the wheel each time.

Tech stack consistency: Technology should amplify your firm, not create confusion. Is your software documented, consistently used, and integrated across teams? Every new hire or client adds complexity. Without clear guidance on what systems to use, when, and how, growth slows and errors multiply. Firms with a well-understood tech ecosystem can scale confidently because everyone knows the tools and workflows they rely on.

Predictable workload: Can you anticipate team workload 90 days ahead? Predictability allows for proactive staffing, efficient delegation, and smooth client delivery. If work allocation is reactive, adding clients simply increases stress and burnout. Firms that forecast workloads accurately can plan resources, hire strategically, and avoid last-minute firefighting.

Workflow visibility and review: Do you have true visibility over your firm's workflow, including what's in progress, what's coming up, and where the bottlenecks are? Can you see start dates, due dates, job owners, and the current status of every task? Workflow visibility isn't just about tracking jobs. It's about understanding capacity, accountability, and momentum across the firm.

Regular workflow review keeps jobs on track, aligns capacity with demand, and ensures your team can adjust as client priorities shift. Firms that maintain this level of visibility don't just react to workflow. They manage it with confidence and control.

Client profitability awareness: Do you know which clients and services are most profitable, not just the overall P&L? Growth that doesn't consider profitability can create "busy" without gain. Tracking profitability by segment allows firms to prioritise high-value clients, prune low-return engagements, and focus energy where it truly drives margin.

Answering "yes" to most of these questions indicates a firm

has the structural resilience to grow sustainably. Answering "no" is not a failure; it's a signal. Growth at this stage would amplify inefficiencies and stress, rather than profit. By measuring readiness, firms can focus first on stabilising operations, clarifying offerings, and understanding capacity, setting the foundation for deliberate and profitable growth.

2. The Five Growth Principles

Have you answered a resounding yes to the previous point and truly feel like your firm is ready to grow? Before you chase new clients, bigger revenue, or a larger team, there are five non-negotiable actions you need to take to ensure growth is sustainable, profitable, and (relatively) stress-free. These aren't just tips; they're the disciplines that separate firms that thrive from those that merely survive. Follow them consistently, and you'll set a strong foundation for expansion that actually delivers results, rather than chaos.

1. **Start with the end in mind:** Define success metrics, whether profit, freedom, or client satisfaction.
2. **Build systems before scale:** Standardise processes, document workflows, then optimise.
3. **Choose clients intentionally:** High-maintenance clients often cost more than they deliver. Be selective.
4. **Empower your people:** Train, delegate, and trust your team. Every partner hour spent on routine tasks costs thousands in opportunity.
5. **Review quarterly:** Growth is never "set and forget." Track KPIs, process efficiency, and profitability every 90 days.

3. Efficiency as the Foundation

Start by mapping every client journey, from onboarding through to delivery and billing. Break each process into discrete steps and assign clear ownership at every stage. Who collects the data? Who prepares it? Who reviews it? What triggers the next step? When each action is clearly defined and owned, accountability increases, errors decrease, and bottlenecks become visible before they cause delays.

Next, measure outcomes at each stage. Track turnaround times, quality metrics, and profitability to identify which parts of the workflow are draining resources or creating unnecessary risk. This isn't about micromanaging staff, it's about building predictable, repeatable processes that can scale without increasing stress.

Technology should serve as an amplifier, not a patch. Systems like Ignition, FYI, or Karbon can automate data collection, task reminders, and communication, but they cannot fix undefined or inconsistent processes. Firms that implement tech before stabilising workflows often see slower output, duplication, and staff frustration.

When efficiency is embedded into every workflow, expansion becomes manageable. Adding clients, staff, or services no longer triggers chaos. Instead, growth becomes predictable, profitable, and sustainable.

4. The Human Side of Structure

Growth isn't purely operational; it's emotional. Even the most efficient processes and clever technology won't deliver sustainable results if your team isn't supported, clear on expectations, and empowered to do their best work. Structure provides certainty, reduces stress, and gives people the confidence to take ownership of their roles.

Start with boundaries. Clear expectations about responsibilities and decision-making authority are essential. Teams thrive when they know who owns what and when they have the freedom to act. This clarity prevents firefighting and constant escalation to partners, which is a hidden cost that silently eats away at profit.

Next, focus on workload balance. Leaders need to monitor how much capacity each team member has and redistribute work before stress and errors accumulate. Growth without workload visibility is a recipe for overworked staff and inconsistent client delivery. Tools like workflow dashboards and regular check-ins help maintain equilibrium, even as client numbers increase.

Culture and communication are equally important. When partners and managers model structured behaviours, using processes consistently, respecting boundaries, and communicating clearly, teams are more likely to adopt them. A structured culture doesn't stifle creativity; it creates space for problem-solving and high-value advisory work.

Finally, growth readiness includes emotional resilience. Staff and partners alike need confidence that the firm can handle more clients, bigger projects, and new challenges without falling apart. Investing in leadership training, team development, and recognition programs ensures your people can scale alongside your firm.

5. Profit as the Driver

To make profit the driver of growth, start by tracking margins at multiple levels. Look at each client, each service, and each team member. Which clients generate the highest return relative to the time and resources invested? Which services consistently deliver strong margins, and which erode them through scope creep or inefficiencies? Which staff roles are underutilised, and which are stretched so thin that quality or speed suffers? Understanding these dynamics allows you to make deliberate choices about where to invest time, resources, and energy.

Next, use this analysis to align your growth strategy. High-margin clients should be prioritised, and low-margin clients should be evaluated. Prune where necessary, adjust pricing where appropriate, and focus efforts on work that delivers the strongest return. Services that are profitable at scale can be expanded, while those that consistently drain resources may need to be redesigned or discontinued.

Finally, integrate profit tracking into regular decision-making. Make it part of every strategy discussion, staffing allocation, and client engagement decision. When profit drives growth choices rather than revenue, the firm scales predictably and sustainably. Growth then becomes a tool to amplify the value you already deliver, rather than a gamble on more work, more hours, or more stress.

6. Growth by Design

Growth shouldn't happen to your firm; it should happen because of your decisions, planning, and structure. Too often, practices chase new clients, revenue targets, or headcount increases reactively, hoping the outcomes will be positive. Growth by design flips that approach: it's deliberate, controlled, and intentional.

To grow successfully, focus on four critical pillars that form the foundation for scalable, sustainable expansion:

- **Clarity on strategic goals:** Define exactly what growth means for your firm. Is it profit, flexibility, client quality, or a combination? Every decision should be measured against these objectives.
- **Systems that support scale:** Standardised, repeatable processes are essential. When workflows are clear and ownership is defined, the firm can handle more clients or services without chaos.
- **Technology that amplifies, not distracts:** Tools should streamline work, reduce manual effort, and integrate seamlessly with your processes. Technology without structure only creates clutter.

- **People empowered to perform independently:** Teams need clarity, authority, and support. When staff can act confidently within structured boundaries, leaders are freed to focus on strategy and advisory work.

Growth shouldn't be reactive or accidental. It should be a deliberate, measurable outcome of structure, discipline, and alignment. When these pillars are in place, every new client, engagement, or service contributes to profitability and efficiency, rather than stress or unpredictability. In short, growth by design transforms expansion from a gamble into a strategic advantage.

Case Study / Example

Firm Y: Growth Without Chaos

Firm Y, a mid-sized suburban accounting firm, had been experiencing steady revenue growth, but the picture behind the numbers told a different story. With a team of twelve handling around 2500 tax returns alongside several advisory clients, the firm appeared busy and successful on the surface. Partners talked confidently about "growth," but the reality was far more fragile. Margins were flat, staff were overworked, client deadlines occasionally slipped, and partners spent more time firefighting than focusing on strategy or advisory work. The firm was caught in a cycle familiar to many practices: growth in revenue without corresponding growth in structure or efficiency.

The leadership team knew something had to change. They wanted to expand, take on more clients, and improve profitability, but they didn't want to scale chaos. The first step was a comprehensive structural audit.

Step 1: Structural Audit

We began by reviewing every client workflow, pricing model, and staffing allocation. The goal was to identify bottlenecks, inefficiencies, and hidden costs that were quietly eroding profit. The findings were eye-opening:

- **Pricing was 15–20% below market:** Firm Y had been undercharging for core services for years, relying on legacy pricing models rather than evaluating value delivered. This meant that even though revenue was growing, margins were stagnant.
- **Scope creep was common:** Without clearly defined service agreements, staff were frequently performing extra work that wasn't billable or captured. These hidden costs were invisible in the P&L but were burning staff hours and reducing profitability.
- **Processes were bespoke:** Every client job required reinvention. There were no standardised workflows, templates, or repeatable procedures. Partners had to constantly step in to review or correct work, creating bottlenecks and reducing overall efficiency.

The internal review provided clarity: Firm Y wasn't failing; it was simply unprepared for growth. They needed operational alignment, disciplined profitability focus, and a cultural shift to handle expansion sustainably.

Step 2: Operational Alignment

With the review complete, we moved to operational alignment. Workflows were standardised and documented, ensuring that every client engagement followed a predictable path from onboarding to delivery and billing. This included:

- Mapping each client journey, identifying who was responsible for each task, and setting clear triggers for the next step.

- Implementing technology to automate repetitive, low-value tasks. Tools, including Xero Practice Manager and FYI were configured to manage client requests, reminders, and document handling, freeing staff to focus on higher-value work.
- Ensuring each team member understood their responsibilities and limits. This reduced unnecessary escalations to partners and clarified accountability across the firm.

By establishing clear, repeatable processes, Firm Y created a scalable foundation. Growth would no longer be chaotic. It would instead be structured and measurable.

Step 3: Profit-Focused Growth

Next, we addressed profitability. The leadership team realised that not all clients contributed equally to the bottom line. Strategies were introduced to prioritise high-value clients and restructure engagements:

- Low-margin clients were either repriced to reflect the true cost of service or offboarded entirely.
- Service tiers were introduced to differentiate offerings based on complexity and value, helping staff manage expectations and clients choose the level of service that suited them.
- Pricing strategies were updated to reflect market value, ensuring that each engagement contributed positively to margins.

These changes didn't just improve profit, they clarified the firm's market position and allowed staff to focus energy where it mattered most. Revenue growth became aligned with margin improvement rather than being a source of hidden costs.

Step 4: Cultural Shift

Operational and financial improvements were paired with a deliberate cultural shift. Boundaries were set and communicated clearly:

- Turnaround times for client work were standardised and tracked.
- Client communication expectations were defined, including response times and escalation processes.
- Partner availability was clarified, reducing the expectation that they were on call 24/7.

The impact on staff was immediate. With clear boundaries and predictable workflows, stress levels decreased, morale improved, and team members felt empowered to make decisions without constant supervision. Partners, freed from routine delivery work, could focus on advisory services, business development, and strategic planning.

Outcome

Within 12 months, the transformation was measurable:

- **Profit increased by 35%** as pricing, scope management, and process efficiencies took effect.
- **Staff turnover decreased**, reflecting improved morale and workload balance.
- **Partner hours in delivery work reduced by 20%**, allowing more focus on advisory and strategy.
- **Client satisfaction scores improved**, thanks to consistent, predictable service delivery.

Firm Y didn't just grow; they grew with structure. Revenue growth was matched by operational stability, improved margins, and a confident, empowered team. Growth was no longer a source of stress; it became a predictable, profitable outcome of deliberate planning and disciplined execution.

The lessons from Firm Y are clear: without structure, growth magnifies problems. With structure, growth amplifies value. Operational alignment, profit focus, and a supportive culture turn expansion from a risky gamble into a strategic advantage. For accounting firms aiming to scale sustainably, this case study illustrates that success isn't measured by client numbers alone; it's measured by the harmony between profit, people, and process.

Implementation Guide: Growing With Structure

Scaling a firm is more than hiring more staff or taking on more clients. True growth happens when operations, people, technology, and profit metrics are aligned. This step-by-step guide walks through exactly how to implement a structured growth plan that drives measurable results within 12 months.

Step 1: Conduct a Growth Readiness Audit

The first step in structured growth is understanding where your firm currently stands. This isn't about ambition or gut feeling; it's about measurable evidence. A growth readiness audit provides clarity on current workflows, team capacity, and profitability, ensuring you know what you can scale safely.

1. **List all workflows by service type:** Start by cataloguing every recurring service your firm delivers. This could include individual tax returns, business advisory and compliance services, bookkeeping, or financial planning. The goal is to see every process in one place.
2. **Map each client journey:** For each service, document the end-to-end journey from onboarding to delivery and billing. Note every step, including client interactions, internal tasks, and review points.

3. **Track timelines, owner responsibilities, and dependencies:** Identify who is responsible for each task, how long it takes, and what must happen before the next step. Highlight bottlenecks or unclear ownership.
4. **Measure current profitability:** Analyse revenue, costs, and time spent per client and per service. Understanding profitability at this granular level allows you to make data-driven decisions about where to invest effort, repricing needs, or client pruning.

By the end of this audit, you should have a clear map of your firm's current workflows, capacity, and profitability, forming the baseline for all growth initiatives. Without this clarity, any growth risks magnifying inefficiency instead of creating profit.

Step 2: Standardise Processes

Once you understand your workflows, it's time to bring order to them. Standardisation ensures work is consistent, repeatable, and scalable.

1. **Create templates for recurring tasks:** For every service, develop templates for emails, reports, and documentation. Standard templates save time, reduce errors, and make it easier for new staff to step in without reinventing the wheel.
2. **Define steps for approvals, review, and communication:** Establish clear checkpoints. Who reviews work before it reaches the client? What approvals are required for billing, client communications, or exceptions? Having these steps documented removes ambiguity.
3. **Document exceptions separately:** Not every scenario fits the standard workflow. Keep a separate log of exceptions and their resolutions to avoid ad-hoc workarounds, which can create inefficiency and margin leaks.

Standardising processes ensures that as you grow, every client receives consistent service, your team can work independently, and partners are freed from routine oversight.

Step 3: Align Technology

Technology can be a growth enabler, but only if it supports clear, standardised processes. Without alignment, technology often creates more work than it solves.

1. **Identify core systems and remove redundancy:** List all software tools in use and determine which are essential. Eliminate duplicates or unnecessary applications to simplify workflows.
2. **Automate where appropriate, but only once processes are clear:** Use technology to reduce repetitive tasks like data collection, reminders, and document management. Tools like Karbon, FYI, or Ignition work best when processes are standardised; otherwise, automation magnifies chaos.
3. **Assign internal "owners" for software adoption and training:** Every tool should have a responsible team member who oversees adoption, updates, and training. This ensures consistency, reduces errors, and builds confidence across the team.

Aligned technology amplifies efficiency, accuracy, and capacity. Misaligned technology, by contrast, can slow growth and frustrate staff.

Step 4: Define Profit Metrics

Profit should be the lens through which growth is measured. Without clear metrics, additional revenue can mask inefficiency or hidden costs.

1. **Segment clients by profitability and growth potential:**

Identify which clients deliver the highest margins and which may require repricing, pruning, or additional services to support their own business goals.

2. **Establish service-level targets tied to margin goals:** Determine the expected return on each service, factoring in time, staff cost, and operational effort.
3. **Introduce regular KPI tracking for teams and partners:** Monitor key indicators such as turnaround times, WIP days, staff utilisation, and client satisfaction. Use this data to guide decisions and maintain alignment between profit, efficiency, and growth.

By measuring profitability and performance consistently, firms can make strategic growth decisions that genuinely improve the bottom line.

Step 5: Empower Your People

People are the multiplier for every system and process. Without a capable, empowered team, even the best workflows fail under growth pressure.

1. **Train team members on new workflows:** Ensure every staff member understands the standardised processes and technology tools. Training should include "why" as well as "how" to build engagement.
2. **Delegate decision-making within clear boundaries:** Empower staff to take ownership while providing clear guidelines on escalation points and authority limits.
3. **Recognise and reward efficiency and ownership:** Celebrate staff who follow processes, improve workflows, or proactively address issues. Positive reinforcement strengthens adoption and builds a culture aligned with growth.

Empowered people reduce bottlenecks, increase client satisfaction, and allow leaders to focus on strategy and advisory work rather than firefighting.

Step 6: Implement Growth Discipline

Growth is never "set and forget." Even with strong systems, discipline ensures sustained results.

1. **Conduct quarterly reviews:** Evaluate workflows, profitability, client mix, and technology performance. Assess whether processes are being followed and whether KPIs are being met.
2. **Prune clients or services that drain resources:** Don't hesitate to offboard clients or discontinue services that consistently deliver poor margins or high operational effort.
3. **Adjust staffing, tech, or pricing as required:** Rebalance team capacity, optimise software usage, and reprice services to reflect real costs and value delivered.

Quarterly discipline keeps the firm agile, responsive, and aligned with profit-driven growth goals.

Pitfalls to Avoid

Even with a strong framework, common mistakes can derail growth:

- **Scaling before standardising processes:** Growth on shaky foundations amplifies inefficiency.
- **Adding technology without process clarity:** Automation magnifies chaos if workflows aren't defined.
- **Treating revenue growth as the sole measure of success:** Revenue without margin or efficiency is meaningless.
- **Ignoring cultural and emotional readiness of the team:**

Staff buy-in is essential; growth without people alignment leads to burnout and turnover.

Tools

To make implementation practical, leverage these tools:

- **Workflow documentation template:** Map every service step, owner, timeline, and dependency.
- **Client profitability calculator:** Track revenue, costs, and time per client to identify high-value engagements.
- **Quarterly KPI dashboard:** Monitor turnaround times, WIP, staff utilisation, and client satisfaction.
- **Staff workload planner:** Forecast capacity, redistribute tasks, and prevent overloading.

Putting It All Together

A structured growth approach ensures that each new client, service, or staff member adds value rather than chaos. Begin with a growth readiness audit, standardise processes, align technology, measure profit, empower your team, and enforce quarterly discipline. Combine these steps with tools and checklists, and you'll create a firm capable of scaling predictably, profitably, and sustainably.

The goal is simple: growth that works **because the firm is prepared**, not despite it. Firms that follow this structured implementation approach don't just expand, they thrive. Margins improve, staff feel empowered, clients are happier, and partners can focus on advisory and strategic work rather than handling constant chaos. With clarity, discipline, and consistent execution, measurable profit growth within 12 months becomes an achievable reality.

Summary & Action Steps

Growth is often treated as a goal in itself, but in accounting firms, growth without structure is a risk. Expanding revenue, taking on more clients, or hiring new staff may look impressive on paper, but if your systems, processes, and people aren't prepared, growth can magnify inefficiencies, increase stress, and erode profit. The firms that thrive are those that grow deliberately, with clarity, discipline, and alignment across operations, technology, profitability, and culture.

The first key insight is that **profit, not size, is the true measure of success**. Chasing revenue, client numbers, or headcount can give the illusion of growth, but without healthy margins, the effort of growth may actually cost more than it delivers. Sustainable growth focuses on high-value clients, profitable services, and efficient delivery, ensuring that every hour spent by your team contributes to measurable outcomes.

Efficiency is the foundation for expansion. Before adding clients, services, or staff, processes must be standardised, repeatable, and well-documented. Technology can then amplify these processes, but it should never compensate for unclear workflows. Tools like Xero Practice Manager, FYI, and Ignition, just to name a few, work best when staff know exactly what to do, when to do it, and who is responsible for each step. Without this clarity, automation becomes a source of frustration rather than a multiplier of capacity.

Equally important is the **human side of growth**. Teams thrive when expectations are clear, responsibilities are defined, and staff feel empowered to act within boundaries. Clear communication, workload balance, and structured decision-making prevent burnout and enable leaders to focus on advisory work rather than firefighting. Boundaries for client communication, turnaround times, and partner availability protect both people and profit, allowing the firm to scale confidently.

Finally, growth must be deliberate, monitored, and reviewed regularly. Firms that grow successfully implement quarterly check-ins on workflows, profitability, client mix, and KPIs. They prune low-margin clients or services, adjust staffing and technology as needed, and maintain alignment between strategy and execution. Growth is never "set and forget"; it's a continuous cycle of measurement, improvement, and refinement.

Action Checklist

To turn these principles into action, start with these six steps:

1. **Conduct a 90-day growth readiness audit:** Evaluate workflows, staff capacity, and client profitability to establish a clear baseline.
2. **Map all workflows and assign ownership:** Document every step in each service and define who is responsible for each task.
3. **Review client profitability and service tiers:** Identify high-value clients, adjust pricing where needed, and prune or restructure low-margin engagements.
4. **Standardise processes before adding new clients:** Develop templates, define review points, and document exceptions to ensure repeatable, scalable workflows.
5. **Implement quarterly review cycles:** Track KPIs, process efficiency, client satisfaction, and team workload, and adjust as necessary.
6. **Communicate boundaries clearly:** Make expectations transparent to clients and team members, covering turnaround times, responsibilities, and escalation protocols.

That's a Wrap!

You can't grow successfully if you aren't structured to grow in the right way. You'll break your clients, your team and yourself! Understand your own goals, be clear with your plan, communicate it, take small, actionable steps and get your internal infrastructure set up for success.

Finally, growth must be deliberate, monitored, and reviewed regularly. Firms that grow successfully implement quarterly check-ins on workflows, profitability, client mix, and KPIs. They prune low-margin clients or services, adjust staffing and technology as needed, and maintain alignment between strategy and execution. Growth is never "set and forget"; it's a continuous cycle of measurement, improvement, and refinement.

CHAPTER 3

The Growth Squeeze – Why Success Feels Heavier as You Scale

Toni Eisenhut

Introduction

Context, the Problem, and Why It Matters

Growth in professional services is often framed as the answer. More clients. More staff. More revenue. In accounting firms, growth is typically treated as a proxy for success and security. Yet for many partners, growth brings an unexpected paradox. The business becomes harder to run, not easier. Days fill with questions, approvals, meetings, and unresolved issues. Strategic thinking is crowded out by operational noise. The work that once defined the role of a partner - judgement, direction, and stewardship - is steadily displaced by intervention. The firm does not feel out of control, but it does feel increasingly dependent on the partners' constant presence.

This experience is what I call the Growth Squeeze.

The Growth Squeeze occurs when systems, leadership capacity, and operating structures fail to evolve at the same pace as the firm's growth. Complexity increases faster than clarity. Decision cycles lengthen. Administrative effort expands. Profitability plateaus or declines, even as activity increases. The partner becomes the default problem solver, decision maker, and safety net.

Importantly, the Growth Squeeze is not a sign of incompetence. It is a predictable stage of maturity. Most accounting firms encounter it somewhere between early success and true scale. What worked when the firm was smaller begins to strain under volume, people, and client expectations. Informal processes that once felt flexible become bottlenecks. Personal oversight becomes dependency. Goodwill substitutes for structure until it no longer holds.

At its core, the Growth Squeeze is a failure of operating experience. What leaders say matters is no longer consistently reflected in how the firm actually behaves day to day. Internally, teams escalate rather than decide. Management roles coordinate activity but lack the authority to hold boundaries. Externally, clients push beyond scope, timelines blur, and expectations creep. Execution falters not because people do not care, but because the operating experience does not support aligned behaviour under pressure.

Operating experience is often misunderstood as a mechanical issue. In reality, it is a human system. How decisions are made, who feels safe to exercise judgement, what behaviour is reinforced under pressure, and how consistently the firm shows up for clients all shape the lived experience of the business. When the operating experience is unclear or inconsistent, capable people hesitate, leaders overfunction, and clients feel the friction even if they cannot name it. Teams disengage not because they lack commitment, but because the system does not support confident ownership. Clients push boundaries not because they are difficult, but because expectations are not held consistently. Over time, partners absorb both the operational and emotional load of the firm, becoming the stabilising force that keeps everything moving.

Growth magnifies everything. Unclear accountability becomes decision paralysis. Meetings multiply to compensate for lack of structure. Partners intervene to keep standards intact. None of this is dramatic in isolation. Together, it creates a business that feels heavy. From the outside, the firm may look successful. Internally, it requires constant attention to keep moving.

This pattern is intensifying across the profession in 2026. Margin pressure is no longer theoretical - it is structural. Clients expect certainty, responsiveness, and consistency while fee sensitivity increases. Talent is harder to attract and retain, particularly at senior levels where judgement and client relationship capability matter most. Technology promises efficiency but often adds complexity without reducing partner dependency. At the same time, many firm owners are thinking seriously about sustainability, succession, and their own role in the business. The question is no longer whether the firm can grow. It is whether growth creates freedom or simply more weight to carry.

Firms that do not address the Growth Squeeze either stall under the weight of execution or grow larger without becoming easier to run. Revenue increases. Profit per partner does not. The business expands, but the partners' capacity to lead it does not expand with it. Eventually, the firm reaches a ceiling determined not by market opportunity but by the partners' ability to personally hold the operation together.

The Strategic Freedom Framework™

How the Growth Squeeze Is Resolved

The Growth Squeeze is not a failure. It is a signal. It signals that the firm has reached a point where execution can no longer rely on partners enforcing it personally. The operating experience must be deliberately redesigned so the business can carry its own weight.

I first recognised this pattern during my time as CEO of a large multidisciplinary professional services firm with an active M&A strategy. As we acquired accounting and advisory firms, a consistent theme emerged. These businesses were well run by conventional measures. They had strong margins, loyal clients, and capable operators. Yet their partners' days were increasingly spent unblocking decisions, resolving exceptions, and personally holding standards together. Nothing was broken enough to force a reset. Everything required their attention to keep moving.

Many of these partners were tired, frustrated, and quietly questioning whether the firm they had built was still serving them. Some were actively looking for a joint venture partner or acquirer, not to accelerate growth, but to take the administrative weight off their plate. The issue was not effort or capability. It was design.

Insight alone does not resolve this tension. In fact, insight without structure often increases frustration. Most partners already know where the problems sit. What firms need is a disciplined way to convert clarity into action and to transfer execution ownership into the firm itself.

This is the role of the Strategic Freedom Framework™.

The framework is designed to move accounting firms from partner-dependent execution to a business that operates with embedded ownership and discipline. It does this through three deliberate phases:

- Refocus
- Simplify and Optimise
- Sustain and Scale

These phases are sequential by design. Capacity must be unlocked before it can be protected. Pressure must be relieved before leadership depth can be built.

Many firms missequence this work. They attempt to scale leadership capability before relieving operational pressure, or they optimise processes while authority and accountability remain unclear. In both cases, activity increases but outcomes decay.

A deeper misunderstanding sits beneath most stalled change efforts. Partners often believe capacity has been reclaimed when calendars briefly clear or firefighting subsides. In reality, busyness and capacity are not opposites. A firm can be busy and still fragile. Capacity is only reclaimed when execution no longer relies on personal intervention. Until authority genuinely transfers with responsibility, relief is temporary. Pressure returns, partners step back in, and leadership depth collapses under load.

This is why many improvement initiatives feel effective initially but fade within months. The partner steps back, observes friction or inconsistency, and re-enters execution to protect standards or client relationships. The team interprets this as confirmation that they were not truly trusted with the decision. Authority retreats. The cycle reinforces itself. What looked like progress was actually just temporary delegation, not structural transfer of ownership.

The Strategic Freedom Framework™ exists to convert reclaimed capacity into protected capacity and to ensure that execution ownership stays embedded in the business rather than reverting to the partners under pressure.

Phase 1: Refocus

Refocus includes resetting strategic intent - who the firm is for, how it creates value, and what leadership capacity must now be protected. This creates strategic clarity and identifies where margin and leadership capacity are leaking. When this phase is done well, partners stop reacting.

At this stage, firms step back to see the system clearly rather than responding to symptoms. This includes examining where partner time is consumed, where decisions escalate unnecessarily, and where misalignment between stated priorities and actual behaviour is costing capacity.

The most common mistake at this stage is trying to fix everything at once. Under pressure, leaders add initiatives, tools, or meetings. Activity increases. Relief does not follow. Complexity compounds.

Refocus requires restraint. Leaders must decide what will not be worked on over the next 90 days. They must also confront which parts of the operating experience no longer support the firm's size or ambition.

When Refocus is skipped or rushed, improvement efforts compete with one another. Direction fragments. Partners remain the default escalation point because clarity never fully settles.

When done well, Refocus produces alignment. Leadership teams agree on what matters now. Competing priorities fall away. Hidden margin becomes visible. Decision fatigue reduces because direction is shared.

Phase 2: Simplify and Optimise

Simplify and Optimise is where the operating experience is deliberately redesigned. When this phase is done well, partners stop intervening.

This phase removes friction while embedding discipline. It addresses how work actually moves through the firm, including operating rhythm, delegation and accountability, decision rights, leadership cadence, and scope control.

The objective is reliability, not efficiency theatre. Simplification strips away steps, meetings, and work that do not create value. Optimisation ensures what remains is reinforced through structure rather than goodwill.

Optimisation fails when authority does not move with responsibility. Without clear decision ownership, processes are bypassed under pressure and partners re-enter execution to protect standards.

When simplification occurs without optimisation, gains fade as volume increases and old habits resurface.

When done properly, behaviour changes without constant vigilance. Boundaries hold because the operating experience supports them.

Phase 3: Sustain and Scale

Sustain and Scale ensures the firm performs without partner dependency as complexity increases. When this phase is done well, partners stop being the system.

This phase focuses on leadership depth and capability transfer so execution ownership stays inside the business. Authority is respected. Operating rhythm holds as volume, services, and headcount grow. Reinforcement shows up through how roles are rewarded, standards are held, and consequences are applied when pressure tests the system.

The distinction here is not documentation. It is reinforcement. When this phase is neglected, early improvements regress. Partners re-enter execution during pressure spikes. Leadership depth erodes because the system never fully carried the load.

When Sustain and Scale are done well, reclaimed capacity becomes durable freedom. The firm carries its own weight.

Case Study

Real-World Proof of the Growth Squeeze

A $1.8M accounting firm appeared successful on the surface. Revenue was stable. Client base was loyal. The team was capable and committed. Yet execution relied heavily on partner intervention. Decisions escalated by habit. Write-offs were creeping upward. Meetings consumed time without producing results. Leadership work happened after hours. Nothing was failing, but everything required attention.

Rather than pursuing growth initiatives or adding resources, the firm committed to a deliberate operating reset.

Over a six-month period, the firm redesigned its operating experience end-to-end. This included the introduction of a clear operating rhythm, clear delegation of authority, and an accountability framework that explicitly transferred decision ownership into defined roles. At the same time, the partners reset the firm's strategic foundations, clarifying purpose, vision, mission, values, market positioning, and ideal client focus.

The client service model was restructured around three clear pillars supported by a redesigned delivery model with consistent client service teams. Low-margin and misaligned clients were deliberately transitioned out. Engagement terms, scope control, and time and billing discipline were strengthened. A values-based reward approach and clarified leadership roles reinforced expected behaviour under pressure.

This work was not delivered as a strategy exercise followed by later implementation. The operating rhythm, decision rights, and reinforcement mechanisms were embedded while the strategy was being actively lived inside the business.

The early months were uncomfortable. Partners had to resist stepping back into execution when decisions were made differently to how they would have handled them personally. Standards occasionally dipped below personal thresholds. The temptation to rescue was constant. What shifted outcomes was discipline. Authority was held. Consequences were allowed to teach. The system was permitted to carry the load.

One partner reflected:

> "We didn't need more effort or better people. We needed the business to operate differently. Once authority actually moved into the firm, everything changed - margin, capacity, and how the team showed up."

Once the new operating model was active, the impact became visible.

Comparing the same period year-on-year, revenue remained broadly stable. However, gross margin increased by **16 percentage**

points, driven by tighter scope control, improved client mix, clearer delivery accountability, and reduced write-offs. The improvement reflected structural change in how work was scoped, priced, and delivered.

EBIT shifted materially over the same period, moving from a marginal or loss-making position to a sustainably profitable one. This represented a **20.4 percentage point improvement in EBIT margin**, achieved without material revenue growth or additional headcount.

Just as importantly, leadership capacity was released. With decisions held at the right level and operating rhythm embedded, the firm freed **in excess of 1,500 hours of partner-equivalent capacity annually**. Time previously absorbed by escalation, rework, and intervention was redirected into strategic leadership, client relationships, and higher-value advisory work.

These outcomes were not the result of working harder. They were the result of operating design. Execution ownership moved into the business. Decisions were made where the information sat. Standards were reinforced through structure rather than rescue.

The shift was not only financial. Managers exercised judgement without escalation. Boundaries held without confrontation. Meetings produced decisions rather than reassurance. Clients experienced a calmer, more consistent firm, regardless of partner presence.

Most importantly, the firm no longer relied on partners to hold the line. The operating experience now reinforced ownership, discipline, and accountability by design. The business began to carry its own weight.

Implementation Guide

How Firms Actually Unlock Capacity Without Creating More Work

The Strategic Freedom Framework™ only works when it is treated as an operating reset, not a project. Firms that approach this work as an initiative to be implemented or a checklist to be completed rarely achieve durable change. The firms that succeed treat it as a leadership decision about where attention, authority, and reinforcement will sit going forward.

This distinction matters. The work is not about doing more. It is about stopping the right things, holding fewer priorities, and allowing the operating experience to reset how behaviour is shaped under pressure.

Phase One: Visibility Without Defensiveness

The first requirement is shared visibility. Leadership teams must see the same picture of where time, margin, and attention are being consumed.

Firms typically discover that partner involvement has become structural in areas where it was only ever intended to be transitional. Decisions that should sit with managers escalate by habit, not necessity. Client relationships that once generated strong margin now quietly erode profitability. Meetings that were designed to drive decisions have become forums for updates and reassurance.

This phase often creates discomfort. Partners may feel exposed. Long-standing patterns become visible. The temptation is to defend individual decisions rather than examine the system that produced them.

The critical leadership move at this stage is refusing to personalise the problem. When framed as a system review rather than a performance judgement, resistance falls away and alignment becomes possible. Most partners are relieved to discover that their experience is shared, that the weight they feel is not a personal failure but a predictable consequence of growth outpacing operating design.

What makes this phase difficult is that visibility alone does not resolve anything. In fact, seeing the problem clearly without a structured path forward often increases frustration. Partners know where the issues sit. What they lack is the discipline and external perspective required to prioritise ruthlessly and hold focus when pressure returns.

Success at this stage is not agreement on solutions. It is agreement on where pressure originates and a shared commitment to address root causes rather than symptoms.

Phase Two: Focus Before Improvement

Once visibility exists, focus becomes the constraint. Most firms fail here by trying to fix too much at once. Well-intentioned leaders layer initiatives, believing momentum requires activity. In practice, this fragments attention and weakens reinforcement.

Discipline matters more than enthusiasm. Effective firms identify which structural constraints matter most and create the discipline to hold focus - a decision that requires external perspective and leadership courage. This often means pausing initiatives that are already underway, even when they are well-designed and generating early results.

The discomfort here is real. Partners are accustomed to solving problems through action. Deliberately choosing not to act on known issues feels like negligence. What shifts this mindset is recognising that diffused effort produces diffused outcomes. Concentrated effort on the right constraint unlocks capacity that can then be applied elsewhere.

Simplification follows focus. Meeting structures are examined for decision value, not attendance. Decision rights are clarified so authority is explicit rather than implied. Low-value work is challenged, even when it feels culturally sensitive or historically significant.

This is where many partners struggle most, because stepping back exposes where the system must now hold. If the operating experience is not redesigned to support decision ownership, simplification creates gaps that partners will instinctively fill. The work appears to regress, not because the changes were wrong, but because the system was not ready to carry the load.

What firms underestimate is the emotional discipline required during this phase. Partners must tolerate imperfection, allow consequences to teach rather than intervene, and trust that capability will develop when authority is genuinely transferred. This rarely happens without structured support and external accountability.

Success at this stage feels like relief. Interruptions reduce. Decisions accelerate. Escalation declines. The partners' calendars begin to reflect leadership work rather than operational problem-solving.

Phase Three: Reinforcement Under Pressure

The final phase determines whether change holds. Early improvements are fragile. Without reinforcement, old patterns return quietly. Partners step back in just this once. Exceptions multiply. Authority erodes.

This is where many firms believe the work is complete, only to discover that sustainability requires different capability than implementation. The operating rhythm that was established under focus and discipline must now hold under volume, complexity, and the inevitable pressure spikes that characterise professional services.

This phase is not about adding structure. It is about holding consistency when pressure returns. Leaders must reinforce decision ownership, support outcomes even when imperfect, and resist the urge to rescue. Simple measures are reviewed to maintain visibility, not to create control.

What derails firms at this stage is the assumption that improved performance means the system is now self-sustaining. In reality, behaviour change in professional services firms is slow and requires persistent reinforcement. The team is watching to see whether the new operating experience is genuine or whether the partners will revert to old patterns when stakes increase.

The partners' role shifts here from driving change to modelling trust. When a decision is made that the partner would have handled differently, the response matters more than the outcome. If the partner steps in to correct or override, the message is clear: authority was never truly transferred. If the partner allows the outcome to stand and uses it as a learning moment, capability deepens and confidence builds.

Stability emerges when execution holds without intervention. The firm performs predictably under pressure. Leadership depth becomes visible in how decisions are made when partners are not present. Client experience remains consistent regardless of who is leading the engagement.

Success at this stage is not perfection. It is predictability. The business carries its own weight, and the partners' capacity is protected even as complexity increases.

Action Checklist

Immediate Focus Areas

1. Track partner time for one full week and identify where intervention has become structural rather than exceptional, noting specifically which decisions escalate by habit versus necessity.

2. Identify the lowest-margin segment of the client base and examine why it persists - whether due to relationship history, scope creep, or misalignment between service delivery and fee structure.
3. Audit recurring meetings for decision value by asking what decisions were made in the last three meetings, not who attended or what was discussed.
4. Clarify which decisions should not escalate to partners under any circumstances and observe where authority exists on paper but not in practice.
5. Review write-offs by service line and identify structural contributors - whether due to scope ambiguity, unrealistic timelines, or insufficient delegation.
6. Identify where partners intervene to protect standards and ask whether the intervention addresses a capability gap or a structural design flaw.
7. Select one structural constraint to address in the next 90 days and deliberately pause other improvement initiatives to protect focus.
8. Define how reclaimed capacity will be used before it is unlocked, ensuring it converts to strategic work rather than filling with new operational demands.

Closing Guide

A Signal, Not a Setback

The Growth Squeeze is not a sign that something has gone wrong. It is a signal that the firm has reached a new stage of maturity. Firms that respond deliberately unlock margin, capacity, and leadership headroom without sacrificing standards or culture. Those that ignore it often grow larger while becoming harder to run.

Execution cannot continue to sit with the partners. It must be designed into the business itself. Capacity recovery is the first step.

Strategic freedom follows when clarity, discipline, and ownership produce consistent behaviour under pressure, for leaders, teams, and clients alike.

When the operating experience supports confidence and accountability, firms regain not only margin and capacity, but belief in how the business is meant to operate.

SECTION 2
TURN EFFICIENCY INTO CAPACITY

Use everyday compliance work as the starting point for better pricing, stronger client relationships and higher-value services.

"Price is what you pay. Value is what you get."
— Warren Buffett

Section introduction by Amy Holdsworth

Once the structure of a firm is clear, the next constraint usually becomes visible very quickly: capacity.

Most accounting firms don't struggle because they lack demand. The opposite is usually true. Work is steady, clients need help, and the pipeline rarely looks empty. Yet despite that demand, many firms feel permanently stretched. Turnaround times creep out. Review pressure builds. Teams stay busy but progress feels slow.

In many practices, capacity is treated as a hiring problem. When pressure increases, the instinct is to recruit. Sometimes that is necessary. But hiring alone rarely fixes the underlying issue. If the operating rhythm of a firm is inconsistent, adding more people often increases complexity rather than relieving it.

Capacity is created when work flows predictably.

That requires three things: clarity of roles, visibility of workflow, and systems that remove friction rather than adding to it. Without these, even highly capable teams spend their time waiting, reworking tasks, chasing information, or escalating decisions that should never have needed escalation.

When that pattern persists, a firm can grow in revenue while remaining trapped in the same operational pressure.

This section focuses on improving efficiency to unlock capacity.

The chapter **Does Your Workflow Work** begins by examining how jobs actually travel from start to finish. Many practices believe they have clear processes in place, but those processes often depend on habits rather than a consistent system. Work may begin before all the information is available. Files move backwards and forwards during review. Team members spend time chasing documents or clarifying instructions instead of progressing the job itself. Over time these small inefficiencies accumulate, slowing delivery, and increasing pressure on the people responsible for completing the work.

Improving workflow does not simply mean documenting steps. It requires understanding where work pauses, where responsibility becomes unclear, and where review is being used to compensate for earlier uncertainty. When those issues are addressed, work moves more predictably and the team gains confidence in how the firm operates.

Once workflow becomes clearer, attention turns to the next issue addressed in **Capacity Is the New Currency**. Capacity in a professional practice is often misunderstood as spare time or unused resources. In reality it describes the ability of a firm to carry its workload without constant intervention from the partners. When roles are defined properly and the team understands how work progresses through the firm, responsibility can be shared more effectively. Partners spend less time correcting or completing work themselves and more time guiding the direction of the business.

Creating that capacity does not happen automatically as a firm grows. It requires deliberate choices about team structure, responsibility, and trust. Without those decisions, growth simply increases the volume of work that returns to the same small group of people.

The final chapter in this section, **From Tech Stack to Profit Stack**, considers the role technology plays in supporting these improvements. Most accounting firms already operate with extensive software tools and many are now exploring automation and artificial intelligence. These technologies can reduce manual effort and improve efficiency, but efficiency alone does not strengthen a business.

Together, the chapters in this section focus on a practical goal: improving the way work moves through the firm so that efficiency creates genuine capacity. When that capacity exists, the firm is no longer operating at its limits and the partners gain the space needed to decide how the business should grow next.

CHAPTER 4

Does Your Workflow Work?

Amy Holdsworth

Introduction

Every accounting firm has a workflow. Few have one that actually works. Most firms don't fail because they lack the right apps or people, they fail because their systems quietly collide with their culture. A workflow isn't just a checklist or a sequence of tasks. It's the day-to-day embodiment of how your team thinks, prioritises, and communicates. When that structure drifts, the business starts working against itself. Small inefficiencies compound quickly: minor miscommunications become missed deadlines, overlooked client queries turn into escalations, and staff frustration quietly builds until it becomes turnover or disengagement.

At Clarity Street, we've seen hundreds of firms insist they "have workflow sorted." Yet the same symptoms reappear every year: unfinished jobs, unbilled work in progress, frustrated staff, and clients waiting longer than ever. The problem isn't the software. It's the way people use it, or don't (to be more exact), and how well the workflow aligns with the firm's culture, priorities, and real-world pressures.

This chapter is a straight-talking guide for firm owners who are tired of being reactive. It's based on real client experiences and nearly two decades of helping practices design, test, and actually stick to workflows that free their people instead of trapping them.

The promise is simple: when your workflow works, you reclaim your time. You deliver faster without burning out. You reduce WIP lockup, grow profit margins, and stop firefighting. But to get there, you have to strip workflow down to what it really is, a living system of accountability, clarity, and rhythm. It's about creating a repeatable, predictable structure that your team trusts and your clients notice.

In the next sections, we'll explore why workflow is the nervous system of your firm, how to identify and fix bottlenecks, and how to embed consistency as a measurable habit. By the end of this chapter, you'll understand how structured workflows can transform stress into margin, chaos into calm, and inefficiency into revenue. You'll see that a workflow isn't a static tool, it's the backbone of sustainable growth and profit in your practice.

Core Framework / Method

Workflow as the Nervous System of Your Firm

Think of workflow as your firm's nervous system. It's not just a sequence of tasks or a list of jobs to tick off, it's the connective tissue that links every client interaction, invoice, conversation, and internal decision. When it functions smoothly, information flows effortlessly, everyone knows what's next, and tasks move predictably from one stage to another. When it misfires, even small glitches ripple through the firm: messages get stuck in silos, duplicate work proliferates, and your most capable team members spend their days chasing emails, reminders, and clarifications instead of adding real value.

The reality in most accounting firms is sobering. Most "workflow" is nothing more than overlapping to-do lists scattered across multiple platforms, Xero Practice Manager, FYI, Karbon, Spreadsheets, Trello, and even whiteboards. Each team member has their own idea of "what comes next," and by the time a job reaches review, there are three competing versions, none of which are entirely trusted. This lack of consistency costs time, diminishes morale, and ultimately hits the bottom line. A working workflow isn't about adopting the "right" software, it's about establishing consistency: one way of doing things, one language for progress, and one cadence for review. Without that unity, every new hire or client adds noise, every process handover introduces risk, and the firm's output becomes unpredictable.

The Traditional Cycle (and Why It's Broken)

Most firms operate within a reactive, stop/start cycle. A traditional workflow typically looks like this:

1. The client emails, asking if it's "time to do the accounts."
2. The job starts, but half the information is missing, prompting a request for additional documents.
3. The firm waits.
4. The client eventually responds—but often with incomplete or incorrect documents.
5. The job resumes; the accountant loses context, queries pile up, and inefficiencies multiply.
6. The job is completed, frequently over budgeted hours, with inconsistent billing practices.

Signing and payment are delayed, causing cashflow stress and administrative follow-up.

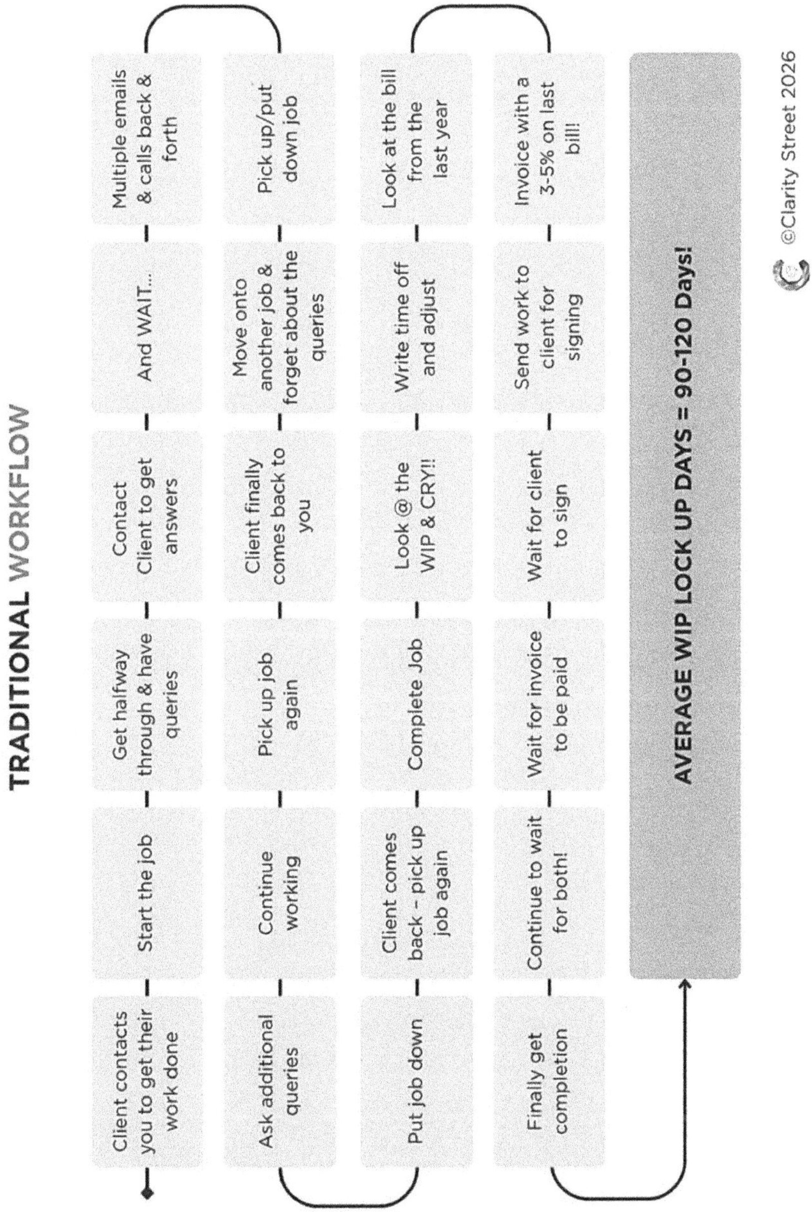
TRADITIONAL WORKFLOW
Client contacts you to get their work done
Start the job
Get halfway through & have queries
Contact Client to get answers
And WAIT...
Multiple emails & calls back & forth
Pick up/put down job
Move onto another job & forget about the queries
Client finally comes back to you
Pick up job again
Continue working
Ask additional queries
Put job down
Client comes back – pick up job again
Complete Job
Look @ the WIP & CRY!!
Write time off and adjust
Look at the bill from the last year
Invoice with a 3-5% on last bill!
Send work to client for signing
Wait for client to sign
Wait for invoice to be paid
Continue to wait for both!
Finally get completion
AVERAGE WIP LOCK UP DAYS = 90-120 Days!
©Clarity Street 2026

The hidden cost isn't just time, it's momentum. Every restart steals 15–30 minutes of re-orientation. Multiply that across hundreds of jobs each year, and you're looking at weeks of lost productivity, reduced realisation, and hidden WIP costs. This "normalised chaos" is the silent profit killer in most accounting firms.

The Perfect Client Life Cycle

The solution is a structured, proactive client life cycle:

- **Proactive scheduling:** Every client's work is scheduled in advance, with clear deadlines.
- **Information request:** Standardised portals or checklists are sent six weeks before work is due to begin.
- **Scoping:** Accountants review submissions, identify gaps, and confirm scope and pricing.
- **Proposal and payment:** Clients approve scoped work via apps like Ignition, with upfront or milestone billing.
- **Preparation:** Work begins on schedule with all required information in place.
- **Review:** Queries are handled in batches, not piecemeal.
- **Signing and billing:** Documents are sent via apps such as FuseSign or Annature for e-signature; invoices trigger automatically.
- **Completion:** Admin monitors payments, closes jobs, and updates dashboards for visibility.

BEST PRACTICE WORKFLOW

Accountant	View & Complete Workschedule + Meeting
Admin	Contact Client for Info – Follow up until arrival into the office
Accountant	Scope the Work
Admin	Prepare Proposal, Send to Client
Admin	PROPOSAL ACCEPTED
Accountant/Admin	**Schedule & Process Relevant Work to ensure 14 DAY (compliance work) TURNAROUND**
Accountant	Queries Answered
Accountant	Review Work
Admin	Prepare Documents for signing
Director/Admin	Meeting to present work to client / Email work to client

The difference isn't complexity, it's discipline. Simple, visible, repeatable steps reduce friction, create predictability, and free your team from the constant stress of firefighting.

Why Most Workflow Projects Fail

Workflow improvement projects often die quietly within six months. It's rarely due to a lack of intelligence, tools, or effort; it's almost always a lack of ownership and accountability. The mistake many firms make is treating workflow initiatives as IT projects rather than as behavioural and cultural shifts. Simply implementing Karbon, FYI, or another platform and assuming staff will follow because "it's in the system" doesn't work. People revert to old habits (typically the use of multiple spreadsheets) if the new process isn't embedded into daily routines, reinforced by leadership, and actively monitored.

A functional workflow balances four critical dimensions:

- **Process clarity:** One documented way of working, written in plain language, so everyone knows the exact steps.
- **Role ownership:** Every task is tied to a position or role, not a single person, ensuring continuity when staff change or are absent.
- **Technology alignment:** Tools are selected and configured to support the process. They don't dictate it or create additional complexity.
- **Cultural rhythm:** Meetings, check-ins, and regular reviews reinforce the workflow and make it a living system rather than a static document.

Miss any of these dimensions, and the workflow begins to drift. Optional or neglected systems always lose to urgent tasks, firefighting, or informal shortcuts. Without anchoring workflow to human habits, communication norms, and firm culture, even the most elegant processes will eventually collapse, leaving the firm back in reactive chaos. The difference between a temporary "fix" and a sustainable workflow lies in ownership, reinforcement, and accountability.

Four Pillars of a Workflow That Works

A truly functional workflow rests on four pillars. Each is essential, and together they transform what is often a static checklist into a living, measurable system that drives clarity, accountability, and profitability.

Process: Start by mapping every client journey from onboarding to completion. Identify and remove points of double handling, unnecessary steps, or ambiguity. Define precisely what "ready for review" looks like, so no task is left in limbo. When processes are documented and standardised, staff know exactly what to do next, reducing errors and delays.

People: Workflow only works when responsibilities are clear. Use a simple RACI (Responsible, Accountable, Consulted, Informed) framework to clarify responsibilities.

: who **does** the task, who **reviews** it, who **approves**, and who ultimately **owns the outcome**. This ensures accountability without micromanagement and creates continuity even when team members are absent. Roles, not individuals, carry the work forward.

Platform: Keep your technology stack lean. Every tool should have a clear purpose, trained users, and documented standard operating procedures. Avoid orphan applications, feature bloat, and overlapping tools, as these add friction and confusion rather than solving it. The right platforms should integrate and amplify your process, not dictate it.

Profit: Workflow exists to serve the business, not just complete tasks. Track key metrics weekly, cycle time, WIP lockup, realisation, and debtor days. These numbers highlight inefficiencies and opportunities for improvement. Profit-focused measurement ensures the system aligns with financial outcomes, not just task completion.

Anchored correctly, these four pillars create a workflow that's visible, accountable, and controlled. Teams operate with clarity, leaders gain insight without micromanaging, and the firm's rhythm becomes predictable, scalable, and profitable. Workflow stops being a source of stress and becomes a strategic advantage.

Resetting Client Expectations

One of the simplest but most overlooked levers for improving workflow and firm profitability is resetting client expectations. Clear, consistent communication saves hundreds of hours every year and prevents small inefficiencies from ballooning into major stress points. A standard script such as:

"Before we begin, we'll request documents (via our portal) by Friday. Once received, turnaround is 14–28 days / 4-6 weeks. Anything outside the agreed scope will be flagged before proceeding."

It may seem basic, but it accomplishes several crucial things. First, it sets boundaries. Clients know exactly what to provide and when. Second, it establishes predictable timelines, removing ambiguity that often leads to repeated follow-ups. Third, it creates mutual accountability: the firm can manage workflow without constantly chasing information, and the client understands their role in keeping jobs on track.

Scripts like this can extend across all client touchpoints: onboarding, scope changes, billing, and sign-off. When every team member uses the same language, the client experience is unified, and staff no longer feel responsible for micromanaging expectations. Over time, this consistency reduces errors, WIP lockup, and client frustration while boosting the firm's credibility.

Technology: Integration Beats Accumulation

Technology should amplify a well-designed workflow, not compensate for poor processes. Adopting software strategically is critical:

- **Workflow:** XPM, FYI, Karbon or AccountKit - pick one and use it consistently.
- **Documents:** FYI or SuiteFiles - standardise structure, access, and naming conventions.
- **Proposals:** Ignition - ensure clients approve scope and pay promptly, eliminating invoice lag.
- **Signatures:** FuseSign or Annature - streamline e-signatures, reducing manual follow-up.

For more app choices, refer to our app stack image on the last page of this chapter. Follow three golden rules:

1. **No orphan apps:** Where possible, every app should integrate, must have a designated owner and standard operating procedures.
2. **No duplication:** Remove overlapping apps to prevent conflicting data.
3. **No stealth rollout:** Pilot in a sandbox, train staff, and launch cleanly to avoid confusion.

Consistency: The Real Measure

Speed alone doesn't impress clients; reliability does. Track these metrics weekly:

- Job Turnaround Time: Average days from job start to completion, < 14-28 days
- Recovery Rate: Invoiced amount vs time cost, > 85%
- On-Time + Overall Lodgement %: Percentage of compliance work lodged by due date, > 95%
- Staff Time Entry Compliance: % of time entries completed daily, > 95%,

Predictability drives profitability. Consistency compounds: fewer errors, faster WIP turnover, improved cash flow, and higher client trust translate directly into stronger margins. By combining clear expectations, disciplined use of technology, and relentless consistency, firms convert workflow from a stress point into a competitive advantage, freeing staff and partners to focus on value.

Case Study / Example

Firm X is a regional accounting practice in Victoria, managing a team of seven people. Their workload included approximately 1500 tax returns annually, alongside a portfolio of advisory clients. On paper, everything seemed manageable, but behind the scenes, the firm was struggling with inefficiencies that were quietly eroding profit, team morale, and client satisfaction. Each partner maintained their own spreadsheets to track work, resulting in multiple versions of the same data. Admin staff were reactive, responding to emails and client queries as they arrived rather than following a structured workflow. Review bottlenecks were constant, creating last-minute fire drills and uneven workloads. Stress levels were high, WIP was locked up, and partner hours were being consumed by routine operational work instead of high-value advisory tasks.

Step 1: Assessment

The first step in transforming Firm X's workflow was a comprehensive assessment of existing processes and bottlenecks. The top three service lines, tax returns, BAS/IAS, and advisory projects, were mapped from start to finish. Each client journey was documented in detail, identifying where work stalled, where duplication occurred, and where errors most frequently appeared.

An audit of the firm's technology stack revealed multiple "orphan apps" and overlapping platforms. For example, separate spreadsheets, and task lists existed alongside Karbon and XPM, but no single system was being used consistently. Removing redundant tools was critical to simplify workflows and avoid confusion.

Ownership of each workflow step was then defined. Instead of leaving accountability with individuals or assuming someone would pick up tasks, every step, from client onboarding to document submission, preparation, review, signing, and billing, was assigned to a role rather than a person. This created clarity and eliminated the guesswork that previously slowed the team down.

Step 2: Standardisation

Once the assessment highlighted gaps and inefficiencies, the firm moved to standardise processes. Weekly workflow huddles were introduced, creating a predictable rhythm where team members could review priorities, check progress, and flag potential delays. This regular cadence reduced reliance on ad-hoc emails and increased visibility across all tasks.

All new work now required upfront acceptance through Ignition, ensuring the scope, fees, and timelines were agreed upon before any work began. Task batching was introduced by type; similar jobs were grouped together to reduce cognitive load and context-switching. Turnaround times were set for each service line, making deadlines predictable and creating clear expectations for both staff and clients.

Standardisation also extended to documentation. Templates were created for recurring tasks, and processes were simplified to remove unnecessary steps. Exceptions were documented separately to prevent adhoc workarounds from becoming the default. Staff were trained to follow these standard workflows, ensuring consistency and eliminating the variability that previously created bottlenecks.

Step 3: Embedding Rhythm

Standardisation alone was not enough; the firm needed to embed a rhythm that made workflow habitual. Short, digestible training videos were created for staff to explain the new processes and tools. Staff could refer to these on demand, which reinforced learning without overloading team members.

Metrics were tracked weekly to monitor the impact of changes. Key indicators included WIP lockup, realisation, debtor days, lodgement targets and cycle times. The bottom 10 percent of clients, identified as low-margin or high-maintenance, were repriced or offboarded. This helped focus resources on clients who contributed positively to profitability and allowed the team to work more predictably.

Cultural changes accompanied the operational changes. Staff were encouraged to batch their work, take advantage of time blocking to focus without interruption, and respect deadlines. Partners reduced micromanagement by trusting that the system would ensure visibility and accountability.

Outcome (90 Days)

The transformation of Firm X's workflow produced measurable results within just three months:

- **WIP lockup** fell by 35 percent, freeing up working capital and reducing stress on admin staff.
- **Partner hours** in routine delivery work dropped by 12 per week, allowing more focus on high-value advisory projects.
- **Team stress levels** decreased, engagement improved, and the workplace became calmer and more predictable.
- **Profit margins** increased by 18 percent due to better efficiency, reduced rework, and repricing of low-margin clients.
- **Client experience** improved as deadlines were consistently met, communication became predictable, and turnaround times stabilised.

Firm X didn't simply adopt software; they embraced rhythm, discipline, and accountability. By linking workflow to culture, they created a system where the process worked for the team, rather than the team working around the process.

Key Lessons from Firm X

1. **Workflow is rhythm, not just software** – Technology supports processes, but only when used consistently within a structured workflow.
2. **Ownership is essential** – Assigning roles rather than relying on individuals creates clarity, accountability, and predictability.
3. **Metrics drive behaviour** – Tracking WIP, cycle times, and realisation weekly reinforces adherence and highlights issues early.
4. **Standardisation reduces friction** – Templates, checklists, and upfront client acceptance eliminate wasted effort and

repetitive queries.

5. **Cultural alignment is critical** – Staff buy-in and habit formation are just as important as technology in making workflow sustainable.

Why This Approach Works

Workflow transformation is often misunderstood as an IT or software project. Firm X demonstrates that the true driver of efficiency and profitability is human behaviour combined with structured processes. By standardising, embedding rhythm, and tracking metrics, the firm turned a reactive, chaotic environment into a predictable, high-performing practice. The results show that investment in workflow, not just people or software, can deliver tangible profit growth, reduced stress, and better client experiences within a very short timeframe.

Implementation Guide

Implementation Guide: 90-Day Workflow Reset Plan

Rebuilding your workflow isn't just about introducing software or creating a few templates; it's about deliberately designing a system that aligns process, people, technology, and profitability. A structured 90-day approach helps embed rhythm, accountability, and measurable results. This implementation guide breaks down the reset into three phases: Audit & Align, Simplify & Standardise, and Embed & Measure.

Days 1–30: Audit & Align

Objective: Understand exactly how the work flows through your firm, where it stalls, and who owns what. This phase is about visibility and clarity.

1. **Map client journeys**
    a. List your top three services by volume and revenue.

   b. Document each step a client takes from onboarding to completion, including all admin, preparation, review, signing, and billing stages.
   c. Include touchpoints like emails, portal submissions, and phone calls.
2. **Identify bottlenecks and delays**
   a. Track where jobs stop or slow down.
   b. Note recurring issues such as missing information, unclear handovers, or duplicate work.
   c. Calculate the average delay time at each stage to understand lost productivity.
3. **Review your tech stack**
   a. List every tool your firm uses for workflow, documents, proposals, time tracking, and billing.
   b. Identify duplicates or "orphan apps" with unclear ownership or integrations.
   c. Decide which systems to keep, consolidate, or remove. Technology should reflect the workflow, not compensate for chaos.
4. **Assign ownership for every step**
   a. Define roles, not individuals, for every workflow step. Use a RACI (Responsible, Accountable, Consulted, Informed) framework to clarify responsibilities.
   b. Ensure that every task has a clear owner who understands what is expected and by when.
   c. Communicate these responsibilities to the team so accountability is visible and unambiguous.

Outcome: By the end of this phase, you should have a complete map of your client journeys, a clear understanding of where work stalls, a streamlined technology stack, and clearly defined ownership across all tasks.

Days 31–60: Simplify & Standardise

Objective: Eliminate variability, reduce errors, and create repeatable processes that the team can rely on. Standardisation is the foundation of efficiency.

1. **Write a one-page workflow playbook**
    a. Condense the mapped client journeys into a simple, easy-to-read document.
    b. Include clear steps for preparation, review, communication, and escalation.
    c. Add exceptions or edge cases on a separate page to avoid adhoc decisions becoming the norm.
2. **Introduce weekly workflow huddles**
    a. Schedule a 30–45 minute meeting each week to review progress, upcoming deadlines, and bottlenecks.
    b. Encourage team members to raise issues proactively rather than waiting for tasks to fail.
    c. Use this time to reinforce standards, celebrate completed work, and maintain rhythm.
3. **Move all new jobs to upfront acceptance via Ignition**
    a. Send proposals with scope, pricing, and timelines before work begins.
    b. Require client approval and payment milestones to lock in commitments and reduce WIP lockup.
    c. Ensure that every new engagement enters the workflow with clarity from the start.
4. **Protect two hours of "maker time" daily**
    a. Block uninterrupted work time for each staff member to focus on preparation and review tasks.
    b. Avoid adhoc interruptions or meetings during these periods to maintain flow.
    c. Encourage batching of similar tasks to minimise cognitive switching.

Outcome: At the end of this phase, your firm will have standardised processes, predictable work intake, fewer interruptions, and a team that understands the rhythm of workflow. Staff confidence and engagement should already be improving.

Days 61–90: Embed & Measure
Objective: Make the workflow habitual, measure its effectiveness, and adjust based on data. Embedding is where discipline meets profit.

1. **Train the team using videos and task links**
    a. Short, accessible training materials ensure everyone knows the new process.
    b. Include SOPs (Standard Operating Procedures), checklists, and task-specific instructions.
    c. Reinforce expectations through repetition and on-the-job practice.
2. **Measure turnaround, WIP, and realisation weekly**
    a. Use a KPI dashboard to track performance metrics, including:
        i. WIP lockup
        ii. Turnaround time for each job
        iii. Realisation rates versus budgeted hours
        iv. Debtor days and payment timelines
    b. Identify areas where performance lags and implement corrective actions.
3. **Prune misfit clients and reprice where needed**
    a. Analyse client profitability and contribution to workflow efficiency.
    b. Offboard clients who consistently require disproportionate effort or reduce profitability.
    c. Reprice low-margin clients to reflect the effort required, aligning revenue with resource allocation.

4. **Celebrate wins visibly**
    a. Recognise teams and individuals who consistently follow the workflow.
    b. Share improvements in metrics with staff to reinforce positive behaviour.
    c. Use small wins to maintain momentum and build a culture of consistency.

Outcome: By the end of 90 days, the firm should have a fully embedded, measurable workflow with clear accountability, predictable client delivery, and improved team confidence. WIP lockup, cycle times, and revenue realisation should show tangible improvement.

Checklists & Tools

To help embed these changes, use these practical resources:

- **Workflow documentation template** – Map every client journey, include roles, steps, and timelines.
- **Client profitability calculator** – Segment clients by revenue, margin, and effort required.
- **Weekly KPI dashboard** – Track WIP, realisation, cycle times, debtor days, and staff efficiency.
- **Staff workload planner** – Assign tasks, protect "maker time," and monitor utilisation across the team.

These tools make the workflow visible, actionable, and measurable, transforming it from an abstract concept into a daily operational reality.

Pitfalls to Avoid

Even with the best plan, firms often stumble if they make common mistakes:

1. **Treating workflow as an IT project**
   a. Workflow is a behavioural and cultural change, not just a software implementation.
   b. Success requires ownership, reinforcement, and discipline.
2. **Ignoring human behaviour and culture**
   a. Staff habits and attitudes determine whether a system sticks.
   b. Engage the team, explain the "why," and reinforce new behaviours consistently.
3. **Adding technology before process clarity**
   a. Don't assume new software will fix inefficiencies.
   b. Define clear processes first; technology should support, not dictate, workflow.
4. **Measuring revenue alone**
   a. Revenue growth without efficiency or margin improvement is meaningless.
   b. Track WIP, realisation, cycle times, and client satisfaction to capture true profitability.

Beyond 90 Days: Sustaining the Gains

A successful 90-day reset is the foundation, not the finish line. To maintain momentum:

- Continue weekly huddles and metrics tracking.
- Review KPIs quarterly and adjust SLAs, tech, or client mix as needed.
- Reinforce culture by celebrating milestones and integrating workflow training into onboarding for new staff.
- Maintain a lean tech stack; avoid adding tools without a clear process rationale.

Sustained discipline and regular review turn workflow from

a reactive, chaotic system into a predictable, profit-generating engine. Firms that do this consistently see faster turnaround, reduced stress, higher margins, and more time for advisory work.

Summary

The 90-Day Workflow Reset Plan is designed to transform your firm from reactive to proactive. Audit & Align clarifies your current state and assigns accountability. Simplify & Standardise reduces variability and introduces rhythm. Embed & Measure ensures habits stick, metrics are tracked, and client profitability is optimised. Using tools, checklists, and disciplined practices, firms can achieve measurable improvements in efficiency, profit, and team morale within just three months. Avoiding common pitfalls ensures workflow remains a living system rather than a forgotten IT project.

By committing to this structured plan, firms turn chaos into calm, WIP into profit, and reactive firefighting into proactive, predictable growth.

Key Takeaways & Action Steps

A functional workflow is the nervous system of your firm. It connects every client interaction, every internal task, and every financial transaction. Without it, work slows, WIP accumulates, and margins suffer. Jobs get lost in email chains, requests go unanswered, and your smartest people spend time chasing rather than delivering. The good news is that this isn't an inevitable state, workflow can be fixed, measured, and optimised.

Workflow is more than just software. It's the combination of **process clarity, role ownership, technology alignment, and cultural rhythm**. Process clarity ensures everyone knows the steps and expectations. Role ownership prevents ambiguity, assigning responsibilities to positions rather than relying on individual memory. Technology alignment ensures tools amplify the process rather than introducing chaos. And cultural rhythm, regular check-ins, huddles, and reviews, keeps the system alive and reinforces accountability. Miss one of these pillars, and the system drifts, optional systems lose to urgency, and chaos creeps back in.

Discipline beats complexity. Simple, repeatable habits such as proactive scheduling, upfront information requests, and batch processing reduce friction and minimise stop/start work. They give staff clarity and focus while giving clients predictable timelines. Scripts for client communications, clear scope agreements, and standardised acceptance procedures eliminate unnecessary follow-ups and reduce misunderstandings. When every job flows according to a known rhythm, momentum is preserved, WIP lockup falls, and revenue becomes more predictable.

Consistency compounds. Clients don't value speed alone, they value reliability. Regular, dependable delivery, predictable billing, and transparent expectations build trust. When a firm can consistently meet turnaround times, process work without rework, and track key metrics like WIP, realisation, and debtor days, efficiency grows and profits rise. Predictability is profit in disguise, and the results of a consistent workflow are cumulative over time: fewer errors, lower stress, and a stronger reputation.

Workflow works when it's anchored to human habits, not just tools. Technology is an enabler, not a solution. Pick a thin stack, train staff thoroughly, and remove duplication. Embed habits through team rhythm, protected "maker time," and visible metrics. Celebrate wins to reinforce behaviour. The workflow should feel natural, freeing your team to focus on value rather than firefighting.

Action Checklist

- Audit workflows for your top three services; map every step, every owner, and every dependency.
- Remove redundant technology and assign clear ownership for the remaining tools.
- Standardise client communication, scope, and acceptance procedures; implement scripts where needed.
- Introduce weekly workflow huddles and protect focused work periods for uninterrupted preparation and review.
- Track WIP lockup, turnaround times, realisation, and debtor days weekly; identify and correct bottlenecks.
- Prune or reprice low-margin clients; focus resources on profitable, high-value engagements.
- Celebrate workflow wins visibly to reinforce adoption and boost team morale.

A working workflow isn't about control, it's about **liberation**. It frees your team from chaos, gives clients clarity and reliability, and maximises profit. Firms that master workflow don't just survive the day-to-day; they grow sustainably, calmly, and profitably. By focusing on discipline, consistency, and alignment, workflow becomes a powerful engine for growth, margin improvement, and long-term firm success.

That's a Wrap!

A working workflow isn't about control, it's about liberation. It frees your team from chaos, gives clients clarity and reliability, and maximises profit. Firms that master workflow don't just survive the day-to-day; they grow sustainably, calmly, and profitably. By focusing on discipline, consistency, and alignment, workflow becomes a powerful engine for growth, margin improvement, and long-term firm success.

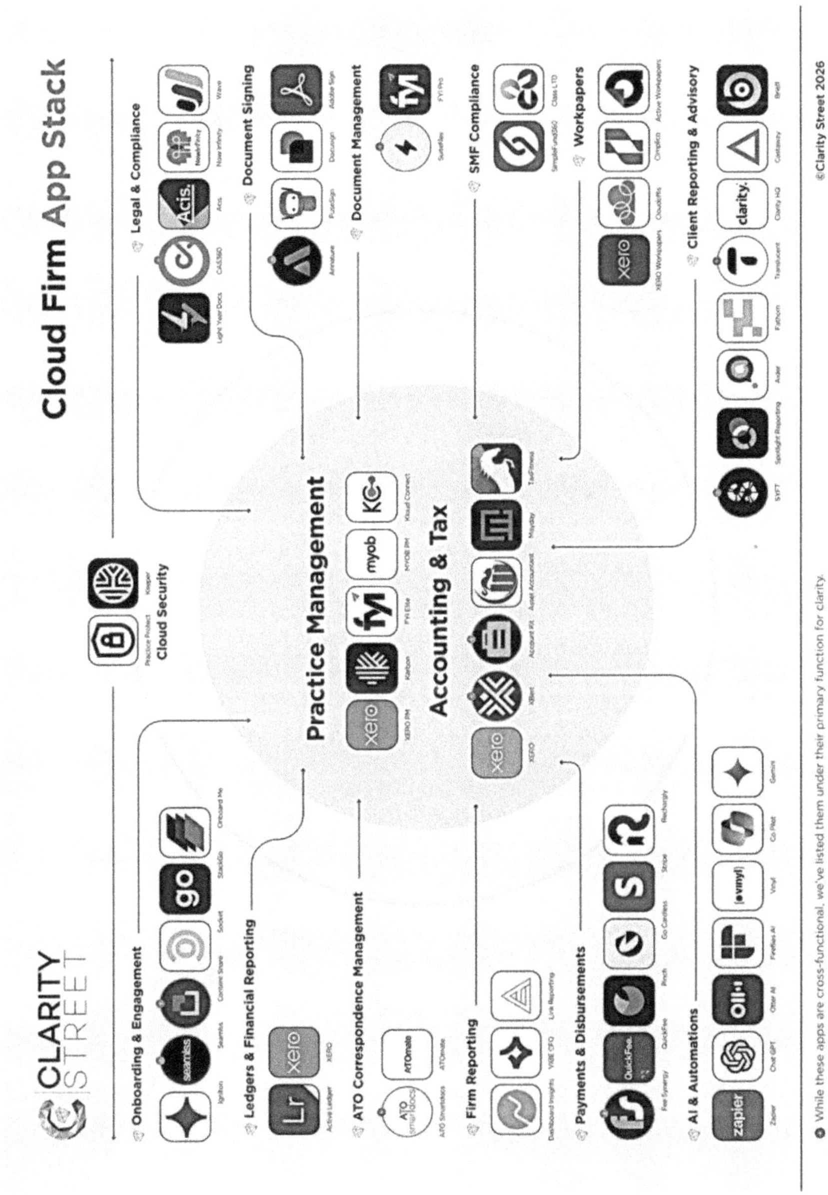
CLARITY STREET
Cloud Firm App Stack
Onboarding & Engagement
Ledgers & Financial Reporting
ATO Correspondence Management
Firm Reporting
Payments & Disbursements
AI & Automations
Cloud Security
Practice Management
Accounting & Tax
Legal & Compliance
Document Signing
Document Management
SMF Compliance
Workpapers
Client Reporting & Advisory
While these apps are cross-functional, we've listed them under their primary function for clarity.
©Clarity Street 2026

CHAPTER 5

Capacity Is the New Currency – How to Build a Team That Runs Without You

Kyelie Baxter

Introduction

The barriers to entry are low. Software is accessible. Cloud systems do most of the heavy lifting. You can be up and running with a laptop, a decent internet connection, and a handful of clients in a surprisingly short amount of time.

That's the good news.

The less exciting news is that running a sustainable firm has never been harder.

Most modern accounting practices are lean by design. Owners run slim teams, keep overheads tight, and run a lot themselves — particularly in the early years. That model works well… until it very suddenly doesn't.

The pressure point usually shows up in the same place:

- Reviews
- Decisions
- Client service

At some point, everything starts to bottleneck with you.

You're the final reviewer.

You're the escalation point.

You're the one clients want to speak to "just quickly" — which, as we all know, is never actually quick.

And while this feels very familiar in accounting, it's not unique to our profession. Ask any partner in a law firm, consulting practice, or professional services business and you'll hear the same story. Hiring one person rarely removes one person's workload in the short term — it usually reshapes it and adds a few new meetings to your calendar.

This is where capacity becomes the real constraint.

Not demand.

Not revenue.

Not even technology.

Capacity.

When firm owners feel stretched, the instinctive response is often to hire. And sometimes that is the right move. But hiring is expensive. Training takes time. And in lean firms especially, adding people often increases review pressure before it relieves it.

You spend more time reviewing.

More time explaining.

More time answering "sorry, just one more question".

And if the hire doesn't work out — which happens more often than we like to admit — the cost isn't just financial. It's cultural.

Hiring fast and firing fast might look efficient on paper, but it leaves scars. Teams become hesitant. Trust erodes. People stop feeling safe to make decisions. And suddenly, even more things come back to you.

The irony is that many firm owners don't actually want to be involved in everything. They just don't see another way to protect quality and client relationships.

So they stay available.

They stay responsive.

They stay in the loop.

And over time, availability quietly becomes dependency.

This chapter is about breaking that pattern — not by disengaging, but by designing capacity properly.

Not so you can disappear… but so the firm can run differently, more efficiently, and so you can redirect your energy to the parts of the business where it genuinely adds the most value.

The Framework

Let's start with a gentle but uncomfortable truth.

If your firm feels busy, stretched, or overly dependent on you, it's probably not because your team isn't capable. It's because capacity — real capacity — hasn't been designed. It's been allowed to evolve organically, which some people may refer to as the polite way of saying "chaotically"… which of course I would never say out loud.

Most firm owners don't set out to become the bottleneck. It just happens, one small decision at a time.

You answer a question because it's quicker.

You review something "just this once" because it's important.

You jump on a call because the client asked specifically for you.

None of those decisions are wrong in isolation. But together, they quietly shape a firm that runs on your availability rather than its systems.

And yes — people often say, "It's just quicker if I do it myself."

I'm not going to argue with you. You're right.

That one time.

But if you use that argument every single time, you are absolutely wrong when you add up the cost over weeks, months, and years.

Doing something yourself might save five minutes today. But documenting it once — whether that's a short Loom video, a walkthrough, or a clear explanation — saves hours of future interruptions, rework, and mental load.

More importantly, our teams want to learn. They want

autonomy. They want to be able to assist clients properly, in real time, without having to "just quickly check with you" every time something slightly unfamiliar comes up.

Capacity isn't just about speed. It's about trust and transfer.

Capacity isn't about headcount.

One of the biggest myths in professional services is that capacity problems are solved by hiring more people.

If that were true, firms would get calmer every time they hired. We all know that's not how it works.

In reality, hiring often reduces capacity in the short term. You spend more time explaining, reviewing, correcting, and answering questions that start with, "Sorry, just checking…"

And suddenly, the thing you hired for — relief — feels further away than ever.

I always have a quiet giggle when people compare accounting firms by headcount. I do it too — just not in the way most people do.

Many assume bigger is better. More staff must mean a better firm.

I look at it differently.

If two firms have the same fee base, and one achieves it with fewer people, I'd argue that firm is often running better systems, clearer workflows, and stronger decision-making — assuming accuracy and service are still high.

Headcount isn't a badge of honour.

Capacity efficiency is.

The Capacity Stack: how teams actually create (or destroy) capacity

Over time, I've come to think about team capacity as a stack. When all layers are in place, the firm runs smoothly. When one is missing, everything slides back to the owner.

There are four layers.

1) Clarity: What does "good" look like without you?

If your team regularly checks in to ask whether something is "right", that's rarely a confidence issue. It's usually a clarity issue.

People can't meet expectations that only exist in your head.

Clarity means:

- consistent standards
- clear review expectations
- shared understanding of what actually matters

Clarity looks like:

- A "definition of done" for each service (BAS, tax, payroll, FBT)
- A clear workflow so people know the next step without guessing
- Templates and examples that show what "standard work" is

Clarity sounds like:

- "I know what the outcome needs to be before I start."
- "I've checked it against our standard and I'm comfortable with it."
- "This doesn't meet the escalation rule, so I'm handling it."

This is also where onboarding matters far more than most firm owners realise.

Onboarding isn't something you get through once someone starts. It's the foundation for whether that person will ever genuinely reduce your workload.

If onboarding is rushed, inconsistent, or treated as something people "pick up as they go", you're almost guaranteed to recreate the bottleneck you were trying to solve.

I always say procedure manuals should be living documents. Procedures aren't meant to just exist — they need to be lived. If they only come out during onboarding or audits, they're not doing their job.

If you find yourself saying, "I'll just have a quick look," that's often a sign clarity hasn't been embedded yet — not that your team isn't capable.

2) Capability: skills plus judgement

Capability isn't just about technical skill. It's about judgement.

It's the ability to understand:

- what matters most
- where risk actually sits
- when to act, and when to pause

I'm completely comfortable with team members saying, "I don't know — I need to check and get back to you."

That's not weakness. That's professionalism.

We work in a complex industry. We are not expected to know everything instantly. What matters is that people know how to find the answer, apply judgement, and come back confidently.

True capability includes knowing when to stop and think.

Capability looks like:

- People knowing the "why", not just the steps
- Staff recognising when something is unusual or higher risk
- The ability to explain something to a client without panicking

Capability sounds like:

- "This is what the numbers are showing, and this is why it matters."
- "I'm comfortable proceeding, but I'll confirm the tax

treatment before we lodge."
- "I've checked the process and here's what I'm recommending."

3) Confidence: trust is a commercial decision

If your team escalates everything, sometimes it's because you've trained them to.

Every time you override a decision without explanation, quietly fix something, or jump in "just to be safe", you send a clear message:

Don't decide. I will.

Confidence doesn't come from telling people to "own it". It comes from knowing they're trusted to make reasonable decisions — and supported if they don't get it perfectly right every time.

This is where sharing the hero work matters.

When people are trusted with meaningful responsibility, they rise to it. And they love it. Confidence grows when teams are allowed to do work that matters, not just tasks that feel safe.

Confidence looks like:

- People bringing you their thinking, not just their problem
- Escalation happening for the right reasons (risk, judgement, client impact)
- Staff being comfortable saying "I'll confirm and come back to you"

Confidence sounds like:

- "Here's what I'm thinking and why — can you confirm I'm on the right track?"
- "I made a call based on our process and documented it."
- "This is within my authority, so I've handled it."

4) Containment: knowing everything vs knowing what matters

Let me be very clear here, because this matters.

I do maintain oversight of client work. Quality, accuracy, and professional standards are non-negotiable. That responsibility ultimately sits with me, and I take it seriously.

What I don't do is involve myself in every operational detail.

- I don't read every file note.
- I don't sit in every client conversation.
- I don't weigh in on every decision that doesn't materially change the outcome.

That's not disengagement. That's intentional design.

The difference is how oversight happens.

I operate at the right altitude.

That means:

- clear standards so the team knows what's expected before work reaches me
- structured checkpoints rather than constant ad-hoc interruptions
- focus on risk, judgement, and client outcomes — not commentary on every step taken

Personally, I use systems that support this visibility. I receive structured file notes and AI-generated meeting summaries with sentiment indicators. It's effectively a triage layer.

Low sentiment doesn't automatically mean there's a problem. Sometimes a client is simply unhappy about paying tax — which usually means the business is doing well.

What matters is context.

When I look at those summaries, I can quickly see whether issues were explained properly, expectations were managed, and judgement was applied appropriately. If something needs attention, I know exactly where to focus.

This is what containment looks like in practice.

The firm doesn't rely on me being involved in everything. It relies on systems, standards, and people doing good work — with clear oversight and accountability.

From hero to designer

The goal of this framework isn't to remove you from the business. It's to change your role within it.

From being:

- the hero
- the fixer
- the default answer

To being:

- the designer of how work flows
- the protector of capacity
- the high-level reviewer who knows where to focus

When you do that, something shifts.

The firm doesn't just run without you — it runs differently, more efficiently, and in a way that allows you to redirect your energy where it creates the most value.

And that's when capacity stops leaking and starts compounding.

Every time capacity collapses back onto the owner, profit is capped. Not because fees are wrong, but because the firm cannot scale its decision-making.

Capacity design is not a leadership preference — it's a commercial necessity.

Designing capacity in a firm where people come and go

Finding and keeping good people has been one of the biggest challenges of running a firm.

Staff are transient. Competition is strong. And even with a hybrid model — where only half of my team works in the office and just one person is fully office-based — change is simply part of reality. Hiring well still matters, but over time it became clear that hiring alone was not a reliable way to protect capacity.

For a long time, my solution was me.

If someone left, I stepped in. I picked up their work, reviewed more, answered more questions, and carried things until we found the next person. In the early days, that approach worked. It felt responsible. It felt supportive.

But as the firm grew, it stopped being sustainable.

It wasn't a solid solution for me, because the load kept increasing.

It wasn't a solid solution for clients, because service became more dependent on one person.

And it wasn't a solid solution for the team, because it quietly reinforced the idea that everything ultimately flowed back to me.

Every time someone left, capacity reset.

That was the real problem.

So instead of asking how we could hire faster, I asked a different question:

How do we design the firm so capacity survives people changing?

That's when we deliberately redesigned how work flows through the business.

We built what we now call our IQ workflow process — a role-based framework that defines what part of the work happens at each stage, rather than who does it. This applies across individual client work and internal business processes, including compliance services like BAS, tax, payroll, and FBT returns.

From the moment work comes in, through engagement and fee proposals, right through to lodgement and billing, each step is owned by a role.

And this distinction matters.

It doesn't matter who is in the role, as long as they are capable of performing it. The role is replaceable. The people are not.

I have enormous respect and admiration for my IQ family. The relationships we have internally matter deeply. But the firm cannot be designed in a way where capacity only exists if specific people are present. That's not fair on the business, the team, or the clients.

Once work moved by role rather than by person, something shifted.

Onboarding became clearer. New team members weren't expected to "just work it out" or wait until they'd been around long enough. They were oriented to how work moves, where decisions sit, and what good looks like in each role.

Review pressure reduced because review stopped being personal and started being structured. Escalation became more intentional. Knowledge stopped living in individual heads.

Clients responded better than expected.

We've always told clients that we work collaboratively, and once the workflow supported that properly, they could feel it. Clients weren't stuck waiting for one specific person to return from leave or come back online. The firm could respond, not just an individual.

As I'm writing this, I'm in another country, working on this chapter from my laptop. Normally, I'd be the person watching these processes closely. But I'm not worried.

Nothing will be missed.

Not because I'm across every detail — but because the process is.

That's when capacity stopped being temporary — and started becoming something the firm could rely on.

This chapter isn't about ripping out your systems, hiring a consultant, or locking yourself in a room for a three-day strategic offsite with coloured Post-it notes.

It's about being deliberate.

The biggest mistake I see firm owners make is assuming capacity will magically appear once they're "less busy" or once they "get the right people". In reality, capacity only appears when it's designed — and then protected.

And yes, that takes a little upfront effort. But it's far less painful than being the solution forever.

Here's how to do it in a way that actually works inside a slim, modern firm.

Step 1: Identify where you are the default solution

Start with honesty. The uncomfortable kind.

Ask yourself:

- Where do decisions still default to me?
- What work slows down when I'm not available or I am the bottleneck?
- What questions do people bring to me because it feels safer than deciding?

If your answer to any of these is "well… most things", congratulations — you're not alone.

Most bottlenecks don't exist because people are incapable. They exist because escalation rules are unclear or unspoken. If people don't know where responsibility genuinely sits, they'll come to you every time.

That's not a people problem. It's a design problem.

Step 2: Redesign workflows by role, not by person

This is the shift that changes everything.

Instead of thinking:

"Jess does this" or "Michael handles that"

Ask:

"What role owns this part of the process?"

Map your core services — BAS, tax, payroll, FBT — from start to finish:

- work received
- engagement and fee proposal
- preparation
- oversight checkpoints
- lodgement
- billing

Each step should be owned by a role, not a name.

Why this matters:

- People change
- Roles endure
- Capacity survives turnover

When work flows by role, the firm becomes far less fragile. Knowledge stops walking out the door. Oversight stops defaulting to the same person. And onboarding becomes faster and far less stressful for everyone involved.

Step 3: Treat onboarding as capacity protection (not a box to tick)

Onboarding is not admin. It's not something you "get through" between client meetings.

Onboarding determines whether a person will ever genuinely reduce your workload — or quietly add to it.

Strong onboarding focuses on:

- how work flows through your firm
- what decisions sit at each role
- what good looks like
- when escalation is expected

If onboarding is rushed or informal, new hires quickly learn that the safest option is to ask you. That habit is hard to undo.

Don't wing this.

Every hour spent clarifying expectations upfront saves dozens of interruptions later — and a surprising number of "just checking..." messages.

Step 4: Redefine oversight — without compromising standards

This is where many owners get stuck.

You absolutely still need to maintain oversight of client work. Quality, accuracy, and professional obligations don't disappear just because you'd like a little more breathing room.

The shift is not whether you oversee — it's how.

Ask yourself:

- What genuinely needs my involvement?
- What can be checked against clear standards before it reaches me?
- Where am I involved in detail that doesn't actually change the outcome?

Oversight should protect quality, not consume capacity.

If you're staying across everything because "it's quicker if I do it", that might be true today. It just won't be true forever — and future you will be quietly annoyed about it.

Personally, I still do a final sign-off on every document that is lodged, but I have other staff do other level checks before some items come to me. Set your own firm up for success in the way that serves your comfort level, your resources, and your risk profile.

Step 5: Set explicit escalation rules

If escalation rules aren't clear, everything escalates.

Be deliberate about:

- What must come to you
- What should be decided at team level
- What only escalates if certain thresholds are met

Example escalation rules (you can copy these and tweak):

Escalate to Owner/Partner if:

- Client is upset, confused, or sentiment is low.
- Tax strategy or structure is involved.
- There is an error with material impact.
- There's a fee dispute or scope creep.
- The team member feels unsure about risk.

Stay with Client Manager if:

- It's a routine query.
- It's process-related (documents, deadlines, status updates).
- It's within the agreed scope and the workflow covers it.

And be prepared to support people when they make reasonable decisions — even if they don't get it perfectly right every time.

Capacity doesn't grow when decisions are flawless. It grows when judgement is allowed to develop.

Step 6: Introduce clients to the firm, not just you

Client handover isn't an event. It's a system.

From the beginning, position the relationship as collaborative:

- clients work with the firm

- the firm works as a team
- access doesn't depend on one person being available

Clients generally respond very well to this — often better than firm owners expect.

They don't like waiting.

They like responsiveness.

They like knowing someone will get back to them without chasing.

When clients trust the firm, not just the owner, capacity becomes much easier to protect.

Step 7: Use systems to support visibility, not micromanagement

Visibility doesn't require involvement in everything.

Use systems that give you:

- clear file notes
- structured updates
- signals about where attention is needed

This allows you to operate as a high-level reviewer, not a constant participant.

You don't need to read everything. You need to know where to look — and when.

That's how you stay across the business without being buried in it.

Step 8: Review capacity quarterly — not daily

You don't need a major overhaul every year. Or every month. Or every Monday morning.

Instead, revisit one simple question each quarter:

Where did capacity still collapse back onto me?

That answer will tell you exactly where design needs refining.

Small adjustments compound quickly — and they're far easier to manage than one big, dramatic change.

You don't need to redesign your entire firm overnight — but you do need to be honest about where capacity is leaking and deliberate about fixing it.

Action Checklist

Use this checklist as a starting point:

- Identify where you are still the default solution (reviews, decisions, client requests)
- Write down the top 5 "quick questions" that interrupt you most often
- Pick ONE core service (tax, BAS, payroll, FBT) to redesign first
- Map that service by role (not by person) from start to finish
- Define what "done" looks like for that service (your standard work)
- Create one example file that represents "our standard work"
- Record one Loom walkthrough of your expectations (10 minutes max)
- Decide what must escalate to you vs what stays with the client manager
- Set escalation thresholds (risk, tax strategy, client sentiment, material impact)
- Introduce clients to the firm, not just you (normalise team contact)
- Build visibility systems (structured file notes, summaries, check-in points)
- Review quarterly: "Where did work collapse back to me — and why?"

Conclusion

Capacity doesn't disappear because people leave.

It disappears because it was never properly designed in the first place.

In modern firms — especially slim, relationship-based ones — capacity is the real currency. It determines whether growth feels exciting or exhausting, whether clients are supported consistently, and whether the firm can function without everything running through you.

Building a team that runs without you doesn't mean stepping away or lowering standards. It means designing work, oversight, and decision-making so quality is protected without your constant involvement.

When capacity is owned, protected, and deliberately designed, it compounds.

And when that happens, the firm stops relying on you as the solution — and starts working the way it was always meant to.

CHAPTER 6

From Tech Stack to Profit Stack – How AI Turns Efficiency Into Earnings

Kyelie Baxter

Most accounting firms believe they have a solid tech stack.

They've implemented cloud accounting software, moved away from paper, and layered in various apps to help with workflow, documents, and communication. On the surface, it looks like the job is done.

But when I'm speaking at events and ask a simple question — "*Who here is completely confident they have the right tech stack for their firm?*" — only a few hands ever go up.

If I'm being honest, mine wouldn't be one of them either.

Not because our systems aren't strong. They are. But technology moves too quickly for certainty to be a permanent state. If I'm not regularly reviewing our software, reassessing pricing, exploring new features, and checking what's changed, then I'm not doing my job properly.

And let's be clear — anyone who tells you their tech stack is "done" is either lying or hasn't logged in properly for a while.

A solid tech stack isn't something you set up once and forget about. It's something you actively manage.

This chapter isn't about choosing software or learning AI tools. It's about understanding how technology and AI change the economics of your firm.

A quick word on where I'm coming from

I've been in public practice for over 25 years. Sadly, as much as I would like to pretend, I am not a digital native. I started my career in the pen-and-paper days — well before scanning, cloud software, or anything resembling a tech stack.

That experience has been a gift.

It's given me a deep appreciation for what technology can genuinely remove from our workload, but also a healthy scepticism of adopting tools without purpose. I've lived through every stage of transition and I've seen firsthand that technology only creates leverage when it's used deliberately.

If I were starting a firm today, I'd be thrilled. The barriers to entry are virtually non-existent compared to when I began. The tools available now are powerful, accessible, and scalable straight out of the box.

But tools alone don't build a profitable firm. Decisions do.

The foundation problem most firms don't talk about

What I see again and again is firms assuming their tech stack is "sorted" because the major systems are in place.

But look a little closer and a different picture often emerges.

Software is underused. Features sit untouched. Teams work around systems instead of letting systems do the heavy lifting. Firms pay for additional apps to solve problems their existing software already handles — simply because no one has stepped back to review what's already available.

At the same time, many firms are layering AI tools on top of their stack without fully understanding the AI functionality already built into the software they're already paying for.

This isn't about doing anything wrong. It's about not being deliberate enough.

If you're not genuinely confident in your tech stack, that's not a failure. It's actually the right starting point.

Because no amount of automation or AI will compensate for a foundation that isn't solid.

Where AI fits (and where it doesn't)

AI has become the loudest part of the conversation — which is exactly why it needs to be handled carefully.

AI is not the tech stack. It sits on top of it. And the quality of what AI produces is entirely dependent on the quality of what it's sitting on.

When the underlying systems are clean, connected, and reliable, AI can be incredibly useful. It can summarise information faster, surface patterns that might otherwise be missed, and reduce the friction involved in turning data into something meaningful.

When the foundation isn't solid, AI doesn't fix the problem. It just helps the problem move faster.

This is where I see firms getting distracted. They invest in AI tools without being clear on what they actually want those tools to deliver commercially. The focus becomes what AI can do, rather than what the firm needs it to do.

And this is the critical point: AI doesn't make business decisions.

AI doesn't decide how a firm prices its work.

AI doesn't decide how capacity is used.

AI doesn't decide what margin looks like or how it's protected.

Those decisions remain human ones.

Used well, AI supports judgement. It strengthens consistency. It reduces preparation time and variability in delivery. All of that supports margin and scalability — but only when there is clarity around the outcome.

Without that clarity, AI simply creates faster activity, not better economics.

Profit doesn't appear because AI exists.

It appears because someone decides what the output of that efficiency is meant to be.

The commercial blind spot: why efficiency rarely shows up in profit

Here's the uncomfortable truth.

Most firms that invest in technology do become more efficient. Work moves faster. Errors reduce. Processes improve.

And yet, when you look at the bottom line, very little actually changes.

That's because efficiency doesn't create profit. It only creates capacity.

Capacity is commercially neutral until someone decides what it's for.

In practice, firms tend to do one of three things with the time they save through technology:

1. They absorb more work without adjusting pricing.
2. They take on more clients at the same margins.
3. They let the time disappear into busyness, meetings, and general noise.

None of those outcomes are *wrong*. But none of them are deliberate.

And when capacity isn't treated deliberately, it never converts into margin. It simply gets consumed.

Saved time is not a side effect — it's an asset.

And like any asset, it needs to be recognised, protected, and intentionally deployed.

Until that happens, technology will make your firm busier, not more profitable.

Let's keep this simple.

Technology makes work faster. That part is easy to see.

What's *not* easy to see (and what catches most firms out) is that faster work doesn't automatically mean higher profit.

It usually just means you've created capacity.

And capacity is commercially neutral until you decide what it's for.

When I'm thinking about technology and AI inside a firm, I'm not thinking about tools — I'm thinking about outcomes.

And one of the biggest outcomes technology creates (whether we notice it or not) is saved time.

So the question I come back to is:

When we save time, where does that time go?

Here's a simple way to think about it.

If you save **15 minutes** on a job and you do that job **30 times a month**, you've just created **7.5** hours of capacity.

Over a year, that's close to **90 hours**.

That time is valuable — but only if you deliberately decide what it will be used for.

If the answer is "nowhere" (or "it disappears"), then the tech stack might be working — but the economics of the firm won't improve.

So instead of chasing tools, I focus on a simple sequence of decisions.

1) Get the foundations right first

Before we go any further, I want to be really clear on something — because I see this confusion everywhere.

Too many people use the terms **"tech stack"** and **"AI"** interchangeably, as if they're the same thing.

They're not.

Your **tech stack** is the foundation: the software and systems that run your firm day-to-day.

AI isn't the tech stack — it sits on top of it.

When your underlying systems are clean, connected, and reliable, AI can be incredibly useful. It can summarise information faster, surface patterns you might otherwise miss, and reduce the friction involved in turning data into something meaningful.

But when the foundation isn't solid, AI doesn't fix the problem. It just helps the problem move faster.

It will accelerate inconsistency.

We all know the saying: **rubbish data in means rubbish data out** — and AI is no different. If the information it's working with is messy, incomplete, or inconsistent, the output will be too.

2) Notice where capacity is being created

Most firms don't lack efficiency. They lack visibility.

Capacity is being created all the time — it's just not being measured or protected.

The signs are usually obvious once you start looking:

- jobs that don't blow out like they used to
- fewer follow-ups and less rework
- less partner intervention in routine work
- bottlenecks that quietly disappear

You don't need to track this down to the minute.

Work in ranges.

If you save 5–10 hours a month through a better process, that's meaningful — and over a year it adds up.

3) Decide what that saved time is actually for

This is the step that changes everything.

Saved time without a purpose will always be absorbed.

So be explicit:

- Is this capacity meant to protect margin?
- Reduce delivery risk?
- Improve pricing confidence?
- Reduce pressure on key people?
- Create space for advisory?
- Or simply make the firm a calmer place to work?

There's no perfect answer.

But there *is* a wrong one — and that's not deciding.

4) Hold your pricing when the outcome hasn't changed

This is where many firms unintentionally give away the benefit of their tech investment.

Work becomes smoother and more predictable, and suddenly the internal question pops up:

"*If this feels easier now, should it be cheaper?*"

Not necessarily.

If the client outcome hasn't changed — and the work is still being done properly, reviewed appropriately, and delivered with professional judgement — then you don't need to discount simply because the delivery feels calmer.

That's not being greedy.

That's protecting margin.

5) Protect the profit so it doesn't leak back out

This is where the "free money" lives.

Not because you've charged more.

But because you've stopped giving margin away through:

- discounting
- rework
- scope creep
- unnecessary partner involvement

Technology and AI can absolutely make your firm more efficient.

But profitability only improves when you make deliberate decisions about what that efficiency is meant to produce.

A real example: why faster work shouldn't mean cheaper fees

When we started using AI within our compliance processes, it wasn't about changing what we offered to clients.

We already do advisory — most firms do, in one way or another. Clients ask questions. We explain outcomes. We highlight issues. That's just part of good service.

This wasn't about layering advisory into compliance or creating new services.

It was about improving the way the work we were already doing was delivered — commercially, operationally, and from a risk perspective.

At a practical level, AI was used to support the thinking around compliance work.

It helped summarise information, surface inconsistencies, prompt questions we would usually ask anyway, and reduce the mental load involved in pulling everything together.

What changed first wasn't speed.

It was consistency.

Reviews became easier. File notes were clearer. Fewer things slipped through because someone was tired, rushed, or juggling too many jobs at once.

The work felt more controlled, and the team felt more confident that issues were being identified reliably — not just when the most experienced person happened to be involved.

Over time, the work did become faster — but that wasn't the point.

The real shift was predictability.

And predictability is where the economics of a firm start to change.

As delivery became smoother, that familiar internal question surfaced again:

"If this feels easier now, should it be cheaper?"

It's a natural thought — especially in firms that have historically priced work based on effort or hours.

But when we stepped back and looked at the broader picture, that logic didn't stack up.

Our people costs hadn't gone down.

If anything, we were investing more — in training, governance, and making sure AI outputs were reviewed properly and used responsibly.

Our technology costs had increased too, with AI features, security, and oversight now part of the cost base of a modern firm.

What AI had reduced wasn't value.

It was delivery risk.

The client outcome hadn't changed.

They still received compliant, accurate work, reviewed by professionals.

What had changed was how consistently and calmly that outcome was achieved.

So we held our pricing.

And quietly, without any fanfare, margins improved.

No new services.

No scope creep.

No dramatic fee increases.

Just fewer leaks.

What that looked like in practice

Even without changing the service or increasing fees, we saw practical improvements that mattered commercially:

- **Less rework and fewer follow-ups**, because issues were

being surfaced earlier and more consistently

- **Cleaner file notes and smoother reviews**, which reduced the mental load on the team
- **Less reliance on "the most experienced person"** to catch things at the last minute
- A noticeable improvement in delivery predictability — which is what protects margin over time.

I'm deliberately not turning this into a time-sheet exercise, because the point isn't to obsess over minutes.

But it's realistic to expect improvements like:

- 10–20% faster review cycles in busy periods (because the information is clearer and more structured)
- fewer interruptions and fewer 'can you just check this?' moments across the week
- a more consistent client experience, because the process is less dependent on individual memory and energy

AI didn't replace judgement.

What it did was support judgement by making information clearer, more structured, and easier to work with.

And by being deliberate about what that efficiency was for, we allowed it to show up where it matters — in the bottom line.

Implementation Guide – step-by-step rollout inside a firm

This chapter isn't about ripping out systems, buying new software, or suddenly "doing AI".

It's about being deliberate.

If you take nothing else away, start here.

A simple 30-day rollout (so you actually start)

If you want to make this real inside your firm without overwhelming everyone, this is a clean way to roll it out:

- **Week 1:** Choose one service + agree on what "good delivery" looks like
- **Week 2:** Identify where capacity is being created (even roughly)
- **Week 3:** Decide what that capacity is for (margin, sustainability, advisory, pricing confidence)
- **Week 4:** Lock in one change (pricing rule, workflow step, or review rhythm) and keep it consistent

You don't need a full transformation.

You need one deliberate decision that sticks.

Step 1: Start with one service — not your whole firm (*Owner/Partner*)

If you try to apply this thinking across your entire firm at once, you'll either overwhelm yourself or do nothing at all.

Instead, choose one recurring service.

Something stable.

Something familiar.

A compliance service is often the easiest place to start because it's repeatable and relatively predictable.

Then review it through a profit lens, not a time lens.

Not how long it takes.

Not how busy everyone feels.

But how it's delivered and what it contributes to the bottom line.

I don't look for perfection here.

I look for movement.

If a small change shifts margin by even half a percent, that matters.

Half a percent doesn't sound exciting — but on a $1 million firm, that's $5,000.

Make a handful of those decisions each year and the impact becomes very real.

Step 2: Be clear on what your tech stack is meant to produce (*Owner/Partner + Senior team input*)

Before you look at numbers, be clear on intent.

Ask yourself:

- What do we actually expect our systems to give us?
- Is it speed? Consistency? Fewer errors? Less rework? Reduced partner involvement?
- If everything was working properly, what would feel easier day to day?

A tech stack that's doing its job should reduce friction for the team and lower delivery risk for the firm.

If work is faster but still stressful, something isn't aligned.

Clarity here matters because it sets the benchmark for every decision that follows.

Step 3: Identify where capacity is already being created (*Senior + Admin — with owner oversight*)

Capacity exists whether you acknowledge it or not.

Look for signals:

- Jobs that don't blow out like they used to
- Fewer follow-ups or second reviews
- Less partner intervention in routine work
- Quieter periods where there used to be bottlenecks

I don't try to calculate this down to the minute.

I work in ranges.

If a process improvement saves somewhere between 5 and 10 hours a month, I ask what that represents over a year — directionally, not perfectly.

At a conservative $150 per hour, that's roughly $9,000 to $18,000 a year.

Once you see capacity in dollar terms, it's much harder to ignore.

Step 4: Decide what saved time is actually for (*Owner/Partner decision*)

This is the step most firms skip.

Saved time without a purpose will always be absorbed.

So be explicit.

Ask:

- Is this capacity meant to protect margin?
- Improve pricing confidence?
- Reduce pressure on key people?
- Create space for advisory or higher-value conversations?
- Or simply make the firm a calmer place to work?

There's no right answer.

But there is a wrong one — and that's not deciding.

Capacity that isn't owned will disappear into busyness every time.

Step 5: Pressure-test your pricing logic (*Owner/Partner OR Client Manager*)

This is where discomfort often shows up.

Ask yourself honestly:

- Are we still anchoring pricing to staff hours?
- Are we discounting because work feels easier?
- Are we undervaluing consistency, systems, and reduced risk?

Pricing based purely on time belongs to a different era.

If your systems reduce delivery risk and improve consistency, it's reasonable — and responsible — to price with more confidence, even if the work takes less effort than it used to.

This is where free money often appears.

Not through fee increases, but through better margin on work you're already doing well.

Step 6: Listen to the team and client signals (*Senior team lead + Client Services*)

When systems work properly, people notice.

Ask your team:

- Does work feel easier?
- Are expectations clearer?
- Is there less rework and fewer fire drills?

And pay attention to clients:

- Are interactions smoother?
- Are questions more focused on outcomes than process?
- Is confidence increasing rather than friction?

These are commercial signals, not soft ones.

Happy teams and calm clients are often the first indicators that margin improvement will follow.

Step 7: Build a simple review rhythm (*Owner/Partner — quarterly*)

You don't need a 40-page strategic plan or a once-a-year overhaul.

Instead, revisit one simple question each quarter:

Did the way we delivered this work justify the fee we charged?

If the answer is "yes, comfortably", that's a signal.

If it's "only just", that's a signal too.

Those signals inform small adjustments — minimum fees, pricing confidence, or decisions about where you no longer discount.

Over time, these micro decisions compound.

And that's how profit actually moves.

Action Checklist

1. Pick one recurring service to review this quarter (start small)
2. Confirm what your tech stack is meant to produce (beyond speed)
3. Identify where capacity is already being created (even roughly)
4. Convert time saved into a dollar estimate so it becomes visible
5. Decide what the capacity is for (margin, pricing confidence, sustainability, advisory)
6. Pressure-test whether your pricing is still anchored to hours
7. Stop discounting simply because delivery feels easier
8. Check the team and client signals (less rework, fewer fire drills, smoother delivery)
9. Review quarterly: "Did the delivery justify the fee?"

Technology will happily make you more efficient.

It won't make you more profitable unless you decide what profit actually looks like.

When you're deliberate about what saved time is for — protecting margin, improving sustainability, doing better work, or simply giving your team breathing room — technology and AI stop being costs you justify and start becoming assets that earn their place.

That's where the free money lives.

Not in working harder.

But in making deliberate decisions about how your firm operates.

That's the difference between having a business — and running it profitably on purpose.

SECTION 3

TURN ADVISORY INTO YOUR PROFIT ENGINE

How tax planning, benchmarking and business advice transform accounting firms into higher-value advisory practices.

"The purpose of business is to create and keep a customer"
— Peter Drucker

Section introduction by Darren Gleeson

For decades, the accounting profession has been built around compliance. Tax returns, financial statements, BAS lodgements and regulatory reporting have formed the backbone of most accounting practices. Compliance work has provided reliable revenue and a steady flow of work for firms across Australia, and for many years, that model worked well.

But compliance work alone rarely creates a highly profitable accounting firm.

The uncomfortable reality is that compliance work is gradually becoming a commodity. Technology is automating tasks that once required hours of professional time. Clients expect faster turn-around times and increasingly question the price of work they consider routine. Competition among accounting firms continues to intensify, and many practices are working harder to maintain the same level of profitability.

Despite these trends, a surprising number of accounting firms still structure their entire business around compliance production.

The outcome is predictable. Firms become busy, partners spend most of their time reviewing work and solving operational issues, and profitability eventually reaches a ceiling. The firm grows larger, but it does not necessarily become easier to run or more profitable.

Compliance work tells clients what happened last year.

Advisory work helps them improve what happens next year.

That difference matters more than many accountants realise.

Accountants occupy a unique position in the business community. They see the financial performance of hundreds of businesses every year. They understand tax law, profitability, cash flow and financial risk. In many cases, they have long-standing relationships with business owners who trust their judgment and value their perspective.

Yet very few accounting firms systematically convert that position of trust into structured advisory services.

Many accountants provide advice informally. They offer suggestions during meetings, answer questions over the phone or provide insights during tax planning discussions. While valuable, this advice is often delivered inconsistently and frequently without appropriate pricing.

In other words, the firm provides insight but fails to capture its true commercial value.

Advisory cannot remain an informal activity inside the firm. It must be structured, systemised and embedded into the way the practice operates. When advisory becomes part of the firm's systems, the economics of the practice begin to change. Instead of simply reporting historical results, the accountant becomes actively involved in helping clients improve their business performance.

Conversations shift from compliance deadlines to strategy, profitability and growth. Clients value those conversations far more than they value the completion of a tax return.

Services such as tax planning, benchmarking and profit improvement discussions allow accounting firms to move beyond compliance and become genuine commercial advisers to their clients. For many firms, this work becomes the most valuable and profitable service the practice delivers.

The challenge for most accounting firms is not recognising the importance of advisory. Most accountants already accept that advisory represents the future of the profession.

The real challenge is implementing it.

The chapters in this section explore how accounting firms can make that transition and embed advisory into the everyday work of the firm. Because when advisory becomes systematic rather than occasional, it does more than create additional revenue.

It fundamentally changes the accountant's role and the firm's profitability.

CHAPTER 7

The 5-Minute Benchmarking System – Turn Every Compliance Job Into a $1,000+ Opportunity.

Darren Gleeson

Introduction

Why Every Compliance Job Is an Advisory Opportunity

Most accounting firms don't have a workload problem. They have a **leverage problem.**

Partners and teams are busy. Compliance work is constant. Tax returns are prepared, financials are signed off, BASs are lodged — and the next job is already waiting. The work gets done. That part works.

What doesn't work nearly as well is the return on effort.

There's an uncomfortable reality sitting underneath this. In today's market, the average profitability of a compliance-only accounting practice is around $340,000 per partner. It's steady, predictable, and familiar. It's also the ceiling for most firms that rely solely on compliance work.

What catches many firm owners off guard is what happens when they try to move beyond that average.

Practices that layer in ad hoc advisory — the occasional tax-planning engagement, a strategy session when a client asks, some bespoke consulting — often end up less profitable, not more. The extra meetings, custom work, and unpriced partner time dilute margins. In many cases, profitability falls by around 30%

compared to compliance-only firms.

The firms that materially outperform don't sit in the middle. They take a different approach altogether.

They don't "do some advisory". They run systemised advisory alongside compliance. Those firms consistently generate two to three times the profit per partner of compliance-only practices. Not because they work harder or know more, but because advisory is delivered through structure, not effort.

The difference isn't capability. It's positioning.

In most firms, advisory still sits outside the compliance workflow. It's treated as something separate — a later conversation, a different meeting, a proposal that may or may not happen. In busy practices, that approach rarely produces consistent results.

Clients don't engage with advisory because it sounds strategic. They engage when they can clearly see a gap between where their business is performing now and where it could be performing if it were run closer to best practice. If that gap isn't apparent, the conversation never really starts.

This is where benchmarking matters — and where it is often misunderstood.

Robert C. Camp, widely regarded as the father of modern benchmarking, was clear that improvement occurs only when performance is measured against best practices, not averages.

W. Edwards Deming captured the same idea succinctly:

"*No process is ever good enough unless it is compared against a higher standard.*"

In business, that higher standard is not the average performer.

It's the top performers.

Top 20% benchmarking compares a business's economic structure to the best-performing businesses in its industry — not just at the profit line, but across the key levers that drive results: cost of goods sold, subcontractors, rent, wages, overheads, owner's compensation, and net profit.

Every compliance job already contains this information. The difference is whether those numbers are reported or used.

The 5-Minute Benchmarking System exists to create that moment inside the compliance work firms are already doing.

When applied consistently, benchmarking stops being a report. It becomes the trigger that turns compliance into advisory — and average firms into top-performing, systemised practices.

The Framework

The 5-Minute Benchmarking System

The 5-Minute Benchmarking System was built to solve a very practical problem inside accounting firms:

How do you move clients from compliance into paid, structured advisory without increasing hours, relying on partner heroics, or giving away free thinking?

Most firm owners already know the reality. The average compliance-only practice earns approximately $340,000 in profit per partner. Many have tried to add advisory on top of compliance and have discovered, the hard way, that ad hoc usually means more work and less profit.

The issue isn't willingness. It's the lack of a repeatable system.

This framework exists to introduce advisory with discipline.

It is designed to:

- Sit inside the year-end compliance process
- Take five minutes per business client
- Identify lost profit
- Lead to a 12-month advisory engagement with clear outcomes, not one-off work

The system rests on three principles.

Principle One: Benchmark Against the Top 20%, Not the Average

Benchmarking only works if the comparison forces a rethink.

Averages don't do that. They reassure. Reassurance kills action.

The 5-Minute Benchmarking System compares a client's business to the top 20% of performers in their industry — the businesses that have already solved pricing, cost control, and profit conversion.

This immediately reframes the discussion.

Instead of: "*Did we do okay last year?*"

The question becomes: "*How far are we from best practice — and what is that costing you?*"

That gap is the starting point for advisory. Not opinion. Not theory. A visible difference between current performance and what top performers achieve.

Principle Two: Focus on the Levers That Actually Drive Profit

The system avoids complexity by focusing solely on the business's economic structure —the levers that determine whether profit increases or declines as revenue grows.

Seven levers are benchmarked, each expressed as a percentage of revenue and compared to Top 20% KPIs:

- Cost of goods sold (COGS)
- Subcontractors
- Rent
- Wages
- Overheads (other operating expenses)
- Owner's compensation
- Net profit

These levers tell the real story.

- If COGS or subcontractors are out of line, the margin is capped

- If rent is too high, fixed costs apply pressure regardless of turnover.
- If wages are inefficient, growth destroys profit.
- If overheads creep, scale delivers no leverage.
- If the owner is underpaid, profit is overstated.
- If the net profit is weak after a proper owner's salary, the business is underperforming.

This is not accounting theory. It is a commercial reality.

Principle Three: Identify the Gap and the Lost Profit

Benchmarking only matters if it makes loss visible.

This system is designed to answer two questions quickly:

1. Where is this business out of line with the Top 20% performance?
2. What is that gap costing the owner each year?

The objective is not to analyse everything. It is to identify the profit gap that matters most.

Once lost profit is quantified, advisory becomes mandatory.

The Five-Minute Benchmarking Process

The process fits cleanly into a year-end compliance meeting. No separate session. No additional preparation by partners.

Step 1: Set the Performance Frame (After Compliance)

Timing is deliberate.

Once the tax return and financials are finalised and explained, the accountant shifts the conversation:

"Now that compliance is done, let's spend five minutes looking at how this business compares to the top 20% in your industry."

Compliance is finished. Performance begins.

Step 2: Compare the Cost Structure to Top 20% KPIs

The client's cost and profit structure is reviewed against the Top 20% benchmarks:

- COGS
- Subcontractors
- Rent
- Wages
- Overheads
- Owner's compensation
- Net profit

This is a scan, not a lecture.

The question is simple: Where is this business materially out of line with top performers?

Step 3: Convert the Gap into Dollars

Percentages explain. Dollars decide.

Once a variance is identified, it is translated into an annual dollar impact.

A 3% wage gap on $3 million in revenue is $90,000. Excess subcontractor costs of 4% could amount to $120,000. Undercompensating the owner obscures the business's true economics.

This is the moment the conversation becomes real.

Step 4: Identify the One Biggest Leak

The system deliberately focuses on a single issue.

Trying to fix everything creates noise. One clear issue creates focus.

The largest profit leak becomes the priority.

Step 5: Normalise Owner's Compensation

Before net profit is assessed, the owner's compensation is benchmarked separately and adjusted to market levels.

This removes the illusion of profitability created by unpaid effort and excessive hours.

For many clients, this is the point where the seriousness of the gap becomes clear.

Step 6: Recommend the 12-Month Advisory Package

When the client asks:

"What do we do about this?"

The accountant responds with a recommendation.

The outcome of the 12-month advisory engagement is to close the specific profit gap identified through benchmarking against the Top 20%.

Nothing generic. Nothing open-ended.

The discussion is tight and commercial:

Outcome	The engagement exists to improve the specific lever identified — for example, reducing wage inefficiency, improving gross margin, correcting rent pressure, or restoring owner compensation — with progress measured against the same Top 20% benchmarks.
Process	The accountant outlines a structured 12-month process: agreed actions, regular review points, accountability, and re-benchmarking against the same standards.
Time	The time commitment required from both sides is made clear upfront.
Cost	The fee is positioned directly against the quantified profit gap. The client is not buying advice; they are investing in closing a known loss.

Advisory work only begins once the client commits.

Why This System Works

This system works because it is disciplined.

The firm's upfront investment is limited to five minutes per business client per year. That work can be completed by junior staff or support team members, not partners.

Advisory time is only invested once a client has:

- Seen the profit gap
- Accepted it is real
- Committed to fixing it
- Agreed to pay for structured advisory support

Not every client proceeds in year one — and that is expected.

Systemised advisory is a premium service. It is for clients who want better performance, are prepared to commit time and effort, and are willing to make changes.

The process is applied:

- To every business client
- At every year-end compliance meeting
- Every year

Over time, repetition builds clarity and trust. Some clients act immediately. Others take longer. Each year, the same gap is revisited against the same Top 20% standard.

For the firm, this creates:

- Consistent advisory conversations
- Higher conversion into paid advisory
- Clear boundaries around premium work
- Protection of partner time
- A scalable advisory model without margin erosion

Used properly, the 5-Minute Benchmarking System is not about selling advisory to everyone.

It is about identifying the right clients, at the right time, and delivering advisory only where it will be valued, implemented, and paid for.

Case Study

Using Top 20% Benchmarking to Identify and Close a $64,011 Profit Gap

Background

Jemma Aesthetics Pty Ltd operates two premium cosmetic injectables and skin clinics under the Skin Société brand in Karrinyup and Ellenbrook, Western Australia.

The clinics specialise in non-surgical aesthetic treatments, including cosmetic injectables, skin rejuvenation, and medical-grade skincare. The brand is positioned at the premium end of the market, supported by strong clinical governance, advanced injector training, and a consistent, high-quality client experience.

The business is led by Jemma Hicks, a Registered Nurse with more than ten years of clinical experience and is family-owned alongside Darren Gleeson. The Karrinyup clinic opened in August 2023, and the Ellenbrook clinic opened in March 2025, making FY2025 a transition year to multi-site operations.

Figures have been adjusted for confidentiality while maintaining accurate performance ratios.

Industry Context

The cosmetic injectables sector is one of Australia's fastest-growing health and beauty markets.

- Average clinic revenue: $1.2 – $1.3 million
- Average net profit: 10–12%
- Top 20% clinics: 20–25%+ net profit

At this level, profitability is not driven by demand. It is driven by cost structure discipline, particularly around COGS and wages.

The Compliance-to-Performance Shift

At the completion of the 30 June 2025 year-end compliance work, the discussion shifted from reporting results to assessing performance.

Using the Top 20% benchmarking framework, the business was reviewed across the core economic levers that determine profitability:

- COGS
- Rent
- Wages
- Overheads
- Owner's compensation
- Net profit

The objective was simple: identify where profit was being left on the table.

Top 20% Benchmark Comparison – FY2025

Item	Actual FY2025 ($)	Top 20% Target %	Top 20% Target ($)	Variance ($)
Sales	1,058,606	100%	1,058,606	—
COGS	323,572	25%	264,652	58,920
Rent	73,790	7%	74,102	(312)
Wages	191,913	23%	243,479	(51,566)
Overheads	128,690	10%	105,861	22,829
Owner's Compensation	140,000	10%	105,861	34,139
Net Profit	**200,641**	**25%**	**264,652**	**(64,011)**

What the Numbers Showed

On average, this business would be considered strong. Revenue had scaled into industry norms, and profitability was already well above the sector average.

Top 20 % benchmarking showed more useful results.

- Rent was on benchmark
- Wages were better than the Top 20%
- Overheads and owner's compensation were slightly elevated but manageable

One issue stood out clearly.

COGS was materially above Top 20% standards, accounting for $58,920 of the total profit gap. That single variance accounted for nearly all of the difference between current performance and Top 20% profitability.

The Turning Point

When the table was reviewed, the conversation sharpened.

Jemma looked at the numbers and asked:

"So this is the biggest thing holding us back?"

The answer was yes.

If COGS discipline could be brought back to Top 20% levels — through tighter product mix control, supplier pricing, and margin management — most of the $64,011 profit gap would be recovered without increasing staff, rent, or marketing spend.

The discussion moved quickly from explanation to focus.

From Insight to Action

With the profit gap clearly identified, the priority for the following 12 months was defined:

- Improve product and treatment margins
- Renegotiate supplier pricing and terms

- Tighten inventory controls and reduce wastage
- Adjust pricing where required
- Measure progress quarterly against the same Top 20% benchmarks

Each action is tied back to the same benchmark that identified the issue.

Why This Case Matters

This case highlights why benchmarking against the Top 20% works.

The entire discussion took five minutes at year-end.

That five minutes:

- Confirmed the business was already performing well
- Identified a $64,011 annual profit gap
- Isolated a single, controllable lever
- Created a clear focus on what mattered most

This is what turns benchmarking into a management tool rather than a report.

It doesn't tell owners what they already know. It clearly and quickly shows them where performance can still improve.

And that is the point of the system.

Implementation Guide

How to Run the 5-Minute Top 20% Benchmarking System at Every Year-End Meeting

This implementation guide shows how to turn year-end compliance meetings into structured advisory conversations without increasing partner hours or drifting into unpaid consulting.

This system works because it is disciplined. It only requires five minutes per business client per year. And it only works if the right benchmark data already exists.

Step 1: Take out a TaxFitness subscription
Goal: access proper Top 20% benchmark data.

Top 20% benchmarking cannot be done using ATO small business benchmarks.

ATO benchmarks are built for compliance and audit risk. They are based on averages, heavily aggregated, backward-looking, and designed to answer one question only:

"Does this business look normal?"

That is a useless question for performance improvement.

ATO benchmarks will never tell a client:

- Where profit is being left on the table
- How they compare to the best operators in their industry
- What structure is holding them back

If you use ATO data, you will never get a meaningful advisory conversation.

To run this system properly — and to do it in five minutes — you need a TaxFitness subscription.

TaxFitness provides:

- Access to 400+ industry-specific Top 20% benchmarks
- Benchmarks based on high-performing businesses, not averages
- A consistent KPI structure across all industries:
    - COGS
    - Subcontractors
    - Rent
    - Wages
    - Overheads
    - Owner's compensation
    - Net profit

Without this data, benchmarking becomes slow, subjective, and inconsistent. With it, benchmarking becomes routine.

Step 2: Standardise account mapping once

Goal: make every benchmark comparable.

Inside the firm, agree once on how accounts are mapped:

- What goes into COGS
- How subcontractors are treated
- Rent treatment
- Wages (including super and on-costs — consistently)
- Overheads
- Owner's compensation (normalised to a market salary)

Do this once. Write it down. Enforce it.

If mapping changes client by client, benchmarking fails.

Step 3: Build benchmarking into the year-end workflow

Goal: make it automatic.

When year-end accounts are ready, the workflow includes:

"Prepare Top 20% Benchmark Snapshot"

Using TaxFitness, this takes around five minutes.

This task:

- Is completed by junior or support staff
- Requires no partner preparation
- Produces a one-page snapshot ready for the meeting

Partners review. They don't build.

Step 4: Prepare the Benchmark Snapshot

Goal: identify the profit gap.

Using TaxFitness:

- Revenue is pulled from the final accounts
- Actual $ and % are calculated for each KPI
- Top 20% benchmark % are applied automatically
- Target $ figures are calculated
- Variances are shown in dollars

At the end of this step, one thing must be clear:
What is the single biggest profit gap?
That is the focus of the meeting. Nothing else.

Step 5: Run the meeting in the right order
Goal: separate compliance from performance.

In the meeting:

1. Finish compliance.
   Explain the tax outcome.
   Finalise the job.
2. Then shift the discussion:
   "Now that compliance is done, let's spend five minutes looking at how this business compares to the Top 20% in your industry."

This change in tone matters. It informs the client that the conversation has shifted from reporting to decision-making.

Step 6: Walk through the benchmark
Goal: create clarity, fast.

Use the one-page snapshot:

- Start with net profit % versus Top 20%
- Identify the one biggest variance
- Translate it into dollars

For example:

"At Top 20% performance, this is costing you about $60,000 a year."

Do not explain how to fix it in the meeting. That comes later.

Step 7: Confirm intent

Goal: qualify who advisory is for.

Ask direct questions:

- "Do you want to close this gap?"
- "Are you prepared to commit time and make changes?"

Some clients will say yes. Others won't.

That's fine.

Systemised advisory is not for everyone. It is for owners who want improvement, not just reassurance.

Step 8: Recommend a 12-month advisory plan

Goal: avoid ad-hoc advice.

When the question comes — "*What do we do about this?*" — the response is structured:

- The outcome is to close the specific profit gap identified
- The work runs over 12 months
- Progress is measured against the same Top 20% benchmarks
- Focus stays on one main lever at a time

The benchmark remains the reference point for the entire engagement.

Step 9: Record and move on

Goal: make it a system.

After the meeting, record:

- The gap identified
- Client intent (now / later / not ready)
- Next step

If they proceed, schedule the first advisory session.

If they don't, revisit the benchmark next year.

Step 10: Repeat every year

Goal: let repetition do the work.

This process is run:

- For every business client
- At every year-end meeting
- Every year

It takes five minutes per client per year.

Some clients act immediately. Others take time. Each year, the same gap is revisited against the same Top 20% standard. Eventually, the cost of doing nothing becomes obvious.

The discipline that makes it work

- Use Top 20%, not averages
- Identify one gap, not ten
- Quantify it in dollars
- Only invest advisory time after commitment
- Repeat every year

This is not about working harder.

It's about using the right data, following a tight process, and letting benchmarking do what it's supposed to do — turn compliance into advisory, without burning partners out.

Action Checklist

Immediate, Practical Actions You Can Take Now

1. Stop benchmarking against averages. Averages create comfort, not improvement. If you're using ATO benchmarks, you're measuring "normal", not "better". Switch your reference point to the Top 20% only.
2. Put the right infrastructure in place. Five-minute benchmarking only works if the data already exists. Make sure your firm has access to reliable Top 20% benchmark data so this doesn't turn into research or guesswork.

3. Lock in your account mapping. Decide once what goes into COGS, wages, rent, overheads, and owner's compensation. Write it down. Apply it consistently. Benchmarking fails when files are treated differently.
4. Hard-wire benchmarking into year-end jobs. Add a non-negotiable task to every business client workflow: *Prepare Top 20% Benchmark Snapshot.*
5. Get it off partner desks. Train juniors or support staff to prepare the snapshot. Partners review. They don't build.
6. Focus on one number that matters. In every meeting, identify the single biggest profit gap. Ignore the rest.
7. Talk dollars, not percentages. Convert the gap into an annual dollar number. That's what gets attention.
8. Separate insight from advice. Use the meeting to identify the gap. Do not solve it on the spot.
9. Run it every year. Same process. Same benchmark. Every year. Repetition does the heavy lifting.
10. Protect your time. Advisory is for clients who want improvement, will commit, and value your time.

Conclusion

Compliance pays the bills. Advisory creates wealth.

Compliance-only firms hit a ceiling. Firms that run structured, systemised advisory don't — they double or triple profitability without adding clients or hours.

- The shift isn't about selling. It's about discipline.
- Use Top 20% benchmarking to expose the gap.
- Focus on one issue.
- Fix it.

Run the process every year and let the results compound.

That's how compliance turns into advisory — on purpose, and on profit.

CHAPTER 8

The 5-Minute Tax Planning Triage System – How to Turn Savings Into Recurring Advisory Revenue

Darren Gleeson

Introduction

Why Tax Planning Breaks Down — and How to Fix It

Most accounting practices claim to offer tax planning.

It's one of the profession's least well-executed services.

For most firms, tax planning gets pushed into April, May, and June. It becomes a last-minute scramble to "see what we can do before 30 June", layered on top of already stretched compliance deadlines. There's no space to think properly, no time to model outcomes, and no capacity to do anything that isn't simple or obvious.

That's not a tax problem. It's a system problem.

Tax planning hasn't been designed to work inside a real accounting practice. It relies on the partner's memory, confidence, and spare time — none of which are reliable. Some years it happens. Most years it doesn't. And when it does, it feels rushed, uncomfortable, and hard to charge for.

Before going any further, it's worth being clear about what tax planning is.

Tax planning is not chasing deductions in June. It's not fixing things after the year is over. Proper tax planning is a forward-looking process that manages tax across a client's business, investments, structures, cash flow, and future decisions — before tax is incurred and before mistakes are locked in. Done well, it improves outcomes over time, not just this year's return.

The way tax planning is usually delivered almost guarantees it will fail.

It's raised too late. Strategies are discussed before the value is quantified. Clients don't know what they're agreeing to, so approval is either vague or never given. Fees are mentioned only after work starts, if at all. Advice leaks out during compliance meetings. By the time June arrives, everyone is tired and risk-averse.

Over time, practices learn the wrong lesson.

They conclude that clients "won't pay for tax planning". The numbers tell a different story. The average Australian accounting partner earns around $340,000 per year in a compliance-focused practice. When firms bolt on ad hoc advisory, including tax planning, that profit typically falls by around 30% — more thinking, more pressure, more responsibility, and very little structure.

But when advisory is systemised, the outcome flips completely. Practices that embed structured, repeatable advisory services routinely generate two to three times the partner profit of compliance-only firms. Same clients. Same technical knowledge. Completely different outcome — purely because of the system used to deliver it.

That matters more now than ever.

Compliance margins are tightening, and they won't be coming back. Automation continues to strip time and value out of basic tax work, and measures like the $1,000 standard deduction are clear signals of where things are heading. Low-value compliance is being simplified, standardised, and pushed further down the value chain. Practices built purely on compliance will feel that pressure year after year — not because they're doing anything wrong, but because the ground underneath them is shifting.

Tax planning, done properly, is one of the highest-value services an accountant can deliver — but only when it's treated as a decision system, not a last-minute favour.

That's what the 5-Minute Tax Planning Triage System is designed to do.

In five minutes, the accountant does three things — every year, for every business client:

- Identify whether a genuine tax planning opportunity exists
- Quantify the potential value and the tax gap
- Secure approval to proceed with a paid, fixed-price tax plan

No strategies are given away.

No work starts without approval.

No guessing.

This is how tax planning stops being something you rush through in June — and becomes a structured, repeatable, and profitable part of how your practice actually operates.

The Framework

The 5-Minute Tax Planning Triage System

Most tax planning problems don't come from a lack of ideas.

They come from a poor structure.

In many practices, tax planning starts too late, runs too long, and is priced too low. Accountants give away thinking before anyone has agreed that the work is worth doing. By the time fees are mentioned, the value has already leaked out of the conversation.

The 5-Minute Tax Planning Triage System fixes that by separating decision-making from delivery.

- This is not a tax plan,
- It's not advice.
- It's a gate.

The system exists to answer three questions only:

1. Is there likely to be a genuine tax planning opportunity here?
2. Is the opportunity material enough to justify proper work?
3. Is the client willing to approve and pay for a formal tax plan?

If the answer to any one of those is no, the process stops.

That discipline is the system.

The Principles Behind the System

A few rules matter.

- **Tax planning is a decision, not a discussion.** Clients don't need education to decide. They need clarity.
- **Value must be identified before work starts.** If you can't point to a dollar range, there is nothing to approve.
- **Nothing is delivered without consent.** Triage identifies opportunity. Delivery is scoped, priced, and paid.
- **Consistency beats brilliance.** This works because it's done every year, the same way, for every client.

Where the Triage Happens

The triage is run **after compliance**, not during the April–June rush.

Usually:

- At the year-end compliance meeting, once the return is explained, or
- As part of a scheduled annual review

The process is capped at five minutes.

That limit is deliberate. It keeps the conversation tight and prevents drift.

Step 1: Set the Frame

Once compliance is finalised, the accountant deliberately shifts the conversation forward.

The wording matters. It should sound like this:

"When we talk about tax planning, we're not talking about last-minute deductions before 30 June. Proper tax planning looks ahead — at structures, cash flow, and upcoming decisions — before tax is incurred. Today, we're not doing a tax plan. We're just doing a quick triage to see if there's anything worth planning properly."

This makes it clear:

- This isn't advice
- This isn't free
- This is a decision point

Step 2: Initial Opportunity Assessment
(Judgement)

This step is about professional judgement.

The accountant quickly assesses who is paying the tax, at what rate, and whether the system is under pressure.

This is not a review. It's a sense-check.

What is considered

Structure and income flow

- Individual, company, trust, SMSF or group
- Where profits are landing
- Whether income is concentrated in one place

Tax rates

- Overall effective tax rate across the group
- By entity:
    - o Individuals at marginal rates

  - Companies at 25% or 30%
  - Trust distributions and where tax ultimately sits

Pressure points

- Profits growing faster than structures have evolved
- High marginal rates across most income levels
- Retained profits with no clear plan
- Assets held personally by default
- Cash flow stress or tax surprises
- Upcoming sales, restructures, succession, or exit

The question being answered is simple:
Based on what we know right now, is this worth checking further?
If not, the triage stops here.

Step 3: Opportunity Confirmation
(Guidance only)

This step strengthens judgment with discipline.

Nothing is being designed, and no advice is being given.

The accountant confirms whether the opportunity identified in Step 2 is real, relevant, and worth quantifying, based on the whole picture, not just the tax return.

This confirmation considers:

Client goals and intent (yes/no, not discussion)

- Minimise tax now and over time
- Increase profit or cash flow
- Grow the business
- Asset protection
- Lifestyle improvement
- Succession or sale
- Finance readiness

Assets and liabilities — business and personal

- Business assets and debt
- Home and mortgage
- Superannuation
- Shares and investments
- Rental property
- Cryptocurrency
- Cash reserves
- Personal debt

To ensure consistency and avoid relying on memory, the accountant runs a short TaxFitness AI strategy selection scan.

This provides guidance only.

No strategies are explained. No solutions are discussed.

Its purpose is to confirm:

- That recognised opportunities commonly apply
- That the opportunity aligns with the client's goals and balance sheet
- That it's worth quantifying properly

If not, the triage stops.

Step 4: Quantify the Opportunity and Show the Tax Gap (Materiality check)

This is where the conversation becomes concrete.

Using a one-page tax summary, the accountant shows:

- Where tax is currently being paid
- How much tax is being paid
- The size of the gap

One page. No clutter.

The summary includes:

- Taxable income and estimated tax payable for:
    - Individuals
    - Companies
    - Trusts
    - SMSFs
- Group totals:
    - Total taxable income
    - Total tax payable
    - Effective average tax rate
- A conservative indicative tax saving range

No modelling. No promises.

The question now is:

Is this big enough to justify doing something about?

If it isn't, the triage stops.

Step 5: Ask for the Decision

Clients will usually ask:

"So what do we do about it?"

Only now does the accountant move forward.

The response is consistent:

"If you want us to explore this properly, that's a formal tax plan. We scope it, price it upfront, and you decide before we do any work."

The tax plan exists to:

- Confirm what's achievable
- Address the tax gap identified
- Set out steps, risks, and timing

If approved, the engagement proceeds on a fixed price.

If not, nothing happens — and no value has been given away.

Why This System Works

This system works because it protects time and value.

The firm invests **five minutes per business client per year** — often prepared by staff — until a client commits.

Not every client will proceed in year one. Some will. Others won't.

That's fine.

You don't need every client to do tax planning.

You only need the clients with:

- A real opportunity
- A willingness to act
- A readiness to pay

Run this process:

- Every year
- For every business client
- The same way, every time

Over time, tax planning stops being rushed and underpriced.

It becomes what it should be — a structured, paid, repeatable advisory service built into how the practice operates.

Case Study

The 5-Minute Tax Planning Triage System – Construction Trust with High Profits

(*Steps 1–3 unchanged for context*)

The numbers (de-identified)

Net trust profit (pre-distribution): $672,000

- Distribution method: 50% husband / 50% wife
- Distribution per individual: $336,000

The 5-Minute Tax Planning Triage (run after compliance)

Step 1 – Set the frame

"Let's take five minutes to check whether this business is paying more tax than it needs to."

Step 2 – Initial opportunity assessment

- High trust profit
- Straight 50/50 distribution
- Individuals in top marginal tax brackets
- No corporate beneficiary
- No planning strategies

Likely opportunity identified.

Step 3 – Opportunity confirmation

- Profit well above individual thresholds
- No tax smoothing or profit capping
- Common, low-risk strategies are clearly applicable

Material planning opportunity confirmed.

Step 4 – Quantify the opportunity (show the tax gap)

Current position (no planning)

Item	Husband	Wife	Total
Trust distribution	$336,000	$336,000	$672,000
Taxable income	$336,000	$336,000	$672,000
Approx. tax & Medicare (top rates)	$155,000	$155,000	$310,000

Outcome: Most of the profit is taxed at 47%.

Indicative position (with tax planning)
Using standard, mainstream strategies:

- Corporate beneficiary to cap tax
- Timing of distributions
- Superannuation optimisation

Item	Amount
Estimated tax payable after planning	$185,000 – $215,000
Indicative annual tax saving	$95,000 – $125,000

No aggressive strategies.
No schemes.
Just using the structure properly.

Step 5 – Ask for the decision
One question:

"Do you want to keep paying roughly $310,000 in tax each year, or do you want us to design a plan to reduce this by around $100,000 legally?"

The decision was immediate.

The outcome
For the client

- Significant reduction in tax
- Improved cash flow
- Greater control over retained profits
- Clear, ongoing plan

For the accounting firm

- $10,000+ annual tax planning engagement

- Defined scope
- Advisory delivered with intent

Why this works

This step matters because:

- Clients don't react to percentages
- They react to dollars lost

The 5-Minute Tax Planning Triage System makes the tax gap visible, fast, and unavoidable.

Compliance first

Five minutes second.

Advisory on purpose.

Implementation Guide

Embedding the 5-Minute Tax Planning Triage System in Your Practice

This only works if it becomes a **process**, not a good intention.

The objective is simple:

Every business client, every year, gets the same five-minute tax planning triage.

Here's how to embed it properly.

Step 1: Lock It into the Year-End Meeting

(*Framework Step 1: Set the frame*)

The triage must be anchored to an existing meeting.

It is run:

- After the tax return is explained, or
- As part of a scheduled annual business review

It is **not** added to April–June tax planning conversations.

Make it a standing agenda item:

1. Compliance done
2. Tax planning triage
3. Decision

If it isn't anchored, it won't happen consistently.

Step 2: Standardise the Language and Enforce the Time Limit
(*Framework Step 1 continued*)

The framing statement is fixed. No improvising.

Five minutes is a boundary, not a guideline.

This is triage — not advice.

The moment the discussion drifts into "what we could do", the system breaks.

Step 3: Structure, Pressure, Goals & Balance Sheet Check
(*Framework Steps 2 and 3 combined*)

To keep this fast, the same inputs are reviewed every time.

This step answers one question:

Is there likely to be a genuine opportunity worth checking properly?

At a high level, confirm:

Structure and tax position

- Entity structure and where profits land
- Group effective tax rate (high level)

Pressure points

- Rising profits and rising tax
- High marginal rates
- Retained profits with no plan
- Division 7A issues
- Cash flow strain or tax surprises

- Upcoming asset sales, restructures, succession, or exit

Client goals and intent (yes/no, not discussion)
- Minimise tax now and over time
- Increase profit or cash flow
- Grow the business
- Asset protection
- Lifestyle improvement
- Succession or sale

Assets and liabilities (business and personal)
- Business assets and debt
- Home and mortgage
- Superannuation
- Investments and shares
- Rental property
- Crypto
- Cash and personal debt

This doesn't need to be perfect. It needs to be *directionally correct.*

Using these inputs, run the **TaxFitness AI opportunity confirmation scan** to sense-check relevance and avoid missing obvious opportunities.

No strategies are explained. No solutions are discussed.

This step exists to confirm whether the opportunity is real enough to quantify.

Step 4: Produce the One-Page Tax Summary
(*Framework Step 4: Quantify the gap*)
This is the centrepiece of the triage.

One page only:

- Taxable income and estimated tax payable by:
  - Individuals
  - Companies
  - Trusts
  - SMSFs
- Group totals and effective tax rate
- A conservative **indicative tax saving range**

No modelling. No promises.
Just a visible **tax gap** that supports a decision.
If the gap isn't material, the triage stops here.

Step 5: Ask for the Decision
(*Framework Step 5*)
Clients will usually ask: "So what do we do about it?"

The response is consistent: "If you want us to explore this properly, that's a formal tax plan. We scope it, price it upfront, and you decide before we do any work."

If approved:

- Issue scope
- Set fixed price
- Get approval
- Book the work

If not, nothing happens — and no value has leaked.

Step 6: Track Usage, Not Just Fees
Track:

- Triage conversations run
- Stops at "no opportunity"
- Stops at "not material"
- Conversions to paid tax plans

This tells you whether the system is being used appropriately — not whether "clients won't pay".

Step 7: Run It Every Year, Without Emotion

Not every client proceeds. That's fine.

You only need the clients who:

- Have a real opportunity
- Want better outcomes
- Will pay for it

Run this process **every year**, for **every business client**, the same way.

That's how tax planning stops being rushed and underpriced — and becomes a structured, repeatable, profitable advisory service inside your practice.

Action Checklist

Turning the 5-Minute Tax Planning Triage System into Reality

Use this checklist to move from intention to execution. Keep it simple. Consistency matters more than perfection.

1. **Decide that every business client gets triaged — no exceptions.**
   If partners can opt out, the system collapses.
2. **Lock the triage into your year-end meeting agenda.**
   Run it after compliance is explained, not during the April–June rush.
3. **Fix the framing language and stop improvising.**
   Use the exact opening words every time. This prevents free advice and keeps the conversation controlled.
4. **Create one internal triage input sheet.**
   Capture structure, tax rates, pressure points, goals, and assets/liabilities in one place — quickly, not perfectly.

5. **Embed the opportunity confirmation step.**
   Use TaxFitness AI as a sense-check, not a talking point. It supports judgment and consistency, nothing more.
6. **Build and template the one-page tax summary.**
   Produce it the same way every time using **TaxFitness**, so it's fast, consistent, and based on real data — not spreadsheets or memory. One page only. No strategies. No promises. Just a clear tax gap and an indicative savings range.
7. **Separate triage from delivery — completely.**
   No tax plan work starts without a defined scope, a fixed price, and written approval.
8. **Delegate preparation, not the decision.**
   Staff prepare the inputs. Partners lead the conversation and ask for the decision.
9. **Track usage, not just fees.**
   Measure how often the triage runs and where it stops. Data beats excuses.
10. **Run it every year, without emotion.**
    Not every client will proceed — and that's fine. Over time, the right clients will.

Do these ten things consistently, and tax planning stops being rushed, underpriced, and uncomfortable — and becomes a structured, repeatable advisory service inside your practice.

Conclusion

Tax planning doesn't break down because accountants don't know enough. It breaks down because there's no system to decide when it's worth doing and when it isn't.

The 5-Minute Tax Planning Triage System fixes that. It creates a simple, repeatable decision point for every business client, every year. In five minutes, you identify whether there's a real opportunity, put a dollar range around it, and ask the client to decide. Nothing more.

No strategies are given away. No work starts without approval. And nothing relies on memory, confidence, or "we'll come back to it later".

When tax planning is treated as a decision, not a discussion, it stops being rushed and underpriced. It becomes structured, predictable, and easy to charge for. That's when it starts working — for the client and for the practice.

CHAPTER 9

Advisory By Design

Richard Francis

Introduction

Once you have decided (as surely you have by now!) to be advisory by choice in pursuit of profit with passion, the fun begins. Being 'advisory by design' is shorthand for designing the organisation, strategy, skillsets, services and methods of delivery for your practice. This is whiteboard/mind-map magic-making of the highest order, and will be an investment in time, brain power and vision that you won't regret.

Designing the Profitable Advisory Practice

Most firms that I have dealt with over the years as Spotlight Reporting CEO have said that they are (or aspire to be) "advisory-led". This is grand, but if the traditional muscle memory and economics of the firm still show compliance-dependency, then some high-level design and strategy questions need to be tackled.

Following my own trial and error of creating an advisory firm from scratch and observing hundreds of others do it with varying degrees of success, the methodology I would follow would be:

1. **Design your advisory practice at a high level** – draw a picture, outline the 'bottom lines' and set some sketch goals.
2. **Determine and detail the key building blocks of the practice** – step through the 7 essentials using my checklist

and 'leading questions' for debate and digression.

3. **Mind the gap(s)!** - having completed steps 1 and 2, perform an honest gap assessment across 5 key baselines to determine critical 'gap-filling' steps to optimise.
4. **Lock in the irreplaceable human ingredients** - and circle back to the starting point of your Why? whilst also considering how the human elements will raise your organisational design above the pragmatic to embrace the passionate.

Design the Future

If you're open to reinvention and change—fantastic. Now it's time to get intentional with your organisational design.

By choice you have either started your own firm, re-positioned yourself within your existing firm, or committed to a new direction for the practice you own. We're ready now to roll up the sleeves and design something special. This is the creative, fun and slightly scary part of the profitable firm journey.

Designing your future business model means more than tweaking the status quo. It often requires a clean slate—psychologically and practically. That means setting aside "how things are done" and imagining how they *could* be—shaped by purpose, efficiency, and alignment with your **Why**.

This process should lock in a decision about what you're really going to become. Is advisory your core identity ("advisory led"), a premium offering ("advisory ready"), or ad hoc reactive ("advisory capable")? This is key for a number of reasons, as we'll explore later in this chapter.

Creating the 'right' value-add service model for you and by you requires research, blue sky thinking, consultation - and a decent white board, too. Drawing a picture just might be worth a thousand words and to be honest, there's nothing quite as visceral as holding a whiteboard marker and staring at the white space of possibility.

So grab a whiteboard or a blank sheet of paper—literally. Start sketching your vision for a business that resonates with your goals, values, and strengths. Whether you're solo or collaborating with like-minded partners, this stage is about imagination and clarity.

My Own Example

When I decided to found my own practice, I realised I needed to start organisational design from scratch. I had seen first-hand how larger firms, built on volume and scale, often struggled to make a meaningful impact. Workload pressures pushed teams into transactional, reactive modes—churning rather than transforming.

I wanted something smaller, smarter, and more personal. I chose to create something new—a boutique consultancy built on advisory foundations, not a traditional accounting firm. Advisory was central to who we were, how we pitched ourselves and our brand equity; compliance was our ad hoc side-line and initially we didn't even promote that we were Chartered Accountants, which was pretty radical at the time.

I envisioned a tight-knit team or 'pod', a modest but ambitious client base, and a culture grounded in depth of relationships over volume. A strong work-life balance and personal fulfilment were non-negotiables, especially as we were planning a family and had a thirst for travel and adventure.

While we didn't fixate on serving a specific niche, we naturally gravitated toward New Zealand's emerging tech and start-up scene—an energetic space full of aspirational businesses that *needed* growth-focused advisory. Our primary target market was locally-based, globally-ambitious and early stage.

Our sweet spot would become delivering high-impact Virtual

CFO services—with just a touch of traditional accounting. We broadened our remit to a range of interesting businesses across a few industries, but holding true to our Client Acceptance Criteria. We slowly built our boutique firm around the clients we wanted to serve and the lives we wanted to lead.

For me, once I had my why of "empowering our customers to achieve transformation outcomes" firmly established and a mantra of "be different", it was easier to create my own **client-centric business model**. I took up the whiteboard marker and drew one image (now flashed up by our designers); and yes, in a nod to a certain space movie franchise that I have followed since I was knee high to a grasshopper, it helped to visualise the shape of things to come.

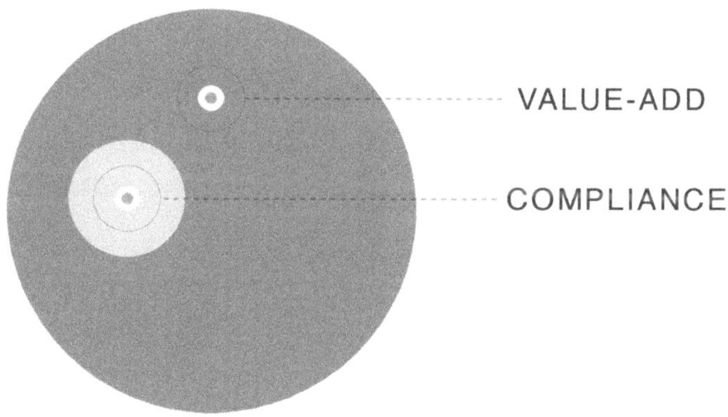

We conceptualised an 80:20 split of advisory vs compliance, with a small but powerful 'compliance' tractor-beam to bring in clients if need be. Advisory was our North Star – and actually it turned out that our advisory and value-add vision and service matrix were more of an attractant to the target clients than the fact we were Chartered Accountants.

Once you've drawn *your* future, the building blocks or core components now need your attention. You have nailed the Why and drawn at a conceptual level the What – but the How is of course equally important.

Building Blocks

Whatever your overall organisation design or visual is, your actual business model – the engine by which vision becomes reality - will need to account for several foundational attributes:

1. **Market**
2. **Customers**
3. **Services**
4. **Delivery**
5. **Team**
6. **Processes**
7. **Culture**

Be clear on what belongs in your model—and what gets left *out*. Avoid simply copying what others are doing. Your model should mix tested ideas with your unique perspective and ambition.

These building blocks will form the shape and direction of your practice. Alongside your vision and mission (or Why and What), this work should coalesce into a kick-arse Strategic Plan.

Key Questions to Ask Yourself

If your goal is to build a profitable value-add practice, consider these 'design' questions:

- Are we **advisory-led, advisory-ready or advisory-capable?** (core, hybrid or ad hoc)
- What **size** do I want my business to be? (Boutique, medium-sized or mega)
- What **target customers** do I want to serve? (and is this a niche or a horizontal play?)

- What **defining attributes** should those customers have? (create a checklist)
- What **services** will we offer—and how will we **price** these? (what energises you and your target market? What is the value creation worth?)
- Which **revenue split** (advisory vs compliance) makes most sense? (set targets across multiple years)
- What will I emphasise in my **messaging and brand**? (seek alignment with the mission)
- What **skills** do I need to develop—personally and with the team? (can we deliver?)
- What **kind of team** do I need to build or grow or resource? (how and who will I hire?)
- What will be our defining **culture and values**? (essential for reconnection on the journey)
- What **tools and processes** will help me deliver efficiently and effectively? (app stack plus customer journey flow)
- Do my answers **align with my Why**—or is it time to re-evaluate or redesign? (an important last step to ensure you're staying true to your defining vision).

These questions are intentionally personal as well as professional. They are not an exhaustive list but should encompass most of the principles of organisation design as well as enabling you to balance that mix of personal, professional and financial aspiration.

Your answers will ultimately need to *connect* to your purpose and what organisation that you aspire to construct and evolve - not just filling out a business canvas. If your responses feel diluted by too many conflicting views or agendas, your design may lose its potency. If you have business partners, collaboration and compromise will be necessary - but don't be afraid to articulate your ideal vision and fight for it.

Structure Meets Strategy

It is so easy to have a misalignment between your strategy and your structural design, especially if you have come from a traditional firm. Most firms, especially the mid to larger ones, have a structure around technical specialism (Compliance Team, Advisory Team, Tax Team, Administrators). This model isn't set up with client-centricity or ownership in mind, but instead creates internal silos, competition and hand-offs that slow service delivery down.

Maisy Harris is a successful two office practice in the north of New Zealand. Co-founder Peter Harris recently spoke to me on the *Advisory Edge* podcast series. Peter confessed that he and Nathan Maisey (who both started in a large logo firm), initially made the mistake of transplanting the traditional organisation design and processes to their young business:

"We followed what we knew and started doing what we thought we needed to do, rather than what we were passionate about. We learnt some lessons the hard way but once we had designed and crafted the firm around our passion and working with clients we wanted to work with, only then did we fly."

This is a common founder story in our profession and one that resonates with those of us who have tried to grow beyond our origin learnings. Maisey Harris are now one of the most respected advisory practices in the region and continue to be advisory-led, structured around the client relationship delivery.

Service Opportunity Matrix

Whether it's increasing profits, building personal wealth, or seizing growth opportunities, your profitable advisory services need to be built to deliver tangible results for clients and you. Being advisory by choice and design raises the bar of expectation and the need to deliver value, always – especially if you are pricing for value (outputs) rather than time (inputs).

Key examples of great value add service options include **Virtual CFO reporting, strategic planning, goal-setting, and budgeting/forecasting.** These should not be seen as optional or ad hoc extras, but essential 'level-ups' for ambitious SMEs that you can position and execute on. When done well, these elevate your role from accountant to **trusted advisor**.

You may choose to specialise or remain generalist. You could build:

- A **Virtual CFO firm** that also handles compliance work;
- A **strategic mentoring practice** for tech start-ups or another industry vertical;
- An **industry specialist** focused on franchising, creatives, or not-for-profits;
- Or a **generalist practice for SMEs** who value advisory services and the investment in their future.

Whatever you choose, make sure your service model makes sense—for both your market and you.

Our basic model looked like this:

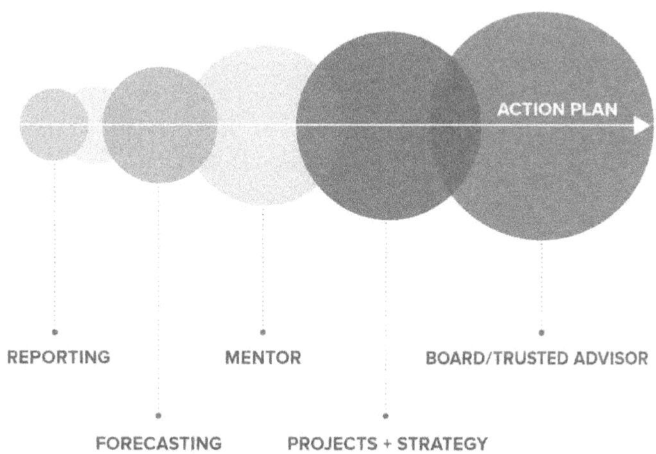

Each and every client got regular management reporting with visuals and recommendations (often the starting point for a deeper relationship), a cashflow forecast and budget (because every business deserves a future view), ongoing mentoring fit-for-purpose (generally monthly or bi-monthly), annual strategic planning (a great anchor service), gnarly projects as needed (often positioned and 'sold' by the client themselves) and – if this was appropriate – an Advisory Board of the wise. Underpinning our services and the understanding between advisor and client were Action Plans to drive momentum and accountability (and this is one reason why we have Action Plans as a key piece of functionality in the Spotlight Reporting app). This approach worked well for most clients, most of the time – and if it didn't, we could refer them to a compliance accountant next door!

Your service mix and model will look different to this of course - and that's a good thing. You do you! The point is to start, not to wait for perfect clarity; the clarity you seek will ultimately come from *doing* and all of the trial and error that is part and parcel of kick-starting your new or (freshly redesigned) firm.

Mind the Gap(s)!

Once you have determined your 'perfect' advisory practice design and shaped the building blocks, you should pause, breathe and consider any mission-critical gaps to fill. Another way to look at this process, is to avoid the pitfalls or trade-offs that you can avoid with some foresight and honesty (a common down-stream regret), whilst also ensuring that you identify and forward plan for the outcomes you aspire to.

Accountants wanting to grow into advisors and/or to run their own practices typically have a mix of the following 'gaps' to consider and close if necessary:

1. Capability Gap
2. Exposure Gap
3. Time Horizon Gap
4. Financial Reality Gap; and
5. Identity Gap.

These are briefly explained below and serve as a good reality check.

1. The "Capability Gap" — your skills don't automatically align with purpose

Explained:

You may have determined your *why* and *what*, but not whether you have (or are actively building) the *skills or attributes* required for the future you want. In other words, what investment in you will *you* need to make?

As Andrew Mattner (Your Success Lab) said in his *Advisory Edge* podcast: "your firm will be limited by the investment you make in yourself."

Considerations:

Does your current role and day-to-day activity deliberately stretch the skills your future self will need?

In an accounting context, this could include:

- Building more **commercial acumen** (not just technical excellence)
- Growing Advisory and **client-facing confidence**
- More exposure to systems for **technology fluency** and/or advocacy
- Communication, storytelling, and active listening (**soft skills** development)
- Growing **leadership** before you have the title!

Many accountants wait for permission or promotion before developing these skills - by then, you'll already be behind the more ambitious and urgent.

2. The "Exposure Gap" — being good isn't enough if no one can see it

Explained:
You may have the capability and the determination, but most likely you'll still need to continue to develop your **visibility and profile**.

Considerations:
Who knows what you're capable of - and who is advocating for you when you're not in the room?

In a business launch context, or career trajectory pivot:

- Progress is accelerated by sponsors or advocates
- Internal and external visibility matters (with clients, team, networks)
- Thought leadership and community presence increasingly differentiates accountants, with social media offering an established opportunity if used wisely.

Accountants can confuse and conflate their competence or tenure with expected career velocity or inherent business desirability to outsiders. They're not the same thing and you will need to plan to smartly bridge the gap.

3. The "Time Horizon Gap" — pivots are forks in the road, not single bets

Explained:

Time horizons allow for multiple pivots or options to play out over time. Early-career growth often benefits from option-building, not all-or-nothing decisions. Even mid to later stage career moves or entrepreneurial flourishes are now quite common and more easily planned for and executed on than perhaps in a more traditional, mono past.

Considerations:

You don't have to choose your 'forever' move yet – it may be better for you to focus on building optionality over a time horizon and iterating as you go. Careers compound; small strategic moves now can create disproportionate freedom or progression later.

Examples of utilising a time horizon wisely:

- Undertaking side projects or advisory pilots inside a firm
- Secondments to other teams, in-industry stints, or portfolio roles
- Education for fresh credentials/courses aligned to future pathways
- Involvement in innovation, ESG, tech, or growth initiatives.

4. The "Identity Gap" — letting go of who you've been

Explanation:

Career acceleration often requires identity change, not just role change. This change is as much about how you perceive yourself as how others perceive you.

Consideration:
Are you willing to let go of being "Accountant X" to become "Advisor Y" who leads, challenges, and creates in the white space of advisory?

Can you move from:

- A recorder of past fact to a story teller and futurist
- Technician to commercial thinker
- Checklist follower to confident on a blank page
- Reactor to initiator?

Many accountants I have worked with over the years have stayed stuck in one swim lane for their entire careers not because of lack of opportunity or even desire, but because of a loyalty to an old self-image and the safety of the known. Often this has been an image bestowed upon them by where they work, the perception of colleagues or management, or a lack of courage to 'fill the gaps' and swim away from the side of the pool. Others have known that they aren't able to (or don't want to) move their identity or are quite happy with the status quo.

5. The "Economic Reality Gap" — purpose and passion still need a runway

Explanation:
Your pivot or plan needs to consider your **financial readiness and appetite-for-risk**, especially relevant for starting your own firm.

Considerations:
In practice:

- Understand your personal financial runway (and sacrifices you feel you can make)

- Understand your personal risk appetite and emotional resilience
- Assess and be honest about lifestyle trade-offs you are prepared to make in the short to medium term (a new firm is not a 9-to-5 gig!).

Plan for financial consequences (good, bad and ugly), don't discount the inevitable stress of starting your own advisory firm and engage your closest stakeholders. Does your 'mind the gap' plan account for financial and emotional resilience, not just intrinsic motivation? Purpose without a plan can turn into pressure - and that's when good people flame out or retreat to safe harbours.

Humans Do Advisory

A final word...don't forget that the human part of the 'advisory by design' equation is the most important part. Now this may seem like a strange statement for a software entrepreneur to make, but whilst cloud software, automation and AI are powerful enablers, they are far from the whole advisory solution. From my experience in the front-lines of the accounting profession delivering advisory services and from supporting thousands of other professionals do likewise around the globe, I remain convinced that technology (yes, including AI) augments rather than replaces the human insight, curiosity, and relationship-building required to sell, deliver, and sustain advisory services.

Technology is a means to an end, albeit an ever-evolving one. It automates tedious tasks, reduces administrative load and provides a process or workflow that supports the humans it should be designed to serve. It can empower (as we aspire to deliver at Spotlight Reporting), get creative (AI) or enslave (the epidemic of smartphone addition) - the choice is ours.

However, the human element of the advisory firm is paramount. Just as my own passion was ignited by creating customer interactions and building purposeful teams, I've observed the most memorable firms paying attention to:

- Shared mission – a belief and vision that the humans will coalesce around
- Interaction – celebrating being together, with clients and with others in the industry or eco-system
- Hiring for heart and purpose, not just technical acumen
- Building relationships that last – combining that sense of loyalty, shared purpose and familiarity.

The 'sweet spot' of Advisory – where passion and profit intersect - is invariably powered by people: professionals who combine expertise with empathy, and tech with trust. It is art and science, ears and heart. Without the right humans in the mix, your advisory model will be built on shifting sands.

Actions:

- Set aside time for focused, creative thinking for high level organisation design. Whiteboard it, sketch it, talk it through.
- Work through the 7 building blocks and start creating your How.
- Answer the challenger questions above to ensure your design is able to be clearly articulated and is deliverable
- Assess and address any gaps that need to be filled
- Deep dive into your human elements of your profitable advisory-led future.

CHAPTER 10
Advisory by Choice

Richard Francis

Two of the biggest obstacles to running a profitable *and* life-affirming accounting practice that I have witnessed during my 30 years in the accounting industry are:

1. The absence a **defining purpose and direction** – personally and professionally for the owners, and organisation-wide for the practice and team; and
2. A lack of **organisational design and operational playbook** for the win.

In other words, the 'rocket-ship' has no co-ordinates set (or clarity as to what the mission destination is in the first place!) and/or the rocket itself isn't fit for purpose and will likely splutter ineffectually on the launch pad, careen off in a crazy trajectory or – worst case – crash and burn. The stakes are high in overcoming these obstacles as early as possible, certainly well before you try to get tactical and operational for profit and growth.

As we know, many firms and their owners are burdened doing the day in, day out busy-work that has accumulated by multi-year osmosis and/or an accept-anything-with-a-heartbeat-and-a-wallet client attribution. This demand-driven, reactive state of affairs results in an unsatisfying and frequently unprofitable mix of client type, volume and demands, sapping the energy and mental health of the owners and eroding the 'bottom line' of accounting practices.

It doesn't have to be that way – and crucially, accounting firm owners or aspirants can be the authors of their own 'mission rewrite'. I have done this more than once myself, and it is one of the most positive processes of rediscovery and reconfiguration that you can invest your time, intellect and soul into.

Running a profitable practice doing *only* the work you and your team want to do isn't easy, but it is possible. It involves conscious choices and 'red lines', ensuring that energy-sappers and profit-eroders are kept firmly at arms' length. In my view, the best firms – whether advisory-focussed, hybrid or compliance-first - are run with passion and purpose, to an organisation 'design' and with established playbooks and expectations around who they work for, why and how.

When I founded my own firm, I embraced this heady mix of passion, purpose and pragmatism most resoundingly in the creation and delivery of advisory services. Crucially, I made an early and clearly defined choice for it to be so.

Like most accountants, I had started out as a compliance workhorse - and if you're reading this, chances are you did too. As a diligent professional, I quietly did my best to keep businesses compliant, organized, and afloat. It was important work (I suppose), but it seemed to me a commoditised and lower-value proposition that was largely mechanical and unstimulating. It was necessary – but was it *enough* for me to jump out of bed in the morning and feel like the outcomes I valued (life affirmation, professional growth *and* monetary reward) were being delivered?

For some of you, the answer to this question would likely be 'Yes'. For me though – in fact, from day one when I found myself blinking in the shock and awe of being in my first job at an accounting firm, complete with hessian-walled cubicles and tax returns piled high on my kitset desk – the answer was a resounding 'No'. This important epiphany in my career happened very early on, triggering my search for greater purpose, passion and 'more' to do or be in my career.

Opportunity Lost?

In the months and years that followed I felt a real sense of 'opportunity lost' in terms of deploying the skills I thought I had, what I knew our firm could do, and across our industry, which was seemingly obsessed with technicalities and reporting standards to the exclusion of all else. It quickly became evident to me that, more than any other professionals, we accountants existed in a privileged position at the fulcrum of commerce, eyeball to eyeball with entrepreneurs and the business owners that power our economies. Compliance put us on the field, gave us access to the ball, but for some reason we didn't want to pick it up and run for the try-line or to hear the delight of the crowd. I just couldn't understand why we didn't really leverage this position or status and our experience and expertise in a way that excited or delighted our customers! Surely this would be good for them – and our accounting businesses and career satisfaction; so why weren't we leaning in on this obvious opportunity to shine?

We've all heard the accountant stereotype: conservative, cautious, and slow to embrace change or swim against the tide. Like many clichés, it contains a kernel of truth – and I'm sure many of us can recognise these traits in colleagues, embedded in the DNA of any traditional firm we may have worked at, or even within ourselves. It was clear that this mindset and the weight of a traditional approach was literally the albatross around our necks, holding us back individually and collectively. In fact, we all know colleagues and commentators who delight in holding back change or who sneer at anything innovative or different to their world view. For others, they are doing just fine thanks on the historic number-crunching, so why bother to get uncomfortable by changing things up?

None of that 'don't rock the boat' thinking resonated with me – especially when I could see clients being under-serviced by us or enticed away by progressive firms, business coaches and worse. So I bided my time, developed my knowledge and skills – a nodding acquaintance with accounting, audit and tax - and eventually reached the level of free agency that comes with solid tenure, long hours, and general competence. This agency led me to a decision: I was, come Hell or high water, going to do transformational, soul-enhancing and intellectual-stimulating work that was of genuine 'added value' to the customer. High value, high margin and profitable work, to boot!

My pathway to advisory by choice resonates and reflects similar journeys made by so many of the progressive advisor-accountants of today. Steph Hinds of Growthwise, Paul Gardner of Fresh Accounting and Andrew Mattner of Your Success Lab are all cases in point.

Steph Hinds' Growthwise firm put the ninja in accounting (check out the website) and made advisory a core offering for her Newcastle clients. Getting to know clients and their goals – through structured sessions, over monthly beers and through Spotlight-empowered interactions meant that Steph not only developed 'sticky' customer relationships but was able to convert traditionally cost-averse clients (tradies, small business owners) into significant investors in their own futures (and Growthwise services).

Paul Gardner flew half way across the world and founded a virtual Finance Team-orientated firm in Hong Kong. Having come from a Finance background (rather than traditional accounting), Paul found it natural to deploy a 'virtual CFO' mindset and was an early adopter of tools such as Xero and Spotlight Reporting that enabled a broader approach to client relationships.

Andrew Mattner started out in a compliance world but realised that he needed work that connected with his passion and made him keen to jump out of bed in the morning. He wanted to do strategy, set goals with clients and truly help them succeed – not just do the numbers. Andrew's firm now has Strategic Planning as the cornerstone 'kick off' service offering for clients that want to invest in themselves and their future success. Smart move.

Advisory Defined

When I rolled up my sleeves and first got all-in on advisory, it wasn't even called 'advisory' - and I don't think anyone really cared. Somewhere I have a yellowed newspaper cutting of the press release by the 'Big 5' firm I worked for announcing my appointment as Consultancy Services Manager. It sounds terribly important and indeed was a significant organisational shift, but I'm not sure "consultancy" necessarily caught the zeitgeist of the era ahead.

For those that need definitions, Advisory Services (or whatever you wish to call them) for me have always have been *Value-add services that go beyond the "must-do" compliance core or customer 'grudge purchase' of most traditional accounting firms. Advisory services step beyond what your client simply needs to be compliant, embracing what they need or want to invest in to achieve their broader aspirations.*

This definition generally takes us into the realms of:

- insight and understanding rather than just opaque accountant-speak financial statements
- looking to and planning the future, not just consuming a stale historic view
- mentoring and guiding proactively, with regular touch-points
- considering the nexus of the business, financial and

personal goals and aspirations of clients – not just the financial outcomes of the business
- providing strategic support and stimulating strategic conversations and thinking
- helping clients execute on and achieve meaningful outcomes in their lives.

It is part art, part science and most definitely not just about filing a tax return and financial statements on time. It is where soft skills balance out our hard-won technical expertise and we connect with clients in different and more proactive ways. Advisory is about possibility and not just what is or has been.

Opportunity Knocks

Going full-monty on advisory was a conscious choice to stimulate and define my career, to be entrepreneurial within the construct of a typical accounting/tax/audit firm, and to surprise and delight our clients. Later, when I hung out my own shingle, it was a conscious choice to construct an advisory-first business model, offering proactive, future-focussed services and to position my boutique advisory firm in a way that would be seen as very different to a typical historical-numbers-and-tax-return shop.

Now before I get into foam-flecked debate with the no-school-like-old-school cohort at the next conference, I am not advocating that an advisory focus is necessarily to the exclusion of or to diminish compliance – and I wouldn't be so bold as to say that many traditional or compliance accountants can't or don't do some of this work (albeit, often reactively when asked or pushed by the client), but for advisory to flourish, a significant mindset shift and a series of choices or decisions need to be made that disrupt the status quo. If advisory services are not a conscious, defined part of the firm business model, strategy or core priority set – rather, it is perhaps seen as an occasional indulgence, ad hoc intervention or even classified as a distraction from the 'real work' of keeping the authorities happy – then it is unlikely you will 'unlock' your true profit and passion dividend.

Looking back through experienced eyes, I can safely say that being advisory by choice was the best career decision I ever made. Once committed to this direction, I found key allies at the leadership level and was empowered to establish an 'Advisory Services' offering at the firm, learning to market, sell and deliver new services to the best and most progressive clients. I learnt by doing, by observation and via accessing external mentors and stimulating resources, but still had to suck up plenty of lessons and earned a bruise or three on the way. Crucially though, it was clear early on and a great 'aha!' proof-point that clients truly valued this work and saw it as a premium offering, which made the work itself more fulfilling as we developed stronger client relationships and achieved better outcomes for all – including profits for the partners!

Global Advisory Trends

I believe that the profession is slowly embracing advisory services as a norm, or at least as an alternative pathway to profit. The latest Global Advisory Trends Report (by Spotlight Reporting, 2025) highlights the distinct evolution towards 'value add' and 'balanced' service offerings. Fully two-thirds of the 1,000+ firms (across 10 countries) in this survey now declare themselves either as "progressive" (i.e. with more advisory revenue than compliance) or as a "hybrid" firm (with a solid balance between the two fee streams). Most firms are also setting growth goals around their advisory work and investing in the tools, team and skill-mix (including training) to execute on this shift.

These trends have accelerated over the 4 years that the Global

Advisory Trends Survey has been tracking firm focus and fee mix. I'm excited by this steady industry shift, especially given that we live in a world marked by uncertainty and economic headwinds. Too often accountants have reverted to safe harbours when the wind starts to howl, but I argue that now more than ever our role should be useful, proactive, and impactful for the SMB's in the 'front lines' - not just accurate and compliant.

Time Is Now

My advisory journey was a few sleeps ago now, and how I salivate at the opportunity new tools, knowledge, and rapidly-advancing technology now provides for accountants wanting to be advisory by choice. Being advisory by choice is faster, cheaper and easier now than ever before.

Timing can be everything as they say. What excites me is the palpable sense that the 'time is now' for forward-thinking firms and existing or aspiring leaders to reimagine their role - not just as compliance professionals, but as strategic partners with customers. Many new entrants to the profession are no longer interested in the status quo either; they want to be change agents, movers and shakers – trusted advisors utilising tools that empower and thinking that stimulates.

One of the joys of my current role as an advisory software CEO is talking to hundreds of practitioners in our great accounting industry every year. From solo bookkeepers to global behemoths, technology and changing consumer expectations are levelling the playing field. Cloud platforms, AI and eco-system software give small and mid-sized firms access to the kind of technological firepower once reserved for global giants. Today, any ambitious practitioner can (with the right mindset, tech stack and support) automate the repetitive, collaborate seamlessly, and streamline their workflows. This massive shift from the world of desktop, paper and disconnection (which were hallmarks of the profession when I entered it), has the potential to free up the time, headspace and imagination for the cultivation and delivery of richer services - all without being tied to a physical office or legacy infrastructure.

Embrace the Freedom

If I had to summarise the biggest difference between the professional opportunity now from when I entered the industry, it would be *freedom*. Old models were locked in, manual, based on patronage and ladder-climbing, with tech sparingly used or not yet available and clients told what to do (generally once per year). Today, we have unprecedented freedom to shape our practices, careers and the industry itself:

- Freedom to rethink and adapt business models - fast
- Freedom to serve clients from anywhere in the world
- Freedom to scale impact without scaling your overhead
- Freedom to share, collaborate and engage with each other and our teams.

This freedom, combined with the disruption from AI, the benefits of more tightly integrated cloud ecosystems, changing client expectations, and a purpose-driven workforce is creating unprecedented opportunity right now. Whilst industry innovation at a macro level may remain gradual at best, entrepreneurial and visionary accountants are getting ahead of the curve to embrace change and create their own reality. And they're doing it right now.

Getting Started

1. Identify and Articulate Your "Why?"

As we heard earlier, I experienced a not uncommon introduction to the coal-face of the accounting profession. I can still recall the visceral dread that descended on day one of being in the 'workforce' as shoeboxes of receipts were dropped on my desk and my allocated office 'buddy' reluctantly showed me the ropes ('induction' was not really a concept back then!). Deadlines were tight (so I was told – this was news to me!), clients were already grumpy (apparently this was a fairly consistent state of affairs), the accounting firm expected results (I wasn't sure which), and I needed to account for every six minutes of my day (what!? And why six?).

Now before I get a letter from the lawyers, I freely acknowledge that I had scored a role at a decent firm with good people. It's just how it was in the profession and at a compliance-first practice.

What kept me sane and hopeful was the belief that our skills and our humanity could actually be used to deliver something more useful. Importantly, the more humans I met the greater the validation of my thesis that our clients actually *wanted* more too, even if they weren't always sure what that could be or whether we were the people to provide it. This belief kept me moving forward one step at a time with my professional radar on full beam searching for those moments of opportunity.

Eventually, I got my 'pivot' opportunity and I was lucky and motivated enough to position myself as the young upstart best given a chance to 'lean in' on this value-adding work. When 'consultancy' work ramped up and our value proposition not only shifted but became my daily focus, everything shifted: I was engaged, energised, and fulfilled. The powers-that-be celebrated a fee jump and clients started to *want* to see me and engage on more than just the backward-looking number crunch. Happy days!

I started to connect my "Why" to my work in the months and years ahead by sitting with clients and asking questions, probing just a bit deeper on a human level. I wanted to understand what their aspirations were and the roadblocks to success; they wanted to share and to jointly chart a positive and proactive course forward.

Years later and like millions of others, I watched the *Start With*

Why? TEDx talk by Simon Sinek (2009) and then bought the book, too. In just a few minutes he hit the nail on the head of how I had been feeling all of those years ago, but also how I had recalibrated my trajectory by defining my own Why? and taking steps to make it a reality in my career.

Sinek captures a powerful human truth: the most successful individuals and organisations are anchored in a clear, compelling sense of purpose; they know their **"Why?"**—and they use it to inspire customers, attract talent, and fuel growth. It might seem obvious, but how many of us have evaluated this truism head-on and looked in the mirror?

One line from Sinek's talk leapt out to me:

"Why do you get out of bed in the morning - and why should anyone care?"

It's a confronting question, especially as you get further into your career and questions of legacy and succession start to whisper in your ear. Can you answer it?

"People don't buy what you do they buy why you do it". I reframe this today as:

- Why does *your* organisation or practice exist?
- Why do *you* do what you do?

These aren't abstract musings. In fact, they're the foundation of your value-add journey. Without a clear North Star (or Southern Cross if you are in my neck of the woods), navigating transformation becomes harder, less meaningful, and far less sustainable.

So I encourage you to reflect, challenge and choose if you truly want to land on the intersection of passion and profit via advisory services. Write down your Why?, draw a picture, review and sleep on it – whatever it takes. This is not a box-ticking exercise - it's a self-reflection, intellectual and emotional investment that could shape your entire future trajectory.

2. Make Today Serve Tomorrow

Now that you have (hopefully) defined and refined your "Why", you can perform some straight forward 'gap analysis' to determine if your today (the here and now) serves your tomorrow (where and what you want to be). Does your current role and/or business model align with your belief, your passion – your *why?*

If it does – fantastic! Congratulations and please move forward to the 'Go' square.

But what if it doesn't? If your driving purpose feels disconnected from:

- the work you do; or
- the direction, nature and/or cultural setting of your organisation...

...then you face a choice. Possibly a big one.

Disconnection doesn't need to mean despair of course; I should know! It does mean **opportunity** though - to rethink, reset, and reclaim your direction. Here are four possible pathways to consider:

1. **Reinvent yourself within your current organisation.** Change your role, mindset, or approach. Pivot, find your tribe or create one.
2. **Design a new future** by moving to another firm that aligns better with you. They'll be out there – ask around.
3. **Start your own firm** or business – build from the ground up! I can recommend this, but it's not for the faint-hearted.
4. **Leave the profession** if it no longer serves you—and channel your skills and passion elsewhere.

If you already own and run your own practice, the great news is you have your hands on the controls and more readily choose or iterate the pathway you are on.

My Leap

I turned down a partnership at the successful 'Big 5' firm I had started at to strike out on my own (after the obligatory late 20's travel years). It was a leap of faith in a pre-cloud world, but what made the leap less scary was I had an 'Advisory By Choice' vision, a stimulating purpose, and (most of) the skills to deliver – not to mention great support behind the scenes from my wife and family. This support made all of the difference and I suggest that you seek advice and consider all options – but having said that, only you can make the decision and take the actions to give your desired tomorrow the best chance of coming to pass.

Action Checklist (Advisory By Choice):

1. Watch Simon Sinek's "*Start With Why?*" on YouTube if you haven't seen it - or read the book
2. Reflect and define honestly: What is your "Why"? Why do you do what you do? What are you trying to achieve in the profession—and beyond?
3. Share these thoughts and dreams with a trusted colleague, mentor and/or loved ones for feedback and refinement.
4. Reflect on how you can make your today serve your tomorrow. Do some gap analysis and identify if reinvention, retraining, or relocation is needed—for you or your team.
5. Lock in your choices and ensure that you have support for the road ahead!

SECTION 4
BUILD A FIRM THAT SCALES

Create the systems, leadership structure and operational discipline required to grow without overwhelming the partners.

"Systems run the business. People run the systems."
— Michael E. Gerber

Section introduction by Monique Parker

For many accounting firms, profitability problems aren't caused by capability, effort, or even pricing. They're caused by something more nuanced: the clients that the firm serves and the way it serves them.

By the time most firms reach this section of the blueprint, they've already done a lot of the heavy lifting. Earlier chapters focus on designing a practice intentionally, improving workflow efficiency, and building advisory capability. Those foundations matter because without them, growth simply creates more pressure.

This section focuses on taking the great work that the firm is doing behind the scenes and making it visible in the market, so that future growth is aligned with internal strategy.

Across the next four chapters, we explore four powerful drivers of sustainable growth.

First, **client attraction**. The goal isn't more clients. It's better clients — businesses that value advice, respect boundaries, and are willing to pay appropriately for expertise. A well-designed marketing framework helps firms move away from reactive referrals and toward intentionally attracting clients who fit their model.

Second, **brand authority**. In professional services, brand is often misunderstood as logos or colours. In reality, it's reputation and perception. It's the reason a client chooses your firm before they even speak to you. A strong advisory brand positions a firm as the obvious choice for certain clients and problems — which naturally supports premium pricing.

Third, **strategic partnerships**. Some of the fastest-growing firms don't rely solely on marketing. They build networks of aligned professionals — bankers, lawyers, financial planners, consultants, and technology providers — who create consistent referral pathways. When partnerships are intentional, they can become one of the most powerful growth engines in a practice.

Finally, **client experience**. Many firms focus heavily on attracting clients but give far less attention to what happens after the engagement begins. Yet client experience is one of the most powerful drivers of referrals, retention, and fee growth. Every interaction — from onboarding to communication to delivery — shapes how clients talk about your firm.

Together, these chapters explore how firms can move from being **technically competent providers** to becoming **trusted, visible, and sought-after advisors**.

Because clients rarely pay premium fees for firms that feel interchangeable.

And the opposite also holds true…

In today's AI-powered landscape, scaling transactional relationships is not a sound strategy to future-proof your firm's profit (or sanity)!

Instead, progressive firms are looking to unlock more profit by maximising the transformational nature of their client relationships and services.

Having a strong brand that stands for something becomes a beacon to the right clients, partners, and team members in a crowded market.

Let's shine a light on how to make that happen in your firm!

CHAPTER 11

A-Class Client Attraction – The Marketing Framework to Secure Better Clients and Fee Uplift

Monique Parker

Introduction – The Right Clients Will Transform Your Firm

The most profitable firms aren't busy "generating leads", they're curating their client bases behind the scenes.

And the least profitable and most stressed? They're doing the opposite.

Somewhere along the way, many firms have accidentally built a client base full of what I lovingly call **D-Class Daves.**

You know Dave.

Nice enough. Been around forever. Pays late. Questions every invoice. Ignores advice. Wants "just a quick call". Refers you to his cousin who is… also Dave.

Multiply Dave by 20–40% of your client list and suddenly:

- You don't even *want* more clients
- Capacity issues are impossible to fix
- Your best staff burn out
- And your best clients quietly subsidise the worst ones

The reality is that there's simply **no room in your firm** for better clients while your worst ones are getting all your attention (and causing all the headaches).

If you've read this far, you already know this.

Deep down, most firm owners know they need to bite the bullet and bid farewell to some troublesome fees.

You can sell off a parcel of fees (there's lots of smaller firms who'd be delighted to take Dave off your hands), increase your prices (Dave magically disappears by himself), or you can send the infamous "Dear John" letters to a percentage of your clients each year.

Regardless of the strategy, you can make these sorts of decisions more comfortably when you have a plan in place to attract more **A-Class Clients.**

A-Class clients are commercially minded. They value time, clarity, data-driven decision making, and expert guidance. They want a firm that looks like it is already helping clients like them achieve the outcomes they want.

Let's make this real.

Meet **Abby**.

Abby is ambitious.

Her business is in growth mode.

Her finances are ready for restructuring.

She knows she needs the right advice – and she's prepared to pay for it.

Let's break down some of the key differences in these client profiles:

Dave	Abby
Chooses an accountant based on price	Chooses an accountant based on value
Wants "just the basics"	Wants insight, clarity, and strategy

Questions invoices	Understands what expertise costs
Ignores advice	Implements advice
Seeking quick fixes	Desires sustainable results
Creates noise and urgency	Creates momentum and progress
Drains team energy	Generates meaningful work
Refers more Daves	Refers more Abbys
Keeps the firm busy	Helps the firm grow

When you display these client personas side-by-side, it's easy to see which one you would choose. Yet, accounting firms put messages out into the market that are (accidentally) appealing to Dave instead of Abby.

Like DIY tax hacks, promises of saving money, generic stock images, and boring advice without any context or depth.

Abby is successful and she's not looking for the cheapest service or a firm with a legacy dating back to 1970, she's looking for **the best firm for her**.

Which is why advertising without a strategic framework doesn't work.

Agencies are incentivised to maximise enquiries while minimising price by using tactics that appeal to the masses. Mostly… Daves.

That approach works for many industries. It does not work for professional services firms trying to attract premium clients.

What you need is a **tactical client attraction plan**.

A marketing "welcome mat" designed specifically for Abby.

Because when A-Class clients are knocking on your door, it's easier to gently close the door to Dave.

Forever.

So let's get started!

Breakout Quote: It's hard to roll out the welcome mat for your ideal clients while you're busy being a doormat to those paying the least.

The A-Class Client Attraction Framework

As you read through this framework, you might think:

"This feels basic."

"This is common sense."

And you'd be right!

But in my experience, around 99% of firms aren't actually implementing any of it.

Not that they can't – but because they're distracted, overwhelmed, or blindly following the advice of marketing experts who don't understand accounting firms.

I get it.

That's why this framework is practical, not theoretical.

In my spare time, I summit mountains and transmit radio frequencies to people around the world. It's a hobby I started to spend more time in nature – and to connect with my dad in New Zealand, who is an official "radio ham".

What do radio frequencies have to do with client attraction?

Everything.

If I transmit on the wrong frequency, my message disappears into static – no matter how good my antenna and equipment is. No matter how many hours I transmit for.

A frequency is a signal.
It directs focus.
It allows you to be found.

That idea inspired the 4WH framework – the 4 W's and the H of client attraction. The framework is the signal that allows your firm to stand out and be found online.

The 4WH framework:

- WHO you want to work with
- WHAT they actually want from you
- WHERE they're already paying attention
- HOW you show up and convert
- WHY they should choose you (and not the firm down the road)

Let's break it down.

1. WHO — Define the A-Class Client (Not "Everyone with a Pulse")

Most firms default to vague definitions of their ideal client.

"Small businesses." "Anyone who needs an accountant."

The real question is not who *could* work with your firm.

It is who *should.*

Some client segments are easier to serve, more profitable, and far more enjoyable than others. Creating criteria gives you a lens for focus – and focus is what allows firms to deliver value consistently.

Here are examples of how to define your "Abby".

Individual Profile Examples:

- Income streams

- Net wealth or family wealth
- Property, assets, investments
- Age, dependents, stage of life

Commercial Profile Examples:

- Industry
- Revenue and/or profit
- Team size
- Structure and complexity
- Business goals and challenges
- Location

Behavioural Profile Examples:

- Ambitious
- Coachable
- Ethical

Some attributes can be screened in advance through your marketing.

Others are shaped by the expectations you set – and the behaviours you tolerate.

Your "who" doesn't just help you attract better clients.

It also helps you clearly identify who no longer belongs in your firm.

2. WHAT — The Outcomes Clients Are Really Buying

Dave pays for his compliance because he has to.

Abby invests in her future.

She still needs compliance – but she wants outcomes:

- Growth
- Profit
- Control

- Less Stress
- A better future

This is where firms get stuck worrying about labels.

Advisory. CFO services. Business planning.

Abby doesn't care what you call it.

She cares about results.

The best firms don't just describe the tasks and functions they perform, they communicate the **impact** of their services.

When you understand what Abby wants (what she really *really* wants!), you can reverse engineer:

- Your service packages
- Your messages in market
- Your first-step offers

And suddenly, your marketing starts doing the filtering for you.

3. WHERE — Being Visible in the Right Places

B2B marketing is not a mass-market game.

It is not the same as what you see Apple, Nike, or ecommerce brands on TikTok do.

Unless your firm is trying to process infinite tax returns, you don't need to be everywhere. You just need to be in the right places.

Strategic visibility is about showing up where decisions are already being influenced:

- Industry ecosystems
- Referral partners
- Niche events, publications, and communities
- Targeted digital platforms

In other words, you need to know what frequency Abby is operating on, tune your firm into that wavelength, and don't worry about the rest.

Ten ideal clients seeing you consistently beats a million random eyeballs every time.

4. HOW — Converting Attention into Currency

Visibility without a conversion mechanism is like fishing without a hook.

You need a clear pathway – a client magnet or system – that turns interest into action.

This might be:

- A survey, diagnostic, audit, or assessment
- A free resource with a high perceived value
- A paid entry-level service
- A workshop, webinar, event or experience

This process isn't just about new clients.

The same approach can be used to generate **fee uplift** within your firm, by creating opportunities for the *Abbys* hiding in your client base to say yes to!

Clients won't magically upgrade themselves.

And yes, this is the part firms often avoid because it feels "pushy".

Done properly, this process adds value, positions your pathway to the desired results, and pulls the right people toward your offers.

5. WHY — The Reason Clients Choose You

Here's the slightly brutal question:

Why would Abby choose *you*?

Lots of firms have slogans like "we're not your average accountants" on their website, but what are you doing to demonstrate that?

Your branding (visual identity, team, proof, positioning, and personality) sends a signal that your ideal clients use to assess in less than 30 seconds if you're the firm for them – or not!

Every firm has a brand, whether intentional or not, and it's either attractive or repellent to the clients (and candidates) that you want.

We'll cover branding in more detail in the next chapter.

Client Case Study

One firm I worked with wanted to sign more ecommerce clients.

Margins in ecommerce are tight, while complexity is high – physical stock, high transaction volume, and international orders.

All ecommerce businesses benefit from sophisticated financial support, but only those that have reached a certain size can afford it (and then, they can't afford not to)!

Following my advice, the firm implemented a minimum revenue benchmark for new ecommerce clients.

Any new client enquiry from a business trading below that number was offered a referral to another accounting firm they trusted.

They didn't fire their existing clients,

They simply became more selective about new ones.

Next, they repositioned their digital presence.

Out went generic blog articles about setting up Xero.

In came industry-specific insights, fashion-led visuals, and ecommerce case studies.

They exhibited at ecommerce expos and partnered with an ecommerce business coach, embedding themselves within that ecosystem.

The 4WH Framework in Action (12-month rollout):

Framework	Tactical Application
Who	Set a **minimum revenue threshold** for new ecommerce clients and added it to enquiry screening calls. Trained admin staff to redirect sub-scale enquiries to a trusted referral partner without escalating to partners. Created an internal reference sheet for client acceptance (both for ecommerce clients and non-ecommerce fees).
What	Created **three tiers of retainer service levels** specifically for ecommerce clients. Rewrote service descriptions to focus on **gross margin improvement, stock management visibility, and cash flow predictability.** Introduced an ecommerce cash audit as an easy paid engagement (for both new clients and to upsell existing clients).
Where	Booked a booth at two national **ecommerce expos** and sponsored one industry breakfast event. Reached out to secure guest speaker spots on ecommerce and fashion founder podcasts and started a **webinar** series with an ecommerce business coach. Prioritised **LinkedIn content** targeted at ecommerce founders over general social posting. Declined non-industry networking events that didn't attract ecommerce decision-makers.
How	Built a structured **discovery session** with an agenda and diagnostic checklist for clients matching the ideal client criteria. Identified financial blind spots and presented next-step recommendations with a 6–12-month roadmap that aligned to levels of the service retainers. Followed up discovery sessions with insights and invited prospects to client networking events.

Why	Replaced stock imagery with fashion and retail visuals reflecting ecommerce brands. Published three detailed ecommerce case studies on their blog showing margin improvement, cashflow stabilisation, and growth. Highlighted the firm's long-term work with ecommerce clients (not just quick wins). Added a "Who we help" section on the website to clearly signal standards and expectations.

Three years on and this firm is reaping the rewards!

Around 70% of their client base fits their A-Class profile.

They have a new client waitlist and only onboard when capacity allows.

Their team is leaner – but happier and more productive.

They regularly increase their fees without resistance.

They attract top industry talent because the work is meaningful.

By consistently transmitting such a **clear marketing signal**, the firm has become the "go to" for ecommerce founders in growth mode.

It was never about chasing more clients but becoming magnetic to the right ones.

Implementation Guide

Let's be clear upfront: I'm not suggesting that you blow up your firm or reinvent yourself overnight.

This is about progressive refinement.

Step 1: Identify Your Current A-Class Clients (and Be Honest)

This exercise is a fact-finding mission to find the gold that already exists.

Questions to ask yourself:

- Who do you enjoy working with the most **and why?**
- What are your firm's areas of expertise or specialisms?
- What work/services are the easiest to deliver relative to the fee?
- Which client types value your higher-level services the most?
- What are common traits among your current favourite clients?

I recommend stepping away from your computer and brainstorming these ideas on a piece of paper.

You may get some immediate insights.

If not, look for the *patterns* in your answers.

Your current ideal clients are the key to identifying and defining your future ideal clients, don't overthink this step or worry about what other firms are doing.

Step 2: Define Minimum Entry Criteria (Not a Niche… Yet)
Start with defining a minimum entry criteria for new clients. This is a *filter*, not a label.

Examples:

- Minimum revenue or profit (businesses)
- Minimum income or net wealth (individuals)
- Minimum entity or structure complexity
- Industries and/or service types you no longer cater for
- Alignment with your values or expectations

Setting standards creates immediate clarity – for both your team and the wider market.

Your criteria can be uplevelled over time and this step does **not** require letting go of existing clients straight away.

At this stage, you don't need to commit to choosing a niche, you're simply becoming more selective about who you want to attract as new clients.

Step 3: Outline the Results You Create for Clients

Write down the core services you'd like to promote and ask a confronting question:

"What does the client actually get from this?"

Not the deliverable.

Not the report.

Not the meeting.

The outcome.

Here's some examples:

- More profit for their hard work
- Security for the future of their family
- Cashflow stability and less stress
- Business growth that outperforms the market
- An exit that sets them up for life

Here's the truth that the coaches and gurus selling overhyped services to your clients know: if the goals and outcomes feel exciting, people will happily pay more.

Now, pressure-test this by making it more specific to your ideal A-Class client.

Step 4: Create Services & Offers for Your Ideal Clients

Make it easy for Abby to say yes!

Rather than bespoke proposals or hourly work that focuses on your process behind the scenes, create clear service packages and retainers that align with the goals and outcomes identified in the previous step.

To help transition clients into these services (and upgrade your current clients) you can add an intentional **first step** that:

- Filters out price shoppers
- Demonstrates your thinking
- Creates momentum toward higher-value work

Examples:

- Strategy or diagnostic session
- Financial health check
- Profit planning workshop
- Paid scoping engagement

Note – you're probably not going to call the first step any of the names above, those are just to help you understand the context. Service names should be tailored to the industry or circumstance of your ideal client.

"Ecommerce cashflow map for growth" sounds more enticing than a "strategy session".

Step 5: Update Your Marketing Welcome Mat

Let's make sure that Abby knows she's in the right place the minute she lands on your website or encounters your firm online.

Ask:

- Does our website clearly say who we help?
- Does it describe outcomes or just services?
- Would Abby feel like this firm "gets" her?
- Would Dave feel slightly uncomfortable?

Your goal isn't to repel people aggressively.
It's to **signal clearly**.

Often, small changes make a big difference:

- Industry-specific examples
- Clear positioning statements
- Fewer services, explained better
- Client results that demonstrate the outcomes ideal clients seek
- Stronger language around standards and expectations

A cheat code to make your marketing more client attractive, is to use the "WIIFM" acronym – "what's in it for me?"

This is where you put yourself in the readers shoes, and ask "so what?"

"*Our firm was started in 1979 by Bob Smith, who has since exited the firm after being bought out by another partner.*"

No joke, I read a variation of this phrase on half of the accounting websites I see.

Seriously – what does this mean for your new ideal clients?

Likewise with generic phrases like "experienced team" and "great service". You need to be clearer about what the benefits are to Abby in particular.

In most cases, you can't see the wood from the trees when it comes to your own business, which is where it's valuable to have an external marketing partner look at your firm with fresh eyes and from a client perspective.

Step 6: Train Your Team to Support the Shift

Client attraction fails when the front desk, managers, or partners aren't aligned.

Everyone needs to understand:

- Who you're trying to attract
- What your minimum criteria are
- How to respond to enquiries that don't fit

This is where internal reference sheets and scripts matter. Not robotic ones — but guidance.

For example:
"We're probably not the right firm for you *yet*, but here's what I recommend."

This protects your brand *and* your people.

Step 7: Use Fee Increases as a Natural Filter
Once A-Class clients start coming in, fee conversations become easier.

Because:

- You're more confident in your value
- You're not operating from scarcity
- You have demand

Strategic fee increases will:

- Improve margins
- Reduce low-value workload
- Create space for better work

And yes — some Daves will leave.
That's progress!

Step 8: Review Strategically, Not Constantly
Client attraction is not a daily decision.

Review every quarter:

- New client quality
- Fee uplift
- Team energy
- Capacity pressure

Refine. Adjust. Improve.

But don't be hasty in changing direction if you don't see instant results – strategy needs time to embed within the firm, and reactive decisions will railroad your momentum.

Action Checklist — Small, Practical Steps You Can Take This Month

This Week

- Pull a list of your top 20 clients
- Highlight the 5 you'd clone if you could
- Write down what they have in common

Next 10 Days

- Define 3–5 minimum criteria for new clients
- Write them down and share them internally
- Decide what you'll say "no" to going forward
- Identify an accounting firm to refer Dave to

Next 30 Days

- Rewrite your service descriptions in outcome language
- Update your website homepage headline
- Add one Abby-style example or case study
- Create an easy first or next step for Abby to engage with your firm
- Review your social media presence – does this stand out to your ideal clients?

Ongoing

- Deploy fee increases strategically
- Track the quality of new enquiries
- Review and refine quarterly

Closing

If your marketing is trying to attract everyone, it's not attractive to *any*one.

Abby isn't inspired by testimonials from Dave – she wants to see case studies that resonate with her situation, and to be supported by a firm that already looks like it understands her world, her pressures, and her ambition.

Some firm owners say they enjoy the variety of working with everyone. That's a valid choice — but be clear on the trade-off. Without focus, systems struggle, margins compress, and burnout becomes far more likely.

You will always find reasons why this approach won't work for you, yet I've seen it work for firms of every size across every location.

If you do the work, it will work for you.

I'll leave you with a final thought: premium clients are like Monarch butterflies.

You can spend your life chasing them in the wild or you can invest the time and resources in cultivating a garden that brings them naturally to you.

CHAPTER 12

Building Your Advisory Brand – Stand Out. Command Premium Pricing. Become the Go-To Firm

Monique Parker

Introduction

The best accounting firms I know used to be some of the industry's best-kept secrets.

Amazing work happening behind the scenes. Deep technical knowledge. Real, measurable client results.

But from the outside?

That was all invisible.

They had same-same websites. Outdated imagery. Generic messaging that could have belonged to almost any firm. Nothing that signalled the depth, sophistication, or impact of the work they were actually doing.

No wonder they weren't attracting clients for advisory work — no one could *see* it.

Meanwhile, your ideal clients (remember Abby?) are being courted daily.

By slick business coaches, influencers with a whiteboard, software providers, and AI tools giving away advice for free.

Standing out in the market with a strong advisory brand is no longer a "nice to have" for accounting firms — it's a commercial advantage.

In a market where compliance is expected, automated, and

increasingly commoditised, **your brand is what signals value beyond the numbers**.

An advisory brand positions your firm as a strategic partner, not just a service provider.

Internally, it matters just as much. A strong advisory brand gives your team a shared narrative — clarity around who you help, how you help them, and why the work matters. It supports talent attraction and retention by positioning your firm as modern, strategic, and forward-thinking — not just busy.

Here's the part most advice about advisory skips… it's not just about what your firm delivers. It's about what people **believe** you can deliver.

That belief is your advisory brand.

Your firm's brand is your overall identity — your logo, colours, website, team vibe, reputation. It's the perception people form before they've even met you. And perception shapes reality.

Your perceived value.

Your perceived expertise.

Your perceived relevance.

Your firm already has a brand, whether you've built it intentionally or not. It's telling a story to the market every day. The question is whether it's the right one.

The firms that grow profitably over the next decade will be unmistakably positioned for human-led, high-trust, high-fee advisory.

As AI continues to streamline transactional work across the accounting function, clients will become more price-sensitive about anything that feels interchangeable.

What will always hold the most value is trusted expertise — and it's far easier to demonstrate this depth and credibility to a *specific* audience than to everyone.

Building an advisory brand is about forming an impression in front of the right people.

It's not marketing fluff.

It's good economics.

If an advisory client is worth $5,000 a year in fees (and many are worth 10X more), then just a handful of new clients or upsold clients can generate a six-figure lift in annual revenue — before you even factor in retention, referrals, cleaner work, and better conversations.

That's why **advisory branding is leverage**.

It's how you turn what you deliver into a brand that creates demand, commands fees, and shapes legacies.

Let's build your brand into a powerhouse.

Framework

Instead of thinking about your advisory brand as a long list of disconnected tactics, it's more useful (and far more implementable) to group it into **four strategic themes**.

Each theme plays a different role. Each one answers a different buying question in the mind of your market.

The four themes are:

1. **Promise** – what you stand for and the outcomes you deliver
2. **Positioning** – how you set expectations, pricing power, and fit
3. **Personality** – why people feel drawn to you specifically
4. **Presence** – how the market consistently sees and experiences your brand.

The Advisory Brand Stack™ visual representation:

BRAND PROMISE		
"Why they believe"		
Mission	Results	Proof
Creates certainty and credibility		
BRAND POSITIONING		
"What they expect"		
Client Profile	Pricing	Visual Identity
Perceived value and profit leverage		
BRAND PERSONALITY		
"Why they feel aligned"		
People Power	POV	Lived Values
Differentiation and resonance		
BRAND PRESENCE		
"What the market sees"		
Promotion	Partnerships	Performance
Visibility and demand creation		

Let's break them down properly.

Theme 1: Brand Promise

(Mission, Results, Proof)

Your brand promise is the headline act. It's what makes someone stop scrolling and think, "This firm gets it."

Most accounting firms undersell their promise. They talk about services instead of outcomes. Processes instead of progress. Let's flip that around!

Your brand promise answers three critical questions:

1. What change do you help clients create?
2. Why should they believe you can deliver it?
3. What evidence exists that this actually works?

A strong promise is made up of three parts:

1. Mission

This is the work you believe matters; this is the impact you're here to make. Not your corporate values poster. Your *real reason* for doing advisory work.

When your **mission statement** is clear, your messaging gains conviction.

"We prepare tax returns" vs "We're here to save the world!" – I am exaggerating this example of course, but you can *feel something* reading the second one.

2. Results

Advisory clients aren't buying effort or information, they want transformation.

These outcomes should be described in *client language*, not accounting language (e.g. "tax minimisation" vs "keeping more of your hard-earned money").

Stating clear results feels bold, which feels risky. But the biggest risk is playing it so safe that your firm is immediately forgettable.

3. Proof

A promise without proof is just marketing.

Proof includes case studies, before/after snapshots, Google reviews, client stories, benchmarks, and patterns you see repeatedly in your advisory work.

New clients want to see their desired state in your proof. Remember that iconic dining scene in the movie "When Harry met Sally"?

You want your ideal client to think: "I'll have what she's having..."

Theme 2: Brand Positioning

(Client Profile, Pricing, Branding,)

Positioning sets the scene. It tells the market: who you're for, who you're not for, and most importantly – what level of conversation you operate at.

This is the **single biggest profit lever** available to most firms, *not* efficiencies (shocking but true – you do the math on the impact of pricing vs productivity on margins)...

Two firms can deliver the same service. One charges $3,000 a year. The other charges $15,000. What's the difference?

It's very rarely technical skill and almost exclusively driven by the perceived value of the service, based on your firm's positioning.

Your firm's positioning is shaped by three factors:

1. Client Profile

Your ideal clients (identified in the previous chapter) should determine the way you position your firm in the market. Speaking to high-net-worth individuals is very different than how you engage scrappy solopreneurs, for example.

They're looking for different services, expect different pricing, and are attracted to a different promise. Your positioning should be polarising: highly attractive to Abby, somewhat repellant to Dave.

2. Pricing

If your brand positioning signals "premium, specialised, outcome-driven," then higher fees feel logical. In fact, higher fees are often *anticipated* and expected.

If your positioning signals "generalist, everyone welcome, beginner-friendly" then pricing pressure is inevitable.

Think of it this way – you wouldn't expect bargain basement pricing for a brand-new BMW and if you can't afford one (or aren't prepared to pay for financing), you won't walk into the showroom!

3. Branding

A powerful brand is consistent and recognisable across every aspect.

We're not just talking about your logo; a *brand* is your firm's identity. Grainy stock images of old men looking at spreadsheets scream "we're out of date", while edgy graphics resonate with a more modern audience.

People do judge a book by its cover, and your aesthetics will influence the narrative about your firm (for better or worse)!

<u>Theme 3: Brand Personality</u>

(People Power, Point of View, Lived Values)

Personality is what makes your firm *memorable.*

In a world of competent advisors, your personality is the differentiator.

People buy from people, especially in professional services. If you're a Fractional CFO or consultant, you *are* the brand. If you run a firm, your brand extends beyond you—but your personality must still be felt. That authenticity is your competitive advantage.

A high-impact brand personality has three drivers:

1. People Power

Advisory is relational. People want to know who they're trusting, and visibility creates a sense of connection.

Faces, voices, and stories matter more than logos. Who are the personalities hiding behind the accountants? The fun facts? The shared wins? *The feeling that you want these people on your team supporting you behind the scenes.*

There are some things that AI will never replace: assurance, guidance, comfort, tough love, real-life examples and lived experience. Human presence is the new premium.

2. Point of View

All the top leaders that you follow online have a clear point of view – one that you resonate with, that's why you follow them!

What beliefs would you die on the hill for? What are you willing to shout from the rooftops? What view do you embody within your firm and through your services?

Marketing material without a point of view or lived personal example is easily replaceable with generic ChatGPT slop.

Beige content blends in. Opinionated content stands out.

Have you ever seen a queue for plain vanilla ice-cream?

3. Lived Values

Values matter most when they're demonstrated in action. Values hung up on the office wall or listed on your website are meaningless unless you're living them.

You want ambitious and coachable clients? You need to be ambitious and coachable yourself – and this must be visible.

If one of your firm's values is "caring", what does that mean in practical terms – to you, your clients, and your team? Your *true* values (not ones you made up in a team planning day) are magnetic to like-minded clients.

Theme 4: Brand Presence

(Promotion, Partnerships, Performance)

Presence is how your advisory brand shows up in the world. Consistently. Strategically.

When people think of the best firm in the industry, they typically think about those that are the most visible.

Not everywhere. But in the *right* places.

Presence includes:

1. Promotion

For most firms, this means your website, social media, newsletters, content, speaking events, webinars, videos, podcasts, free resources, email nurture sequences, referral campaigns, etc.

Promotion should be about positioning your firm for better clients, not necessarily more – so advertising should only be tackled after the basics covered in this chapter are in place.

2. Partnerships

Strategic partnerships let you borrow trust. And audiences.

When aligned properly, partnerships accelerate credibility, reduce acquisition effort, and elevate your positioning.

Choose partners who:

- serve the same clients
- don't compete with you
- share your standards
- reciprocate(!)

3. Performance

You don't need to put premium 98 unleaded fuel into a car that can only go 70km/hour. But if you want to hit top speed? Then yes, you'll need to invest more time and money into your branding strategies.

Performance is less about measurement and more about assessment: to ensure that you're spending the right amount of effort into the right strategies.

But a word of caution: don't obsess over ROI too soon. Most

accountants quit before their marketing activity ever has a chance to compound.

Case Study / Example

Kate runs a firm that isn't trying to be liked by everyone.

She's sharp, commercially minded, and impatient with busywork. Her clients don't want hand-holding — they want decisions, speed, and an accountant who understands what they need to scale.

Her focus is narrow by design: ambitious startups sitting between $500k-$1M in revenue, ready for mega growth.

But here was the problem: you'd never know that from her marketing.

Her firm looked safe. Neutral. Polite.

The kind of brand signal that attracts "nice" small businesses — not startup founders juggling cash burn, hiring pressure, and investor expectations.

So Kate made a deliberate choice: **build a brand that looked like it belonged in the startup ecosystem — not the suburban accounting lane**.

The first move was visual, and it set the tone for everything else.

Kate scrapped stock imagery and booked an editorial-style photoshoot with a clear brief: *tech-adjacent, founder-led, modern.*

The shoot took place in a co-working space and an industrial warehouse studio with exposed concrete, natural light, clean lines. No desks. No files. No accounting props.

The goal wasn't "approachable accountant" — it was *commercial operator*. A team that founders would trust in a boardroom, not just a tax meeting.

Those images replaced every client-facing asset within weeks:

- the website
- advisory proposals

- pitch decks
- LinkedIn banners and profile images
- email signatures

The effect was immediate. The firm stopped looking like a service provider and started looking like a **growth partner**.

Next, Kate tightened the brand positioning, from vague promises to a homepage headline that was a clear line in the sand:

We work with founders building fast — and who expect their accountant to keep up.

Kate introduced a dedicated advisory page for startups in the $500k–$1M range, with visible pricing and a fixed-fee growth diagnostic as the entry point.

No fishing calls. If a founder wasn't ready to invest, they self-selected out.

Visibility followed — but only in the right rooms.

Kate didn't chase broad exposure. She focused on being **seen where startup founders already gathered**.

She partnered with a local accelerator to run quarterly "numbers for growth" sessions and appeared on four of the top startup business podcasts. (It turns out, they don't get many opinionated accountants knocking on their door, so it was an easy win).

Personality was the final lever and Kate didn't dilute it.

She posted LinkedIn content about cash burn, hiring too early, and the brutal realities of funding — written in the same tone she used in advisory meetings.

Some posts polarised. Some were secretly screenshotted. A few clearly annoyed the wrong people.

Good.

The right founders leaned in.

Within 18 months:

- Generalist enquiries dropped off
- Advisory became the default, not the upsell – included in all minimum retainers
- The firm became known as "the accountants startups talk to when they're ready for fast growth"

Unlike other firms, when they say they're "*not your average accountant*" they meant it — and it's apparent across every experience in their firm, including their brand.

Kate and her team now charge fees that accountants who've been in business 20 years longer are quietly jealous of.

Are there risks in this approach – yes.

Was it worth it? Also, yes.

Because Kate doesn't need to explain her value.

Her brand does that before the first meeting even starts.

You don't need to specialise your whole firm like Kate did. If you have a larger firm, you can create dedicated campaigns and internal teams by function or client/service type. The principles are the same, the execution depends on your operating context.

Implementation Guide

Don't worry, this isn't the section where I tell you to start dancing on TikTok.

The opposite, in fact!

This rollout plan is designed for real firms. Busy firms. Firms with client work, deadlines, and a team who didn't sign up to become full-time content creators.

The goal is to build an advisory brand that runs like a workflow.

Phase 1: Foundations (Week 1–2)

1) Focus on your ideal client profile

Pick ONE ideal client type as a point of focus for the next 90 days. Not forever. Just for now.

Examples:

- Builders and trades with lumpy cash flow
- Healthcare professionals with high income and complexity - Agencies scaling from 5–20 staff
- Rural businesses needing better forecasting.

Document their top 3 pain points, top 3 goals, and common objections to advisory fees – the words they actually use (steal these from emails and meeting notes).

2) Define your advisory brand promise

Condense your thinking into a simple structure:

We help [ideal client profile] **who are stuck with** [pain] **to achieve** [outcome] **using** [your method / cadence / tools].

This is your promise – the bolder you can make it, the better.

3) Decide your "visible experts"

You need at least one face of advisory. Founder, partner, senior advisor—someone credible and comfortable enough.

If they hate visibility, don't force it. Support them. Make it easy.

But be honest. If *nobody* is visible, your advisory brand will stay small.

Phase 2: Marketing Assets (Week 3–4)

4) Build your minimum viable asset suite

You do not need 47 brochures. You need a small set of assets that do the heavy lifting.

Minimum set:

- an advisory services page on your website (clear outcomes, clear next step)
- a "snapshot" offer (benchmark review, diagnostic, advisory discovery)
- one lead magnet (free resource) tailored to your ideal client, with an email sequence or follow-up template that invites a consult
- a simple case study format (so you can collect proof consistently)

5) Use high quality photographs

Schedule lifestyle photography for your team – capture images that look more like an editorial feature in a business magazine than awkward corporate head shots.

Of all the steps to take, this is the one that has the biggest and most immediate impact on your brand positioning. Words tell, images sell.

First impressions takes less than a second, so make sure yours counts!

Team photographs need to be included in all your marketing collateral. It may feel awkward, but there's a reason that the top Real Estate agents do it (and they are making more money than the partners at a small firm).

Can you use AI images? Yes, but… very, very selectively. You don't want to instantly erode the trust that you're working so hard to build.

6) Develop your brand style

Create a one-page brand "style guide" for your firm that includes the firm's logo, fonts, colours, and any stylistic or graphic elements to be used.

This document should also include a summary of the key messages and your advisory brand promise for ease of reference.

Consistency creates coherence, and this creates consumer confidence in your brand.

Hashed-together graphics and social media posts that look nothing like the rest of your brand will devalue all your hard work.

Phase 3: Develop Your Brand Rhythm (Week 5–6)

6) Assign marketing roles like you assign client work

Marketing dies when it's left sitting on the partner's desk… and given how busy you are, you're going to need external guidance and implementation support (that's where I usually come in).

The function of branding and marketing needs at least one internal "champion" to help facilitate projects and initiatives, but there should be third party accountability and a way for your firm to fast-track results – like done-for-you elements or access to the templates and resources I offer inside my marketing club.

After all, you're accountants not marketers!

7) Commit to a simple marketing cadence

Aim for consistency over volume.

A realistic baseline:

- 1-2 social media posts per week
- 1 monthly "anchor" piece (webinar, video, article, or client story)
- Monthly or quarterly newsletter
- Seasonal promotions based on client type or service type (e.g. tax planning, EOFY reviews, etc)
- 1-2 key initiatives within a calendar year: Google review push, strategic partner promotion, in-person client event, website refresher, team photos
- 1 free resource and automated email nurture sequence (set up once, then set-and-forget)

Your anchor content becomes the source reference for your brand eco-system – where all activity is aligned and building momentum together, not competing.

Phase 4: Build Momentum (Ongoing)

8) Keep marketing on, manage capacity with process

When demand increases, don't disappear. Control intake.

Options:

- new client waitlists –
- staged onboarding (monthly intake days)
- "next available start date"
- limiting new offers to a set number per month

A stop-start approach to marketing is like constantly taking your foot on and off the gas – you'll never get to top gear (even if your brand is a high performance sportscar)!

The biggest mistake I see well-intentioned firms make is to stop marketing when they get busy. Go back to step 6 and make sure that you have someone helping you deliver marketing with the same commitment that you have to delivering client work.

9) Measure, refine, and scale

Once you have the basics in place, you can review what's working and start to dial up the volume on your brand frequency.

You can begin investing in advertising to get your message in front of more ideal clients, remembering to focus on quality over quantity.

You convert fees from your brand activity by implementing robust internal follow-up processes with clients and prospects – not just by generating more noise!

10) Use AI like an assistant, not a substitute

I'm passionate about helping firms embrace AI, but the caveat here is that it must be used discerningly.

And keep the human parts human.

Advisory work is personal. Clients are inviting you into decisions that affect their livelihoods, families, team, and future.

The market must feel a *human* behind the expertise.

Action Checklist

These are the highest-impact actions (for the least amount of effort) that you can make in the next 30 days:

1. Book a team photoshoot. Even if you had one a few years ago, your online presence and social media requires fresh energy regularly.
2. Update the visuals on your website – new team photos if you have them, or carefully curated, premium-looking stock images. While you're doing that, tweak the headlines on the home, about, and service pages.
3. Craft your advisory brand promise and use this as the "North Star" reference for all marketing and branding decisions and activity.
4. Decide your minimum marketing rhythm and create a calendar of activity dates (e.g. newsletter goes out on the 1st of the month, etc).
5. Assign marketing ownership and seek the right support externally. This one action can get the brand-building ball rolling throughout the year.

That's enough to get your firm in motion!

Conclusion:

You may have heard the saying "your vibe attracts your tribe."

If you want to appeal to the best clients, then your *vibe* – your brand – needs to signal to the market that you are the best at what you do.

It may seem unfair, but it's true: those that get paid the most aren't the best at what they do, they're the best at *promoting* what they do.

If you don't want to spend your life selling (because, who does?) then **your brand needs to do the talking for you**.

The most profitable firms understand this and invest in their brand – sometimes intentionally, sometimes because it's in their firm's DNA.

Either way, the firms that don't build their brand will find themselves at the mercy of a shifting market, while firms with a strong brand position can design their own destiny. The choice is yours!

CHAPTER 13

Strategic Partnerships – The O.U.T.S.T.A.N.D.I.N.G. Method for Explosive Growth

Taryn Holman

He was my netwalking partner, and he was looking down as we walked and was not really saying much. He was obviously exhausted. Not the "I've had a long week" kind of tired, it was the running on fumes, "I'm not sure how much longer I can do this" vibe.

I should probably let you in on what netwalking is first though, shouldn't I?

The Seamless team and I came up with the concept of net-walking because we became tired of attending events where you did nothing but sit around, drinking alcohol and eating fried, fatty foods.

Don't get me wrong, those events can be heaps of fun, but not all the time...

The Seamless team and I wanted to come up with a way that brought like-minded people in our community together, whilst encouraging them to be healthy.

It needed to be a free event too, so it was accessible to everyone and that is how one of our most popular, monthly events was born. Networking + walking = netwalking.

But I will share more on how to cultivate your own engaging events later, let's get back to my exhausted friend...

As we walked, he started to share his story with me.

His practice had grown, but not in a way that gave him the freedom that he wanted. He was working longer hours than ever. He was making the least money he had made in years. His wife was constantly frustrated because she and the kids only received his leftovers; barely seeing his children, let alone being there for all the milestone moments that a father should be present for.

He had gone into business for freedom, both financial and time, but unfortunately his reality was the complete opposite.

"I feel like I'm failing everywhere," he confessed quietly.

"No matter what I do, I'm always behind. My clients want more. My team wants more. My family wants more. And I just… don't have anything left to give."

I've heard variations of that sentence hundreds of times in my career. So many people I meet are drowning but I knew that he didn't have a business problem. He had a capacity problem. A connection problem. A trying-to-do-everything-alone problem.

So, instead of trying to "sell" him anything, I asked one question:

"What would life look like if you had the right people around you?"

Not more people, like more employees to train or more contractors to manage.

Just the right people. The right partners and the right support. The right ecosystem.

He looked up, and for the first time since we started walking, I saw a flicker of hope in his eyes.

That was five years ago.

Today? He works fewer hours than he did when he started his firm. His revenue has surged. He's happily married and he has ample time to see his kids, EVERY DAY. His business runs smoothly, because he no longer tries to do it all himself.

Instead, he built what I call his 'Strategic Partnership Engine' and it transformed everything.

If I could share one thing with business owners across the globe it would be this:

You will never scale alone! You will only scale through the right people. The partners who lift your capacity, your energy, your value, and your brand.

For 25 years, across multiple industries, I have lived and breathed one core principle:

Your network is not just a list, it's your leverage.

Your partnerships are not "nice extras" they are profit drivers.

Your relationships are not soft skills they are the hardest currency you will ever possess.

This chapter is about teaching you the exact frameworks the Seamless team has used to:

- Build a national firm
- Grow Seamless SMSF from 350 SMSFs to 31,267 SMSFs and counting
- Create an ecosystem of raving fans (clients and cross referrers) who have become my "sales team" and recommend us because they genuinely love us
- Build a national community of accountants, advisers and industry leaders
- Generate millions in recurring revenue
- Create growth through connection, not pressure

Because people miss this fundamental point:

Partnerships aren't just about "working together."

They're about creating an experience that people can't shut up about.

I've always understood that people don't remember facts and figures. They relate to your authentic stories, and they remember how you made them feel.

That's why we don't invite people to a standard lunch in a restaurant; we fly them to a waterfront mansion for a Long Table Escape. They are picked up by a chauffeur and transferred to a beautiful private property on the waterfront, where they are greeted by Seamless team members who show them to their rooms and carry their bags. On the bed they find Sheraton robes that are embroidered with their name and 'Seamless Chateau', so they have a keepsake from the fun getaway. They enjoy a lunch prepared by a private chef and are served delicious food and decadent wine, sharing invigorating conversation about life and business with the Seamless leaders.

We don't do networking events, we create experiences like fun days at the Australian Open, helicopter rides to wineries where we have a private tour and tasting, or parties on 80ft yachts with DJ's and saxophone players.

And it's not about glamour either. It's about the feeling that we want to create. We want our clients and community thinking:

"WOW this is OUTSTANDING. I can't get this feeling with anyone else. I really matter here and I am valued"

This is the foundational mindset of elite partnerships.

If you want explosive growth, you must create an ecosystem that people are proud to be part of.

The thing is, no accountant can prove they are "better" than the accountant down the road. The work is regulated, and the standards are set. The differences are marginal and to be honest the consumer has no real idea whether the actual accounting work that you are doing is good or not.

So, what sets you apart?

It's the experiences you create and the relationships you build. It's the partnerships you nurture and the way people feel when they interact with you, both digitally and in person.

This chapter will teach you the complete blueprint for doing exactly that through:

THE OUTSTANDING METHOD

Your step-by-step approach to creating unforgettable client and partner experiences.

If you take nothing else from this chapter, let it be this:

Partnerships are the fastest path to profit when they are built with heart, not hype.

But before we begin, let's be real for a minute. Most accountants aren't exactly known for being "wow" makers. And that's fine, it's not their fault. The work is technical, compliance-heavy, and often measured in numbers rather than experiences.

But experiences are what sells. People will forgive small mistakes if they feel cared for. They will pay more if they feel they are getting value and are being valued. And they will refer to you endlessly if you give them a reason too.

That's where the OUTSTANDING Method comes in. It's simple, but it works like magic, because it's human. And let's face it, in this ever-evolving landscape of regurgitated AI communication, the businesses that prioritize people will be the winners every time.

O.U.T.S.T.A.N.D.I.N.G. isn't just a word we use at Seamless SMSF, it's our playbook for every single client and partner interaction. Here's how it breaks down.

O – Observe

Pay attention to the little things. The devil is in the details.

I'm talking about birthdays, hobbies, favourite drinks, partners and children's name, or whether someone hates yachts (yes, it happens). Most firms don't notice these details and that's why you will stand out when you do.

For example, one client in passing mentioned that it was their birthday, (a detail that you as an accountant would already have access to by the way) and it was promptly recorded in our CRM. We then set up an automated birthday video email that is sent out to people on the morning of their birthday. The video is updated yearly too! When we film the birthday video, the room is set up like we are having a big party just for them. There are streamers, party hats and a happy birthday sign. The whole team are there singing happy birthday. We blow out the candles, tell them to make a wish, so when they open the email on their birthday it's a full birthday celebration just for them! How special do you think that makes them feel? And the best part is, if you don't have the time to set up an automation or a CRM that provides you with a notification that it is their birthday, then you can put it in your calendar and pick up the phone to wish them a heartfelt happy birthday instead.

Observation isn't just nice; it's profitable. It shows you care. And when people feel cared for, they remember you.

U – Understand

Ask questions and really listen.

Not just "how's the market?" or "how's business?" Dig deeper. Find out what's stressing them out. What keeps them awake at night? What do they wish they had more of?

When I first met the accountant from the opening story, he told me about his chaos: overwork, family strain, and a sense of failure. I listened. I didn't try to "fix" him immediately. I understood.

And once you understand, you can tailor your solutions in a way that actually makes a difference.

T – Tailor

This is where the magic happens.

You now know who they are, what they care about, and what matters most. Take that information and design experiences that feel personal.

At Seamless, it might be a Long Table Escape with a private chef, a wine tour where you are transported in a helicopter, or a golf day with PGA legends. At your firm, it could be something smaller - a personalised email, a team hamper, or a handwritten thankyou card. It could be a teabag stapled to a letter that you send saying you can't wait to have a cuppa with them over your next virtual meeting. The point is to make them feel special in some way. Because remember, they are special! Make them feel seen.

Tailoring isn't expensive, it's just being creative and thoughtful. And thoughtfulness is unforgettable.

S – Surprise

Give people more than they expect.

Even small surprises create huge impact. A handwritten card after they complete a big project. Their favourite coffee delivered to their office. A quick follow up phone call just to check in.

At Seamless, surprises are bigger now, yes, we do yachts and private chefs, but it wasn't always like that. We did small, thoughtful things that our clients loved and as we have grown, so too have the surprises. The principle is the same though, no matter how big or small: exceed expectations. Your clients and partners should leave every interaction thinking: "*Wow. That was OUTSTANDING.*"

T – Timing

Timing is everything.

A well-timed call, email, or gesture is far more powerful than a big gift at the wrong moment. Notice when something matters most to your clients. Maybe it's the end of a financial year or achieving a financial goal. It could be their birthday, or their child graduating. Whatever it is, you need to know about it to then act.

The accountant who saved his business? I reached out with a solution before he even knew what he needed. The timing made all the difference.

A – Appreciate

Never underestimate gratitude.

Say thank you. Mean it and do it often. And to really stand out, do it creatively!

A simple thankyou card can turn into a decade-long relationship. A thoughtful gesture can turn a satisfied client into a raving advocate. Appreciation multiplies everything. It multiplies loyalty, referrals, and goodwill.

N – Nurture

Relationships don't end once the invoice is paid.

Keep in touch, follow them up and celebrate milestones. Check in when it's quiet. Go and visit your clients at their workplaces. Get to know their teams and spend time with them in their environment. You will be shocked with how many more insights you can gather by doing this. The photo on the wall of them spear fishing. The trophy they display because they won a championship. The kids picture they have hanging on the wall. These are the gems that give you information about who your client really is and how you can get to know them better and therefore better support them.

Plus, your clients and partners will notice the consistency. It's not about being pushy; it's about being present.

At Seamless, we've built an entire ecosystem of touchpoints. We host monthly networking events, webinars, community gatherings and client functions. Why? It's all designed to nurture relationships and create long-term loyalty from everyone in our network. We are here to play the long game and develop deep, meaningful relationships.

D – Deliver

Promises mean nothing if you don't deliver.

Be precise. Be reliable. Be fast. Whether it's a simple email, or a meeting or an important deadline. Make sure you deliver it with excellence.

Your word is your bond. Always under promise and over deliver. If you say it, do it. If you deliver, people will trust you. If you don't, nothing else matters, you are just like everyone else.

I – Innovate

Innovation isn't just about tech or processes.

It's about finding ways to surprise, delight, and exceed expectations. How can you make the ordinary extraordinary? How can you have a routine meeting and make it unforgettable?

Every helicopter, every Long Table Escape, every yacht day started with one question: *How can we make this unforgettable?* There is someone in my network that sprays the same scent every time someone walks into their office. They all dress in suits, ties and look impeccable. There is a full drinks menu and someone in the office takes the clients order. They serve it in a certain way, matching it with certain biscuits. They only use the best coffee and the best products. They don't just remember the clients name, they know their whole families names including their pets. They know their hobbies, their likes, their dislikes and they speak to them like they are their best friend, because their clients are! None of that is overly expensive, it is just having the discipline to always pay attention and to action it.

N – Network

This is where strategic partnerships come into play.

Your clients aren't just clients, they are connectors. Introduce them to others. Help them grow. Invite them into your ecosystem. When you genuinely give without expecting, the law of reciprocity takes care of the rest.

At Seamless, every happy client is effectively a salesperson. They refer, they advocate, they share. That's the multiplier effect of networking done right.

G – Grow

Finally, always look for growth, theirs, yours, and theirs again.

Every interaction, every relationship, every partnership is an opportunity to expand capacity, create value, and multiply impact. The accountant I mentioned at the start of the story… He's now thriving not just because of outsourcing, but because we built an ecosystem around him that allowed him to grow without burning out.

The OUTSTANDING Method isn't theory. It's what's behind 10x growth in 10 years. It's why Seamless SMSF went from 350 SMSFs to 31,267 and counting. It's why clients love us, are engaged and refer others to us, and have stayed with us for a decade.

It's not about being flashy, it's about being intentional, human, and unforgettable.

Now that you know the **OUTSTANDING Method**, let's get practical. You don't just want to *read* about it, you want to take action and **do** it.

Here's how you can bring it to life in your firm, step by step.

Step 1: Start with Observation

- Make a list of your top 20 clients or referral partners.
- Note personal details you already know. You want birthdays, family, hobbies, favourite wines, preferred communication style.
- Keep this in a simple CRM (yes get one and ditch the spreadsheet! Hubspot is our favourite because you can keep all the information you need and automate SO much of it, which helps as you scale!)

Quick tip: Ask your clients or cross referrers lots of questions casually in conversation or via email to ensure they give you valuable information. People love to talk about themselves and as I always say to my team, you have 2 ears and one mouth for a reason! I want you to do twice the listening that you do talking and when you apply this you can't go wrong. You will have more information than you ever need to support the people in your network with whatever they need.

Step 2: Understand Deeply

- Schedule 15–20 minute regular "check-in" meetings with each client or partner.
- Use open-ended questions: "What's keeping you up at night?" or "If we could make one part of your business easier this year, what would it be?"
- Take notes. Seriously the devil is in the details and they matter.

Why: When you understand their pressures and goals, your solutions hit harder. You move from a service provider to a trusted advisor to confidant and friend.

Step 3: Tailor Your Interactions

- Pick one personalisation tactic for each client each month. Examples:
  - o Send a hand-written card for a milestone.
  - o Offer a tailored resource, like a report or article relevant to their business or personal interests.
  - o Organise a small experience. It could be a coffee delivery, lunch, or a local experience they will appreciate.

Remember: Tailoring isn't expensive. Thoughtful beats flashy every time. An example is when I found out someone loved drinking coca cola. It was his favourite drink. Not whiskey, not coffee, good old fashioned coke. I organised for two cans of coke to be dropped off before our virtual meeting. He was so impressed that I even remembered, let alone that I went to the effort of delivering it. It's not hard or expensive to be thoughtful, but you do need to pay attention in order to become creative and provide these type of experiences.

Step 4: Add a Surprise

Identify moments when they least expect it but will appreciate it most.

- You could deliver their favourite coffee on a Monday morning during their peak busy period, with a note telling them that you know they are under the pump and you hope this let's them know that you think they are amazing, whilst also helping them with the daily grind.
- Or you could buy a massage voucher when you know that they have just gone through a really stressful or challenging time, sharing that you want them to have some much needed 'me time' and you are there if they need you.

Why: Firstly, because it is nice and kind to treat people like this when you genuinely care for them and hopefully that is how you feel about everyone of the people in your network. Also, people remember emotions, not invoices. Surprises create emotional "stickiness." People can easily break up with a service provider, but they find it more difficult to break up with a friend.

Step 5: Master Timing

- Mark important dates in your calendar/CRM: financial year-end, birthdays, anniversaries, kids birthdays, goals, holidays etc.
- Plan follow-ups or small gestures around these dates.

Why: The right gesture at the right moment is exponentially more impactful than the same gesture at the wrong time.

Step 6: Show Appreciation

- Always say "thank you" both verbally and in writing, or with a thoughtful gift.
- Celebrate wins: theirs and yours. Did they hit a business milestone? Did a partnership pay off? Acknowledge it and celebrate it like they are your best friend!
- Send a small recognition to their team if appropriate. Big hampers that the whole crew can enjoy are a favourite of ours. It let's everyone feel appreciated.

Pro tip: Consistency matters more than extravagance.

Step 7: Nurture Continuously

- Schedule regular touchpoints. Whether it is weekly, quarterly or yearly, make it known that they will have your undivided attention and ask lots of questions. Provide

them with an opportunity to give you real time feedback on what they need and more importantly what they are or aren't loving.
- Invite clients to webinars, networking events, or casual catch-ups.
- Keep them engaged without being pushy.

Why: People don't leave relationships they value, they leave relationships where they aren't getting what they need.

Step 8: Deliver Excellence Every Time

- Set your standard high. Our word is OUTSTANDING and if it is anything but that, we need to make an adjustment. I will never forget when I first started at Seamless SMSF and there was an email that I was sending out. Mike, the principal of the firm, called me in to his office and said "Hey buddy, I just want to talk to you about this email. It's not outstanding." As the new kid on the block, I can tell you that I started to sweat just a little. I was sure that I triple checked it before sending it to him for review. I read it again, but for the life of me I could not see what he was referring to. "Ok fill me in, because it looks fine to me. Why isn't it outstanding?" He proceeded to tell me that the font of the email was one shade different to my email signature. And I can assure you that from that day on, I questioned everything I did through the lens of, "is this outstanding?" Holding yourself and your team mates to a high standard is a great way to consistently deliver excellence.
- Be prompt, accurate, and precise.
- Under promise and overdeliver where possible.

Your mantra: "Every interaction and thing you do should feel OUTSTANDING.

Step 9: Innovate Where You Can

- Look at every interaction and ask: "How can I make this better? How can I surprise, delight, or exceed expectations?"
- Think creatively: lunch doesn't have to be in a boardroom. Meetings don't have to be in your office. Experiences, even small ones, are memorable.
- We installed a golf simulator, pool table, tennis table and dart board in our office. It is there for the team to enjoy but also for our clients. Instead of inviting our clients in for a sit-down meeting at a board room table, we have a hit of golf at 'Pebble Beach' golf course and discuss SMSF's. Or we have a laptop on the table next to the pool table, taking notes about process improvements.
- Business doesn't have to be boring.

Step 10: Build Your Network

- Treat every client as a potential connector.
- Ask for referrals, testimonials and google reviews in a thoughtful way.
- Collaborate with non-competing professionals in your space to offer extra value.

Example: Seamless SMSF doesn't just provide audits, we create experiences that connect our clients to others in professional services. The ripple effect is massive.

Step 11: Grow

- Review what's working quarterly.
- Identify relationships and pursue the people that you genuinely love and want to help. That is the best way for them to become more strategic, as it is authentic.

- Invest time and energy where there is a win/win for both of you. That is when the payoff is the highest and they are the relationships that scale your business organically.

Action Checklist

Start Today

Here's a simple, doable list you can implement immediately:

1. List your top 20 clients/partners and record personal details.
2. Schedule 15–20 minute check-ins with each.
3. Pick one tailored interaction for each client this month.
4. Identify one surprise or unexpected gesture to implement this week.
5. Mark important dates in your calendar for follow-ups.
6. Send a handwritten thank-you to one client today.
7. Invite a client or partner to a small, thoughtful experience in the next 30 days.
8. Check that every client interaction this week hits your "OUTSTANDING" standard.
9. Brainstorm one creative improvement for a recurring process.
10. Ask one happy client for a referral or testimonial.

Implementing even a few of these steps creates a chain reaction: clients feel valued - they tell others - you gain referrals - your ecosystem grows - your business grows.

It's simple. It's practical. And it's proven: the accountant from the opening story, our Seamless SMSF growth from 350 to 30,519 SMSFs, and hundreds of client stories all came from doing this consistently.

Your mission: Start small. Be intentional. Be human. Be OUTSTANDING.

Please don't read this and forget about it. This is a framework that turns clients into advocates, partners into collaborators, and your business into a growth engine. But only if you take action and use it!

You will see phenomenal results because this is genuine. It's not manipulative or a gimmick. It's you caring enough to create experiences that matter and that are tailored to each individual contact you have. And when you care that much, people notice and they stay, they refer, they grow with you.

By applying the OUTSTANDING Method, you are not just building relationships. You are building an ecosystem where everyone benefits: your clients, your partners, your team, and ultimately, your business.

Your challenge for the next 30 days:

- Pick one client or partner.
- Apply at least three steps from the OUTSTANDING Method.
- Make them feel truly valued.
- Watch the ripple effect begin.

Because the moment you start treating every interaction as an opportunity to be **OUTSTANDING**, growth stops being a goal and it becomes a byproduct of the way you do business.

Remember: growth isn't just about numbers. It's about **people, relationships, and experiences**. When you get that right, everything else follows naturally.

And that's how explosive growth happens, one thoughtful, human, outstanding interaction at a time!

CHAPTER 14

The Client Experience Multiplier – Turning Every Interaction Into Raving Fans

Melissa Voss

Introduction

The relationship between an accountant and their client is unlike almost any other professional relationship.

We are invited into people's lives at deeply personal moments - when they are starting a business, selling one, dealing with cash-flow pressure, planning for retirement, navigating family change, or trying to make sense of decisions that carry long- term consequences. Clients trust us with their numbers, yes - but also with their decisions, their worries, their hopes, and often their identity. In many cases, we're the steady hand in the background when life feels anything but steady.

That level of trust should never be taken lightly.

And yet, in many firms, client experience is accidental rather than intentional.

Not all accountants think about relationships in the same way. For some, client connection sits at the core of what they do. For others, the focus is technical excellence, deadlines, workflow and output. Neither approach is inherently wrong - but only one creates long-term momentum.

After starting my career in practice as a Chartered Accountant, I spent the last decade taking that background and co-founding FuseWorks - a software business built to help accountants free up time, enhance client experience, and spend more energy on the human parts of the job that actually create loyalty. What I've learned over those years is that an accounting firm and a software business are surprisingly similar. You have clients. You have a product or service. You deliver outcomes. And you scale through trust and relationship. You can have the best 'product' in the world, but if the experience is clunky, inconsistent, or impersonal, it won't grow.

Having experienced working alongside more than 2,000 accounting firms over recent years, its taught me something really simple: in a market where most compliance work looks and feels the same, technical competence is no longer a differentiator. It's the baseline.

What separates firms is the experience wrapped around that competence.

We all know the easiest revenue to grow is from existing clients. The firms that build strong relationships and deliver consistently don't just retain clients - they expand services naturally. They have better conversations. They get invited into bigger decisions. They're trusted earlier. Clients who feel genuinely cared for also become far more forgiving when something goes wrong, because they've banked trust.

But the biggest commercial lever is this: clients who are 'wowed' by you talk.

They talk over a barbecue. They talk at kids' sport. They talk over coffee with a friend who is frustrated with their accountant. Most referrals don't come from a formal request - they come from a client feeling proud to recommend you.

The opportunity most firms miss is that those "new client" feelings don't have to fade. Many firms win a client, woo them at the start, then quietly drop into transactional delivery. The relationship becomes "annual accounts, BAS, tax return, invoice."

The client isn't unhappy - but they're not impressed either. They become passive. And passive clients don't advocate.

Client experience isn't about expensive gifts or luxurious gestures. It's about being deliberate - understanding what matters at each stage of the relationship and designing the experience so it can scale across a busy firm.

That's what this chapter is about: a practical framework that helps you turn everyday interactions into moments that matter. Moments that build trust, create raving fans, and ultimately drive referrals and loyalty without you having to chase them.

The Framework

I like to think about client experience the same way I think about relationships.

Specifically - a new boyfriend or girlfriend.

Stay with me.

At the beginning, everything matters. You show up on time. You listen. You remember details. You follow through. You don't leave things vague. You're clear about expectations. You're trying - consciously - to make a great impression.

Over time, if you're not careful, effort fades. Assumptions creep in. Communication drops. And suddenly the relationship that started strong feels… average. Not because anyone is bad, but because no one has designed what "good" looks like after the honeymoon stage.

Client relationships follow exactly the same arc.

So I break client experience into three stages:

1. **The First Date** – the new client meeting
2. **The First 90 Days** – where promises are tested
3. **The Ongoing Relationship** – where most firms either compound trust or quietly lose momentum

Stage 1: The First Date – The New Client Meeting

This is where trust is formed - or quietly lost.

Too many new client meetings are either:

- a technical data-gathering exercise, or
- a rushed handover from sales to delivery.

Neither creates confidence.

A strong new client meeting should do a few things *clearly*.

1) Set expectations both ways

This is where you remove uncertainty. It should be crystal clear:

- what you're committing to
- what the client is committing to
- what "good" looks like from both sides

When expectations are vague, clients fill in the gaps with assumptions. That's where disappointment starts.

2) Explain how the relationship works

Clients want to know:

- who they'll be working with day-to-day
- who to contact for what
- how communication will happen
- what your response times look like
- how proactive you will (and won't) be

Even if you're a high-touch firm, clients need clarity. Especially when they've come from an experience where they've felt ignored, confused, or surprised.

3) Clarify technology expectations

Technology can be a brilliant experience enhancer - or a pain point. Make it easy:

- what platforms you'll use
- why you use them
- how it makes things smoother for the client
- what you expect from them (timely approvals, uploading info, signing, etc.)

When you frame tech as "removing friction," clients feel looked after, not forced.

4) Remove pricing surprises

Clients hate unexpected bills. Even more than they hate paying.

This doesn't mean you undercharge or avoid scope changes. It means you set clear expectations:

- what's included
- what isn't
- what triggers additional fees
- how you'll communicate changes

Transparency builds trust fast.

5) Introduce the broader capability of your firm

Most clients only know "tax return." They don't naturally understand all the value your team can deliver. The new client meeting is a perfect time to gently show:

- your wider services
- your network (financial planning, legal, lending, etc.)
- what's possible when they work with you long-term

This isn't selling - it's showing the client what they've gained by choosing you.

6) Make it human

This is the part that turns a good meeting into a memorable one.

Ask what matters to them. Not just financially, but personally:

- what's important about their business right now
- what keeps them up at night
- what they're trying to build
- what "success" means to them

And yes - capture the details: children's names, milestones, coffee orders. It sounds small, but it tells a client: *you matter to us.*

Clients may not remember everything you explained, but they will always remember how you made them feel.

Stage 2: The First 90 Days – Where Promises Are Tested

The first 90 days has an outsized impact.

This is where clients subconsciously decide:

- "Did I make the right decision?"
- "Are these people actually different?"

This is also where you have the best chance to uncover technical opportunities. When you win a new client, they're open. Trust is high. Their guard is down. And because they've made the decision to work with you, they're far more receptive to improvements and advice.

This is why I strongly recommend a deliberate deep review early, where relevant:

- alignment of structures
- opportunities to minimise tax
- asset protection
- planning for unforeseen circumstances
- any compliance clean- up that will make everything easier going forward

Do this early and you create that internal client reaction:

"Yes - I've made the best decision ever."

And that reaction gets shared.

This is when clients talk to friends and family - because the relationship is fresh, and they're excited about what's already been improved.

Practically, the first 90 days should include:

- delivering on every promise made in the new client meeting
- making progress visible (don't assume clients "know" you're doing a good job)
- a proactive check- in: what we've done, what's next, what we've already improved
- going deeper into understanding them, their business, and their family affairs
- where possible, visiting their business (or doing a walk-through) to get context

This is where trust accelerates - not from doing *more* work, but from making the right work visible.

Stage 3: The Ongoing Relationship – Where Most Firms Slip

This is where things often become unstuck.

Not because firms don't care - but because life gets busy. Workload is full. New clients take priority. Long-term clients get pushed back because they're "safe." The relationship becomes transactional and reactive.

Clients don't usually leave because of one big failure.

They leave because of silence.

So ongoing client experience needs intentional design. This is where you need repeatable actions that keep the relationship warm and valuable:

- regular proactive contact

- phone calls that aren't tied to invoices
- site visits at home or business
- gifts or acknowledgements for milestones
- asking for feedback and acting on it
- asking "what else can we be doing?"
- inviting clients to special industry events or internal events
- connecting the dots on budget updates, tax changes, and opportunities *before* they hear it from neighbours or friends

And here's an important point: technology should be doing the heavy lifting in the background, so humans can do the human work. When routine tasks are automated, delivery is consistent, and branding is clear and professional, clients feel looked after - and your team has more time for the relationship-building that actually drives loyalty.

That's the multiplier.

Case Study

A mid-sized accounting firm I worked closely with was technically strong and genuinely well-intentioned. Compliance work was efficient. Deadlines were met. The team was busy. On paper, everything looked healthy.

But referrals had slowed to a trickle.

The partners felt it - that subtle shift where new clients weren't coming in through word of mouth anymore. When they did come in, it was more price-driven. And while long- term clients stayed, they were quiet. Loyal, but passive. They weren't advocating.

When they stepped back and looked through a client experience lens, the issue wasn't capability.

It was intentionality.

New clients were onboarded professionally, but quickly absorbed into the general workflow. The first meeting happened, but expectations around communication, proactivity, and what the relationship would feel like weren't clearly set. The first 90 days were technically sound - jobs completed - but progress wasn't made visible. Clients didn't feel momentum.

And long-term clients mainly heard from the firm when something was due.

The firm didn't need a dramatic overhaul. They needed a few deliberate shifts.

First, they reworked the new client meeting agenda. Not to add fluff - but to add clarity: how the relationship would work, who to contact, how communication would happen, and how scope and pricing would be handled.

Second, they formalised the first 90 days. Every new client received a proactive check- in that made progress visible and highlighted early wins - including a deeper review of structure and tax opportunities where relevant.

Third - and most importantly - they rebuilt ongoing contact. Each partner identified a small group of long-term clients and committed to proactive touchpoints that weren't tied to a deadline: a call, a quick update, a relevant insight.

Referrals started to come back, but not through awkward asking.

They followed moments of impact.

After a meaningful tax saving or structural improvement, partners confidently said:

"We love working with you and improving your circumstances. If you know of anyone else in a similar situation, we'd love you to refer them to us. We're keen to work with more clients like you and are actively looking to grow."

Then they closed the loop.

Every referral received a personal thank you - a handwritten card, a bottle of champagne, or something aligned to the client's preferences. The message was simple: "Thank you for your trust."

The result wasn't just more referrals. It was deeper loyalty, stronger engagement, and a culture shift inside the firm where client experience became something the whole team owned - not just the partner with the best relationships.

Implementation Guide – Step- by- step rollout inside a firm

Great client experience doesn't happen because a firm has good people.

Most firms have good people.

It happens because expectations are clear, behaviours are consistent, and responsibility is shared - not left to individual personality.

Here is a practical rollout that works inside real firms.

Step 1: Map the client lifecycle (keep it simple)

Document three phases:

1. New Client
2. First 90 Days
3. Ongoing Relationship

This becomes your operating framework. Everyone in the firm should know what stage a client is in, because each stage has different priorities.

Step 2: Create checklists of non-negotiables at each stage

This is the difference between "we try to do that" and "we do that."

New Client checklist (examples):

- structured meeting agenda (consistent every time)
- set communication expectations

- confirm scope and pricing approach
- introduce team roles
- outline technology workflow
- capture personal details + priorities
- confirm next steps and first 90- day plan

First 90 Days checklist (examples):

- deliver what was promised
- deep review of affairs (structure, tax minimisation, asset protection, risk)
- proactive check- in meeting or call
- make wins visible
- document opportunities for future work
- confirm cadence for ongoing contact

Ongoing Relationship checklist (examples):

- proactive touchpoints scheduled (not "when we remember")
- milestone recognition (birthday, business anniversary, major event)
- annual/biannual "bigger picture" conversation (not just compliance)
- invite to events where relevant
- proactive updates about changes that affect them
- feedback loop (simple and consistent)

Step 3: Assign ownership by role (so it doesn't fall through cracks)
Client experience fails when everyone assumes someone else is handling it.

A simple ownership model:

- **Partners:** lead key relationship conversations, set tone, ask for referrals at the right time

- **Managers:** maintain momentum, ensure checklists are followed, identify opportunities
- **Admin/Client service:** protect consistency, manage touchpoints, track milestones, ensure referral thank-you's happen

You can be a relationship-led firm and still be scalable - but only if ownership is shared.

Step 4: Use technology to remove friction, not replace humanity
Technology should never replace relationships.

It should protect them.

The best use of tech in client experience is when it removes the irritating stuff:

- back-and-forth chasing signatures
- confusion about documents
- inconsistent communication
- manual admin that steals time from real conversations

Digital signing, document automation, clean templates, and consistent branding create professionalism and trust. Clients don't always say it out loud, but they feel the difference between a firm that is polished and consistent, and one that is messy and reactive.

The point is not to become "more automated."

The point is to create capacity for the human parts of the job - the calls, the insights, the relationship moments.

Step 5: Build in a culture of internal sharing (this is where scaling really happens)
This is a big one - and it's often missed.

If you want your team to replicate what's working, they need visibility of what "good" looks like.

Build time into training, meetings, or internal communication channels to share:

- What wins are we having with clients?
- What conversations are landing?
- Who is referring - and why?
- What triggered the referral?
- What simple actions created a "wow" moment?

When your team understands the patterns - the moments of impact, the behaviours that build trust - they can spot similar opportunities across their own client base.

Client experience becomes cultural, not accidental.

Step 6: Create a simple referral system (ask + acknowledge)

Referrals shouldn't be awkward. They should be a natural extension of value.

Make it a firm habit:

- ask after a genuine win or improvement
- keep the language confident and human
- be clear that you're actively looking to grow with more clients like them

Then make your "thank you" process non-negotiable:

- handwritten card
- a thoughtful gift aligned to the client
- quick and sincere follow- up

This is how you turn one referral into many.

Step 7: Review quarterly and refine

Treat client experience like any other system.

Quarterly, ask:

- what's working?
- what's slipping?
- where are clients most engaged?
- where are we becoming transactional?

Small refinements compound over time. That's how you build a client experience culture without burning your team out.

Action Checklist – Immediate, Practical Takeaways

You don't need a full transformation plan to improve client experience. Small, deliberate actions - applied consistently - create momentum quickly.

1. **Identify clients to re-ignite.** Who haven't you proactively contacted in the last 6–12 months?
2. **Audit your new client meeting agenda.** Does it clearly set expectations on communication, scope, pricing, and "how we work"?
3. **Formalise the first 90 days.** Create a checklist that ensures visible progress and at least one meaningful win.
4. **Look for early technical opportunities.** Use the onboarding period to review structure, tax, asset protection, and risk while trust is high.
5. **Schedule proactive, non-billable touchpoints.** Calls that aren't tied to an invoice matter more than you think.
6. **Track milestones.** Birthdays, business anniversaries, big wins - capture and acknowledge them.
7. **Ask for referrals at the right moment.** After impact, confidently ask for introductions to others in similar situations.
8. **Always close the loop.** Thank every referral personally - handwritten note + thoughtful gesture.
9. **Share what's working internally.** Make client wins and referral stories part of team rhythm.

10. **Help the team connect the dots.** When everyone knows what "wow" looks like, they can spot it across their client base.

Pick two or three and start this quarter. Consistency beats intensity.

Closing Guide

Client experience isn't about doing more.

It's about being deliberate.

When you intentionally design how clients are welcomed, supported, and engaged over time, trust compounds. Loyalty deepens. Referrals follow naturally.

The firms that stand out aren't louder or flashier. They're clearer. More consistent. More human.

Whether you're running an accounting firm or another business, the principle is the same: relationships scale when systems protect what matters most.

Treat every interaction as an opportunity to reinforce trust - and growth stops being something you chase.

It becomes something you earn.

SECTION 5

PREPARE YOUR FIRM FOR THE FUTURE

Technology, advisory and the forces reshaping the accounting profession.

"It is not the strongest of the species that survives, nor the most intelligent, but the one most responsive to change."
— Charles Darwin

Section introduction by Toni Eisenhut

There is a version of success that traps you.

It looks like a full client book, a busy team, and revenue that keeps climbing. From the outside, the firm is thriving. From the inside, you are the reason it works and the reason it can't grow without you. Every decision of consequence finds its way back to you. Every pressure spike pulls you back into delivery. Every attempt to step back quietly unravels the moment things get hard.

This section is about breaking that pattern for good.

The firms that escape it share something in common. They have stopped treating their problems as personal failures of effort, resilience, or time management and started treating them as design problems. And design problems have design solutions.

It starts with ownership. Not ownership as a mindset or a motivational concept, but ownership as an operating condition, something that is built, reinforced, and protected by structure. Most firms believe they have delegated accountability because roles are defined and responsibilities are documented. In practice, authority collapses the moment pressure increases. Partners step back in. Decisions travel upward. Teams learn, quickly, that ownership is conditional. Until that pattern is interrupted at a structural level, until decision rights are explicit, authority travels with responsibility, and the operating experience holds under pressure rather than just when conditions are calm, no process improvement will stick. Optimisation without ownership is motion without progress.

Culture is the second pillar. Not the kind that lives in framed values on a wall or gets revisited at the annual planning day, but the kind that shows up on the busiest days, in the hardest conversations, and in the decisions made when no one senior is watching. High-performing cultures are not accidental. They are engineered through shared goals, visible performance, collective rewards, and leaders who are prepared to hold the line with their teams and with their clients, even when it is uncomfortable. When culture is designed deliberately and protected consistently, something shifts. People stop needing to be managed closely. They self-correct. Standards become self-reinforcing. The business gets easier to run, not harder.

And then there is the question of sustainability. The accounting profession has normalised exhaustion in a way that few others have. Long hours, constant availability, and the quiet pride of being indispensable have become so embedded that burnout is often mistaken for commitment. It is not. Burnout is feedback. It is a signal that the business model is asking too much of one person, too often, for too long. It does not resolve through willpower. It resolves through redesign, clearer boundaries, fewer energy drains, systems that support consistent delivery without constant oversight, and the deliberate protection of the time and recovery that good leadership actually requires.

Ownership. Culture. Sustainability. Each one matters on its own. Together, they form the foundation of a firm that performs reliably, not because the owner is always present, but because the business has been built to function without depending on that presence.

That is the firm this section will help you build.

CHAPTER 15

Ownership Before Optimisation – Why Accountability Must Precede Efficiency

Toni Eisenhut

Introduction

When Optimisation Fails Because Ownership Is Unclear

Once firms recognise execution strain, their instinct is to optimise. Processes are reviewed. Systems are upgraded. Roles are clarified. Meetings are restructured. Dashboards are introduced. Visibility improves. On paper, it looks like progress.

In practice, the same issues return. Decisions still escalate. Partners remain involved in delivery. Exceptions multiply under pressure. Improvements hold briefly, then decay.

This is not because firms are poorly run. It is because optimisation has been attempted before ownership is secure.

Most execution problems are not caused by inefficiency. They are caused by unclear accountability. Optimisation assumes ownership already exists. That decisions are held at the right level. That authority travels with responsibility. That outcomes sit with defined roles rather than defaulting upward. In many firms, that assumption does not hold.

Accountability exists on paper, but not in behaviour. Responsibility is assigned, but authority remains conditional. Partners remain the final decision maker, risk absorber, and safety net. Teams sense this immediately. They escalate early. They hesitate under pressure. They seek reassurance rather than exercising judgement.

Not because they lack capability, but because ownership is fragile.

Over time, firms mistake motion for progress. New systems create activity, not reliability. Process changes shift work around, but do not change who ultimately carries risk. Until accountability holds when it matters, efficiency initiatives will continue to fail quietly.

My preceding chapter names the Growth Squeeze. This chapter isolates one constraint underneath it: ownership that collapses under pressure.

The pattern is difficult to interrupt because each instance feels justified in isolation. A partner steps in to protect a client relationship. Another approves an exception to maintain standards. A third resolves a dispute to keep a project moving. None of these interventions appears problematic. Collectively, they signal that ownership is conditional and authority is borrowed, not held. Teams adapt accordingly. They escalate earlier, decide less, and wait for confirmation that never builds their capability.

This dynamic has intensified across the profession in recent years. Technology promises efficiency but often creates more decision points requiring judgement. Client expectations for responsiveness increase pressure on delivery teams. Talent scarcity means firms cannot afford to lose capable managers who feel disempowered or underutilised. At the same time, partners are thinking seriously about succession, sustainability, and whether the business they have built still serves them. A firm that cannot execute without constant partner intervention has limited strategic options and even more limited market value.

You cannot optimise execution until ownership is real.

The Strategic Freedom Framework™

Ownership as the Precondition for Execution

Ownership is often treated as a leadership trait. Something individuals either have or lack. In reality, ownership is an operating condition. It is created, reinforced, and protected by design. When design is weak, even capable people struggle to hold accountability under pressure.

What is often misunderstood is that ownership does not collapse because people lack intent or courage. It collapses because the operating experience does not protect authority when it is tested.

Most firms believe they have delegated accountability because roles are defined and responsibilities are documented. In practice, authority is rarely reinforced in moments that matter. When pressure increases, client stakes rise, or outcomes feel uncertain, partners step back in. The system teaches the team that ownership exists only when conditions are calm.

This is why optimisation so often targets the wrong problem. Firms attempt to improve workflows, tighten controls, or introduce better reporting, believing execution is failing due to inefficiency. In reality, execution is failing because no one feels safe to hold decisions without approval. The system rewards escalation rather than judgement.

Ownership, then, is not a behavioural aspiration. It is an operating condition. It exists when decision rights are clear, reinforcement is consistent, and consequences sit where authority resides. Without these elements, accountability becomes symbolic. Responsibility flows downward. Risk flows upward.

This distinction matters because optimisation assumes stable ownership. Processes only work when someone can confidently apply them. Systems only reduce friction when decisions do not need to be checked. Efficiency gains rely on authority holding under pressure, not just being granted on paper.

This is why the Strategic Freedom Framework™ must be applied through an ownership lens before optimisation is attempted. Until authority is structurally embedded and behaviourally reinforced, every efficiency initiative will be fragile. Improvements may appear to work, but they will not hold when volume, complexity, or pressure increases.

This chapter applies the Strategic Freedom Framework™ through a different lens. Not to unlock capacity, but to anchor ownership so execution can finally transfer. It is not a growth model. It is a decision-ownership model.

The same three phases apply, but the objective shifts:

- Refocus: identify where ownership collapses
- Simplify and Optimise: align authority with responsibility
- Sustain and Scale: ensure ownership holds under pressure

Without this sequencing, optimisation efforts will not stick. Firms that attempt to improve efficiency before securing ownership find that processes are bypassed, systems are ignored, and partners remain the default problem solver regardless of how well the improvement was designed.

Phase 1: Refocus

Identifying Where Ownership Breaks

The first step is not improvement. It is clarity. Firms must identify where responsibility exists without authority and where decisions consistently travel upward.

This includes examining which decisions partners still make by default, where escalation occurs despite defined roles, where managers coordinate work but hesitate to decide, and where outcomes are revisited after the fact.

The most common mistake at this stage is assuming ownership

exists because roles exist. Under light pressure, delegation appears to work. Under real pressure, it collapses. Partners step back in temporarily. Decisions are revisited. Authority becomes situational. Over time, delegation becomes symbolic. Responsibility flows downward. Risk flows upward.

What firms discover during this phase is often confronting. Decisions that were delegated months or years ago have quietly returned to partners. Managers who appeared confident reveal they are seeking informal approval before acting. Authority that was explicitly transferred has been implicitly reclaimed through repeated partner intervention under pressure. The gap between stated accountability and actual behaviour is often wider than leadership teams expect.

People escalate when past reinforcement has taught them that exercising authority carries personal risk.

This is not a failure of intent. It is evidence that ownership was never structurally reinforced and pressure exposed the fragility. When a manager escalates a pricing decision that sits within their defined authority, it is rarely because they do not understand the policy. It is because past experience has taught them that exercising that authority without checking carries risk. Perhaps a previous decision was questioned publicly. Perhaps an exception was approved that contradicted their judgement. Perhaps they observed a partner step in to handle a similar situation and concluded that ownership was not genuinely theirs.

Refocus requires honesty about where ownership fails in practice, not where it is intended to sit. When this phase is skipped, optimisation targets the wrong problem. Processes are redesigned to solve efficiency issues when the real constraint is that no one feels genuinely authorised to execute them.

Phase 2: Simplify and Optimise

Aligning Authority With Responsibility

Once ownership gaps are visible, the work becomes structural. This phase is not about efficiency. It is about decision design. Authority must be explicit. Decision rights must be clear. Escalation paths must be deliberate, not habitual.

Key areas addressed include which decisions partners will no longer make, where authority sits for recurring decisions, how exceptions are handled under pressure, and how decision cadence reinforces accountability.

The difficulty in this phase is not technical. It is emotional. Partners must explicitly name which decisions they will no longer make and trust that outcomes will be acceptable even when different from how they would have decided. This requires confronting the belief that partner judgement is inherently superior, that standards will slip without oversight, or that clients will notice the difference.

In most cases, none of these fears are realised. What clients notice is faster decisions, clearer accountability, and greater consistency. What teams experience is permission to own outcomes rather than coordinate approvals. The shift is cultural as much as structural.

Optimisation fails when authority does not move with responsibility. Without clear decision ownership, processes are bypassed under pressure and partners re-enter execution to protect standards. A manager may have formal authority to approve scope variations within defined parameters, but if that authority has been questioned or overridden in the past, they will continue to escalate. The process exists. The ownership does not.

When simplification occurs without optimisation, gains fade as volume increases and old habits resurface. When optimisation occurs without ownership, complexity is entrenched. Systems are added. Reporting expands. Meetings multiply. None of it changes who ultimately holds risk.

When done properly, behaviour changes without constant vigilance. Boundaries hold because the operating experience supports them. A scope conversation is handled by the engagement manager without partner involvement because the authority is clear, the boundaries are explicit, and past experience has demonstrated that exercising judgement within those boundaries is supported rather than second-guessed.

Phase 3: Sustain and Scale

Ensuring Ownership Holds Under Pressure

Ownership that only exists when conditions are calm is not ownership. This phase ensures accountability holds when pressure increases.

The distinction here is not documentation. It is reinforcement. Ownership holds when decisions are supported once made, when authority is defended even when outcomes are imperfect, when escalation decreases during peak periods, and when partners are informed rather than involved.

The true test arrives during peak periods, unexpected client issues, or situations where the outcome carries reputational risk. This is when partners feel the strongest pull to step back in. The operating experience must be designed to hold under exactly these conditions, not just during calm periods.

What distinguishes firms where ownership is durable from those where it remains fragile is how leadership responds when decisions do not match what partners would have chosen. If the partner steps in to correct or override, authority collapses. The message to the team is clear: ownership was conditional, and when it mattered, the partner did not trust them. If the partner supports the decision and uses the outcome as a learning moment, capability deepens. The team learns that authority is genuine, that imperfect outcomes are part of development, and that exercising judgement builds competence rather than inviting criticism.

The reinforcement pattern matters more than the individual outcome. A single override can undo months of delegation. Consistent support, even when outcomes are suboptimal, builds the confidence required for ownership to become reliable.

When this phase is neglected, early improvements regress. Partners step back in just this once. Exceptions multiply. Authority erodes quietly. The firm returns to the pattern it was attempting to leave: responsibility sits with managers on paper, but risk and decision-making revert to partners under pressure.

When Sustain and Scale is done well, ownership becomes durable. Execution remains stable even as complexity increases. This is where execution finally transfers. The firm can handle volume, growth, and pressure without defaulting to partner intervention because accountability has been structurally embedded and consistently reinforced.

Case Study

When Ownership Was Fixed Before Anything Else

A mid-sized accounting firm was experiencing sustained execution pressure. The team was capable. Roles were defined. Systems were functional. Yet decisions escalated constantly. Managers coordinated work but hesitated to act. Partners approved exceptions, resolved disputes, and intervened to protect delivery standards. Nothing was failing. Everything required attention.

The firm had already invested in optimisation. Systems had been upgraded. Workflows reviewed. Reporting improved. Visibility was not the issue. Execution still relied on partners.

Rather than optimising further, the focus shifted to ownership. The leadership team identified where decisions routinely escalated and clarified which decisions partners would no longer make. Authority was explicitly aligned with responsibility. Patterns of partner intervention were deliberately removed.

The engagement was structured around intensive leadership discipline over 90 days. Partners committed to weekly accountability sessions where their own intervention patterns were examined openly and without defensiveness.

The first month was uncomfortable. Decisions were made that partners would have handled differently. A client scope discussion was managed by a senior manager without partner involvement, and the outcome was less commercially favourable than the partner believed it could have been.

What shifted the pattern was the decision to hold the line. The partner did not override the decision. Instead, the outcome was reviewed as a learning moment. The senior manager reflected on what they would do differently and why. Capability developed because consequence sat where authority resided. The manager's judgement improved in subsequent conversations because they owned the outcome rather than being rescued from it.

One partner described the shift:

> "I realised my intervention was preventing growth, not protecting standards. Once I stopped rescuing outcomes, the team stopped waiting for me. The quality of decision-making went up, not down."

The cultural shift was as significant as the operational one. Managers reported feeling trusted for the first time in years. The broader team understood that accountability was genuine, not performative. Clients experienced faster decisions and clearer communication because approval cycles had been removed. Conversations that previously required multiple touchpoints and partner sign-off were resolved in a single interaction.

No new tools were introduced. No additional optimisation initiatives were launched. When decisions were made within agreed authority, they were supported. Even when outcomes were imperfect.

The impact was immediate. Escalation reduced by more than 60 percent within the first quarter. Decision turnaround time shortened materially. Managers reported increased confidence and clarity about what they were authorised to decide.

Within six months, partners reclaimed approximately 450 hours previously absorbed by approvals and intervention. Those hours were reallocated to client delivery and new business development, contributing directly to revenue growth without increasing headcount. Margin improved not because efficiency increased, but because partner capacity was freed to focus on work that only partners could do.

Optimisation efforts that had previously stalled began to hold. Not because processes changed, but because ownership finally did.

Implementation Guide

Making Ownership Real Without Creating More Work

Ownership does not fail because firms lack intent. It fails because pressure exposes weak design. The Strategic Freedom Framework™ works here when treated as an operating reset, not a leadership initiative.

Phase One: Visibility Without Defensiveness

Leaders must see where ownership collapses under pressure. This includes identifying decisions that consistently return to partners, roles carrying responsibility without authority, and situations where outcomes are revisited after the fact.

The critical move is refusing to personalise the problem. When framed as a system review rather than a performance judgement, alignment becomes possible. Success looks like agreement on where risk currently sits.

What makes this phase difficult is that visibility creates discomfort before it creates clarity. Partners often discover they have been absorbing risk they believed had been delegated. Managers realise they have been seeking approval for decisions they thought they owned. The gap between perception and reality can be confronting.

The most common derailment at this stage is defensiveness. Partners explain why each intervention was necessary. Managers justify why escalation was appropriate. The conversation becomes about individual decisions rather than systemic patterns. This is where external perspective matters most. An outside view can hold the frame on system design rather than allowing the discussion to collapse into performance evaluation.

Firms that succeed in this phase create shared language about where ownership currently sits versus where it needs to sit. They identify specific decision types that consistently escalate and examine why. They notice patterns in when authority is exercised confidently versus when it is checked. They observe how pressure changes behaviour and where the operating experience fails to support accountability when it matters most.

The output is not a solution. It is shared clarity about the problem. Leadership teams must agree on what they are seeing before they can agree on what to change. Without this foundation, subsequent phases will be undermined by misalignment about what the actual issue is.

Phase Two: Focused Authority Reset

Firms must resist the urge to fix everything. Effective teams select a small number of recurring decisions and explicitly reset ownership. Other initiatives are paused to protect focus.

The discipline required here is saying no to good ideas in order to protect focus on the right constraint. Firms often want to reset authority across all decision types simultaneously. This fragments attention and weakens reinforcement. Better to select three to five recurring decision types where ownership will be explicitly reset and hold that focus for 90 days.

The partner's role shifts from decision maker to decision supporter. This is harder than it sounds. When a decision is made that the partner would have handled differently, the instinct to step in is strong. The operating experience must be designed to interrupt this instinct. This often requires structured accountability where partners review their own intervention patterns weekly and commit to holding boundaries even when outcomes feel suboptimal.

What firms underestimate is the time required for new ownership patterns to feel normal. The first 30 days are uncomfortable. Decisions feel slower or less polished. Partners question whether the change was wise. This is where many firms regress. They conclude the team is not ready, when in reality the system has not yet stabilised. Persistence through discomfort is what separates firms where ownership transfers from firms where it remains symbolic.

This often feels uncomfortable, particularly for partners accustomed to rescuing outcomes. The temptation is to interpret early imperfection as evidence that delegation was premature. In reality, imperfection is evidence that capability is developing. Judgement improves through consequence, not through observation.

Success feels like relief. Fewer interruptions. Faster decisions. Reduced escalation. Partners begin to notice space in their calendars that was previously consumed by approvals, clarifications, and exception handling.

Phase Three: Reinforcement Under Pressure

This phase determines whether ownership holds. Leaders must support decisions once made, resist stepping back in when outcomes differ from their preference, and allow consequences to sit where authority resides.

The measure of success in this phase is not whether decisions are perfect. It is whether ownership holds when pressure increases. During peak periods, unexpected client issues, or high-stakes situations, does authority remain where it was designed to sit, or does it flow back to partners?

Firms discover the answer by observing behaviour during the next busy season, the next difficult client conversation, or the next operational crisis. If escalation increases during these moments, ownership has not yet transferred structurally. If decisions continue to be made at the designed level and partners are informed rather than involved, the operating experience is holding.

What reinforces ownership most powerfully is how partners respond when outcomes are imperfect. If the partner steps in to correct or override, the message is clear: authority was conditional. If the partner supports the decision, examines the outcome without blame, and uses it as a capability-building moment, ownership deepens. The pattern of reinforcement matters more than any individual result.

Stability emerges when execution continues without intervention. Ownership becomes reliable, not heroic. The firm performs predictably under pressure because accountability is structural rather than dependent on individual heroism or partner availability.

Action Checklist

Leadership Attention Points

1. Track escalation patterns for two weeks and identify which decision types consistently travel to partners, noting whether escalation is driven by policy, habit, or lack of clarity about authority
2. Identify three to five recurring decisions that partners will explicitly stop making, and communicate this change clearly to the team with explanation of why ownership is being reset
3. Observe where managers seek informal approval before acting, even when formal authority exists, and examine what signals in the operating experience have created this behaviour
4. Review the last month of partner interventions and categorise them: which were necessary due to genuine risk, and which were driven by preference, anxiety, or habit
5. Clarify decision rights explicitly for the three to five decision types selected for ownership reset, including what requires escalation and what does not
6. Notice behaviour during the next pressure spike - busy season, difficult client situation, or operational crisis - and observe whether ownership holds or authority flows back to partners
7. Reinforce decisions publicly when ownership is exercised well, even when the outcome differs from how partners would have decided, to signal that authority is genuine
8. Examine where outcomes are revisited after decisions are made and ask whether this is creating learning or undermining ownership

Closing Guide

Ownership Comes Before Everything Else

Efficiency does not fail because firms lack intelligence, effort, or tools. It fails because ownership is fragile.

Ownership is the foundation. When ownership is real, execution transfers. When execution transfers, capacity returns. When capacity returns, partners regain the space to lead, grow, and choose how they spend their time.

This is not about doing more. It is about designing the business so it no longer depends on partners to hold it together. Once ownership is secure, the firm can optimise with confidence, build operating rhythm that reinforces accountability, and scale without increasing partner dependency. But without ownership as the foundation, every other improvement will remain fragile.

CHAPTER 16

Culture That Creates Champions – How to Build Committed, Accountable Teams

Melissa Voss

Introduction – Why Culture Is King

Culture is king.

Get the culture right and everything else falls into place.

I know that firsthand.

One of the comments I hear most often in my business at FuseWorks - from clients, partners, and people outside the business - is: "*Your team are amazing.*" Or "*You're so lucky to have such a great team.*" Sometimes it's said with genuine admiration. Sometimes with a hint of envy.

And I always push back on the word lucky.

What we have at FuseWorks isn't luck. It's the result of deliberate choices, made consistently, from day one.

Our team doesn't perform at a high level by accident. They show up, support one another, and deliver because culture has been built into the core of how we operate. It's why people stay. It's why they care. And it's why they genuinely enjoy the people they work with.

That alignment doesn't happen organically once a business reaches scale. It happens because expectations are clear, values are lived, and everyone understands what they're working towards.

For the second year in a row, our business has been recognised as a *Great Place to Work*, with scores well above benchmark in their Great Place to Work Certification. I'm proud of that - but more importantly, I'm protective of it. Because culture doesn't sustain itself. It requires ongoing investment, reinforcement, and leadership.

As we've grown - doubling our team size in two years - culture has been one of the biggest risks we've actively managed. Growth puts pressure on everything: communication, trust, accountability, and alignment. Without intention, culture fragments quickly into silos, "us and them" thinking, and quiet disengagement.

I've seen this play out inside many accounting firms. Many firms are technically strong and commercially successful, yet struggle with disengaged teams, turnover, or a lack of ownership below partner level. People show up, but they don't always *step up*.

The common thread is almost always culture.

Early in my career in an accounting practice, I was fortunate to be trained and mentored by a Chartered Accountant who had a deeply selfless approach to leadership. He introduced me to the principles of *The Great Game of Business*, developed by Jack Stack - a philosophy built on teaching people the rules of the game, letting them know the score, giving them a stake in the outcome, and rewarding them when they win. That philosophy stayed with me.

Profit matters. Growth matters.

But what matters more is helping your team understand why the work matters, how it helps clients, and how their individual contribution connects to the bigger picture. When people understand the game they're playing - and believe it's worth winning - they play differently.

That belief sits at the heart of how we run our business today - through clear values, shared goals, visible metrics, and collective rewards. It's why we talk about our people as a team, not staff. It's why transparency, trust, and accountability are non-negotiable.

This chapter is about building a culture that creates champions - not just high performers, but people who care, who own outcomes, and who want to win together.

The Framework – Culture as a Team Sport

If culture feels soft, it's because you're not managing it properly.

High-performing cultures are not accidental. They are engineered.

They are built through clarity, consistency, and courage - clarity about what matters, consistency in how it's reinforced, and courage to lead when it's uncomfortable.

The biggest myth about culture is that it's about perks, personalities, or positivity. It's not. Culture is simply the behaviours you tolerate, reward, and repeat.

In growing firms, culture either compounds - or it fractures.

I've seen both. And the difference always comes back to leadership.

Principle 1: Leadership Sets the Ceiling

Culture never outgrows its leaders.

As a two-director business, one of the most critical decisions we made was building a structured leadership team that lived and breathed our values. Not managers in title only - leaders in behaviour.

This means three things:

- Values are defined clearly
- Leaders model them consistently
- Leaders are prepared to call people out - including high performers

If your leaders don't live the values, no one else will.

This is where many firms get stuck. They want harmony.

They avoid tension. They tolerate behaviour that undermines the culture because the person is 'good at their job'.

That's a short-term win and a long-term loss.

Strong cultures don't avoid accountability. They normalise it.

Principle 2: No "Us and Them" Mentality

The fastest way to kill culture is to create separation.

Partners versus staff. Management versus team. Decision-makers versus doers.

When people feel like passengers rather than participants, they disengage. Quietly at first. Then visibly.

One of the most deliberate choices we've made is language. We don't talk about staff. We talk about team.

That's not semantics. It's intent.

Everyone is shooting for the same outcome. Everyone wins or loses together. There is no "head office" and "the rest".

If you want people to think like owners, you have to treat them like adults.

Principle 3: Teach the Game (The Great Game of Business)

The Great Game of Business, created by Jack Stack, is built on a simple but powerful idea: people perform better when they understand how the business actually works.

The core principles are:

- Teach people the rules of the game
- Let them know the score
- Give them a stake in the outcome
- Reward them when they win

Most accounting firms unintentionally violate these principles.

Teams are expected to care about results they don't understand. They're asked to hit targets without visibility of how the business is tracking or why those targets matter.

At FuseWorks, we've deliberately applied Jack Stack's principles through open-book management and shared scorecards. We give our team full visibility of business performance (excluding wages) - not because transparency is trendy, but because it creates trust and removes fiction.

When people understand how the business is performing, there's no room for false narratives about success or failure. Everyone is grounded in the same reality.

That shared understanding drives better decisions, stronger accountability, and genuine ownership.

It creates alignment. And accountability.

Principle 4: Shared Goals Beat Individual KPIs

Individual KPIs matter - but they don't build culture.

Shared goals do.

One of the most powerful cultural levers we've used is a single, clear business goal that everyone rallies behind.

For example, when we set an X% recurring revenue growth target, that number became *the* number. Not a sales goal. A business goal.

Support, development, retention, delivery - everyone played a part.

We tracked it monthly. We reported progress openly. Leaders reinforced it constantly.

And when we hit it, we celebrated together - as an entire business. Even team members who had only been with us for a few months shared in the reward.

That matters.

It tells people: *you belong here.*

Principle 5: Rhythm Builds Discipline

Culture doesn't live in speeches. It lives in cadence.

Annual planning days. Quarterly check-ins. Monthly reporting. Regular leadership conversations.

These rhythms create predictability, focus, and momentum.

If your goals only exist in a document no one looks at, they don't exist.

Championship teams know the score, know the plan, and know what winning looks like - at all times.

That's not pressure. That's clarity.

Principle 6: Reward the Right Wins

Rewards should reinforce behaviour - not entitlement.

We are clear: if we hit the goal, we celebrate. If we don't, we don't.

That's not harsh. It's fair.

When rewards are tied to collective outcomes, people support one another. Silos break down. Excuses disappear.

The reward itself matters less than the meaning behind it. It is about shared achievement.

That's how cultures turn teams into champions.

Case Study – FuseWorks: Building Culture at Scale

When we talk about culture, it's easy to talk in theory. It's much harder to protect it when the business is growing fast.

At FuseWorks, culture became a conscious leadership priority when our team doubled in size over a two-year period. Growth was exciting - but it also introduced real risk. New people, new roles, more complexity, and more pressure. Without intervention, this is the point where many businesses quietly slip into silos, politics, and disengagement.

We knew that if culture fractured, performance would follow.

So rather than leaving culture to chance, we doubled down on clarity.

The Challenge

As a software business serving accountants, we rely on trust - internally and externally. Every part of the business affects the client experience: sales, onboarding, support, development, delivery. If one area disconnects from the rest, clients feel it.

The risk wasn't poor intent. It was misalignment.

People could easily focus on their own function and lose sight of the bigger picture. And as directors, we were conscious that "us and them" thinking could creep in quickly if information, context, and accountability weren't shared.

The Shift

We anchored culture around three non-negotiables:

1. Shared visibility

We adopted open-book management, sharing the business's financial performance with the team (excluding wages). Revenue, growth targets, progress - all visible. This removed speculation and replaced it with understanding.

2. One clear business goal

Rather than fragmented targets, we set a single, collective goal: a clear, collective recurring revenue growth target. That number became the focus of the entire business - not just sales.

Support teams understood their role in retention. Product teams understood how delivery impacted growth. Everyone could see how their work connected to the goal.

3. Rhythm and reinforcement

Progress was tracked monthly and shared openly. Leaders reinforced the goal constantly. Wins were acknowledged. Challenges were discussed without blame.

The Outcome

When we hit the target, we celebrated together for a weekend on Hamilton Island with all team members and their families

The reward became part of the story of the business.

The reward wasn't reserved for a select few. The entire team shared in it - including people who had joined only months earlier. The message was clear: if you contribute to the win, you share in the reward.

Long after the reward itself, the impact continued.

The Hamilton Island experience became a shared reference point inside the business. It's still talked about - in team meetings, in onboarding conversations, and informally between team members. That ongoing chatter and excitement reinforced what the reward represented: shared effort, shared success, and shared ownership.

The result wasn't just hitting a number.

Engagement increased. Accountability strengthened. Teams collaborated more naturally. And culture - rather than being diluted by growth - became stronger.

What stood out most was this: people started thinking like business owners. Conversations shifted from "my role" to "our business". Problems were raised earlier. Ideas came from everywhere.

That's what a championship culture looks like in practice.

Implementation Guide – How to Build a Championship Culture Inside an Accounting Firm

Strong culture doesn't come from motivation speeches or team events.

It comes from structure.

The firms that build committed, accountable teams don't rely on personality or goodwill. They put clear systems around leadership, communication, accountability, and reward - and they run those systems consistently.

This implementation guide breaks that down into practical steps that work inside real accounting firms.

Step 1: Define the Culture You Are Actually Willing to Enforce

Every firm says culture matters. Far fewer are prepared to protect it.

Start by clearly defining your core values - but don't stop at words. Values only matter when they are translated into behaviours.

Ask yourselves:

- What behaviours do we expect when things are going well?
- What behaviours are unacceptable when things are under pressure?
- What are we prepared to call out - even if it's uncomfortable?

If you're not willing to enforce a value, it's not a value. It's a preference.

Write these behaviours down. Socialise them. Refer to them in decisions.

Culture clarity starts here.

Step 2: Build a Leadership Team That Lives the Values

Culture is not owned by HR. It is owned by leaders.

As firms grow, relying on partners alone to carry culture is not sustainable. You need a structured leadership group - managers and senior team members - who understand that leadership is about behaviour, not title.

This leadership team must:

- model the values visibly
- reinforce expectations daily
- address behaviour early, not months later

When leaders avoid hard conversations, culture erodes quietly.

When leaders step up, culture strengthens.

Step 3: Introduce Shared Business Goals

If you want people to think like owners, you must give them something meaningful to own.

That starts with a clear, collective business goal.

This is not about removing individual KPIs. It's about creating a unifying target that everyone can see themselves contributing to.

For accounting firms, this might relate to:

- revenue growth
- client retention
- service mix
- operational efficiency

Choose one primary goal.

Make it visible. Talk about it often. Explain how each team contributes.

Shared goals break silos faster than any workshop.

Step 4: Make the Scoreboard Visible

People engage when they know the score.

You don't need to run full open-book management if that doesn't suit your firm - but you do need transparency around performance.

At a minimum, teams should understand:

- how the firm is tracking against its main goal
- what's helping or hindering progress
- where focus is needed

Monthly updates are enough - as long as they're consistent.

When performance is hidden, stories fill the gap. Transparency removes speculation and replaces it with trust.

Step 5: Create Operating Rhythm

Culture lives in cadence.

High-performing firms run on predictable rhythms:

- annual planning days to set direction
- quarterly check-ins to adjust course
- monthly updates to maintain momentum

These rhythms are not about control. They are about alignment.

When people know where the business is going and how it's tracking, engagement increases.

Step 6: Design Meaningful Team Rewards

Rewards should reinforce behaviour - not entitlement.

Link rewards directly to collective outcomes.

Be clear upfront:

- what the goal is
- how it will be measured
- what happens if it's achieved
- what happens if it isn't

This clarity removes resentment and builds fairness.

When teams win together, they bond.

Step 7: Build Culture from Day One

Culture starts before a new team member does any work.

Strong onboarding sets expectations early.

Consider:

- a clear employee handbook explaining who you are and how you operate
- a personal welcome process
- time with the team before full autonomy
- early clarity around expectations and accountability

First impressions compound.

Step 8: Review, Reinforce, Repeat

Culture is not a set-and-forget exercise.

Review it regularly:

- what behaviours are we seeing?
- where are standards slipping?
- where are leaders stepping up?

Culture stays strong when it's talked about - not when it's assumed.

Action Checklist – Immediate, Practical Takeaways

Building a strong culture doesn't require a full restructure. It requires deliberate action, taken consistently.

Here are practical steps you can start implementing immediately:

1. **Define the behaviours you will enforce**
   Review your values and write down the behaviours that support them - and the behaviours you will no longer tolerate.

2. **Audit your leadership team**
   Are your leaders modelling the culture you want, or just delivering results? Address gaps early.
3. **Remove "us and them" language**
   Pay attention to how you talk about your people. Language shapes culture faster than policy.
4. **Set one clear, shared business goal**
   Choose a single outcome the whole firm can rally behind and explain how every role contributes to it.
5. **Make performance visible**
   Introduce a simple monthly update so the team knows how the business is tracking.
6. **Create rhythm**
   Lock in annual planning, quarterly check-ins, and monthly communication - and protect them.
7. **Reward collective wins**
   Design rewards that reinforce teamwork, not individual heroics.
8. **Strengthen onboarding**
   Treat Day One as a culture moment, not an admin task.
9. **Share stories internally**
   Talk openly about wins, challenges, and behaviours that reflect your culture.
10. **Have the hard conversations**
    Culture erodes when standards aren't enforced. Address issues early and directly.

Pick two or three and start this quarter. Culture changes when behaviour changes.

Closing – Culture Is the Ultimate Competitive Advantage

Culture is not a side project.

It's the system that determines how your people think, behave, and perform when you're not in the room.

Firms with strong cultures don't just get better results - they get better effort. Their teams show up, step up, and take ownership because they understand the game they're playing and believe it's worth winning.

Building a championship culture requires clarity, courage, and consistency. It means involving your team in the journey, holding the line on standards, and rewarding collective success.

When culture is designed deliberately, growth becomes sustainable, accountability becomes normal, and high performance becomes part of how the firm operates - not something you have to chase.

That's how cultures create champions.

CHAPTER 17

Building Award-Winning Team Culture – Strengthen Client Relationships and Lift Performance

Taryn Holman

Introduction

When I first started working with Seamless SMSF, one of the things that stood out immediately was the quality of our team and our clients.

They were fun, respectful, smart and appreciative. They were the kind of people you genuinely enjoy working with and many beautiful friendships have been born with colleagues and clients, that will last a lifetime.

But there was one client who didn't fit that picture at all.

On paper, he was a great client. Lots of SMSF's which meant high fees and his funds were evenly spread throughout the year, which was great for workflow.

But in reality, he was difficult. He called the team always making unrealistic demands, swore, belittled staff, and spoke to people in a way that left them feeling deflated and anxious. You could feel the shift in energy whenever his name was mentioned.

I remember thinking at the time: *I wonder how this will be handled.* It was one of our biggest clients, so I was extremely curious to see if it would be addressed or we would continue to put up with this behaviour because of the revenue that we would lose if he took his business elsewhere.

So, I raised it with the principal of the firm. I explained what the team was experiencing and asked how we wanted to handle it.

His response was swift and unwavering.

If the client couldn't demonstrate our values, then he wasn't the right client for us, and we would politely introduce him to some other providers that might be better aligned.

At Seamless SMSF the business values are something the team and I live daily. They aren't written on a piece of paper, that has gathered dust from being stuck in a drawer somewhere. They are displayed on the walls in every office and they are displayed by the leadership team and discussed regularly.

Two of our core values are **fun and respect**.

And while 'fun' might sound fluffy, it's a value that we take very seriously, as it means people feel safe, human, valued and are actually enjoying themselves. Respect, of course, is non-negotiable.

The message was clear. If working with this client was no longer enjoyable, and if he couldn't treat our team with basic respect, then we would politely help him find another auditor.

That moment crystallised something important for me.

Most accounting firms believe their biggest challenges are compliance pressure, staffing shortages, regulation, or fee sensitivity. But underneath all of that sits culture.

Culture determines how teams show up under pressure.

Culture determines how clients and team members are treated when things go wrong.

And culture ultimately determines whether a firm grows through loyalty and referrals or burns energy managing tension and issues.

In a world where software can be copied, pricing can be matched, and processes can be replicated, culture remains one of the few advantages that cannot be duplicated, so you better design it rather than letting it happen by default.

So how do you do design an award-winning culture?

Mike, the principal of Seamless SMSF, was crystal clear from the outset about what type of firm he wanted. He wanted to create a business that was described as OUTSTANDING by anyone that interacted with the firm.

He wanted people raving about us because they genuinely love every interaction they have with us. At the centre of it, the culture he wanted to create was a clear idea: **outstanding isn't an aspiration, it's the minimum standard.**

Outstanding had to be defined though and in order to arrive at our mission, and the values that will drive our business, these three questions were asked:

- How would your colleagues describe you?
- In an ideal world how would you want our business described?
- What behaviours must we display if we are to be this ideal business?

Pondering on these questions lead to what our mission is 'To be an OUTSTANDING business and valued supporter to our clients: a business we can be PROUD of because of how we care for our clients, commit to our values and conduct ourselves in business'.

And to accomplish that mission we need to demonstrate these values:

Respectful	all people are treated with respect regardless of their position
Precision	we seek excellence in everything that we do and always look for ways to improve
Brave	we enjoy facing our industry's challenges and embrace progress with open arms

Conviction	everyone involved with the business is fully committed and gives 100% effort
United	we support and care for each other, our clients, and collaborate always
Fun	we balance work and life with enjoyment, enthusiasm and laughter. We don't take ourselves too seriously.
Considered	we strive for good commercial outcomes for all parties – clients, suppliers and ourselves
Integrity	we uphold high standards of behaviour, have deep respect for honesty and always work within the rules.

So, everything we do is through this very clear lens. To accomplish this mission, we need to always demonstrate behaviour that aligns with our values.

If a team member rushes through a task and is careless, we can refer back to the cultural agreement and identify that they haven't been considered and that behaviour needs to improve.

If they come into the office and aren't pleasant, are snappy or being rude, after investigating to see if they are ok, we can remind them that the behaviour isn't very respectful or fun and we need to see an improvement.

If they are 3 minutes late to a meeting, we can remind them that precision is one of our values and that it is unacceptable. Next time they must arrive 5 minutes early so we can start the meeting on time.

And the same goes for our clients.

When standards aren't explicitly outlined, people don't rise, they default. But on the flip side, when there is a framework and it is clearly visible, outlined and discussed regularly, people are empowered to succeed.

Fun became a strategy too, not a perk. When people feel relaxed, connected, and safe, they think better, communicate better, and show far more patience with clients.

Energy is contagious and clients can feel that immediately. The emotional tone of the team becomes the emotional tone of the business. Like Richard Branson always says, "Take care of your team and they take care of your clients and business takes care of itself!'

That combination of clear standards, human connection and benchmarking everything against our word OUTSTANDING became the foundation of how we operated.

And most importantly, it became the filter for every decision.

So, let's get back to that difficult client. We didn't blame him or give him a lecture.

We didn't threaten to walk away and kick him out.

What we did was ask him a question when he was having another rant. "Are you having fun right now?" He sneered and shot back "No I am not! I am pissed off". I was then able to simply explain that the way he was speaking to the team didn't align with how we worked. That two of our most treasured values was fun and respect and that I wasn't having any fun either, so if he couldn't uphold those values together, we might not be the right partner for him and that we would be more than happy to introduce him to another provider if he wanted.

What happened next surprised even us.

He paused and reflected on his behaviour. He opened up about some personal struggles and acknowledged that his behaviour hadn't been ideal. He realised that his frustrations weren't warranted and he loved working with us. He didn't want to work with anyone else and he changed.

Not only did the relationship continue, but he became one of our favourite clients to deal with.

That experience reinforced a critical lesson: culture doesn't repel good clients it attracts them and educates them.

Your culture teaches people how to treat you. And when you hold it consistently, relationships don't weaken, they deepen.

That experience also highlighted something many firms struggle with.

Culture isn't what you say in values documents or onboarding packs. It's what you tolerate on your busiest days.

Defining standards clearly, revisiting them with the team, embedding them into recruitment, and being willing to have uncomfortable conversations when behaviour slips, with both your team and your clients, that's where culture actually lives.

It also requires leaders to go first. To model the behaviour they expect. To address issues early rather than letting resentment build. And to understand that protecting culture and holding people accountable is not unkind, it's responsible.

We have a very clear leadership development plan. It is:

- Develop your self awareness
- Test your values under pressure
- Find your "sweet spot"
- Build your support team
- Integrate all aspects of your life
- Know your leadership purpose

And if our team member wants to BE a leader they need to:

- Model trademark behaviours
- Reward trademark behaviours
- Challenge counter-productive behaviours (remember right way, right time, right place)
- Attend all Monthly Management meetings and team functions when requested to as a leader would do.

Not every client or team member will align and that's OK.

What matters is dealing with misalignment kindly, clearly, and quickly because weak links quietly erode trust and morale far faster than leaders realise.

When culture is protected, something interesting happens. People stop needing to be managed as closely. Teams self-correct and clients adjust and that is when the business becomes easier to run, not harder.

So let's give you the blueprint to create an award-winning culture.

Step 1 – Define the culture you want

Culture exists whether you design it or not, so the first step is to sit down and decide:

- What do we want this place to feel like?
- How do we want people to treat each other?
- What do we want clients to say about us?
- What behaviours will never be tolerated?

If you don't define the standards, the weakest link will.

Step 2 – Run a whole-team Cultural induction and implement that for all new team members

Gather your team. For the first time (or the first time in a long time) and walk them through:

- Who you are as a firm
- Why culture matters
- What OUTSTANDING (or your word of choice) looks like
- How it benefits them personally
- The behaviours expected
- The behaviours not accepted

People can only hit expectations they understand. Get them to sign a cultural agreement at the end, so it can be used as a reference point in the future if required.

Step 3 – Create a repeatable Culture induction for every new team member

Every new team member should receive the same cultural grounding as your existing team.

This needs to be a non-negotiable.

If your recruitment looks like "skills test + quick chat," your culture will erode.

At Seamless, we use the **Two-Hour Beer/Coffee Test:**

- 4 team members meet the candidate and if all four unanimously like them and think they could enjoy a beer or coffee for a couple of hours hanging out socially *then* they get a formal interview
- Because we hire on will before skill.
- You spend a minimum of 8 hours a day with people that you work with, so make sure you have a no DH policy.

Step 4 – Implement a Cultural Agreement (signed by every employee)

This is the game-changer.

A cultural agreement:

- Defines acceptable behaviour
- Defines unacceptable behaviour
- Makes expectations visible
- Gives you permission to discuss behaviour, not personalities
- Gives the team a shared cheat code to an award-winning culture

Every employee signs it and every leader must model it.

When culture is written down, culture becomes real.

Step 5 – Make culture visible every day

Don't hide it in the induction pack.

Culture should be:

- on walls
- in meetings
- in celebrations
- in feedback
- in hiring
- in decision-making
- in the stories you tell

You get what you talk about.

Step 6 – Build High Trust Habits

At a conference we heard one of the speakers talk about Amy Edmundon, a Harvard school professor who coined the term psychological safety, say that high-trust organisations experience a **400% increase in profit**.

High trust is built through:

- Transparency
- Vulnerability
- Clear communication
- Shared goals
- Celebrating wins
- Owning mistakes quickly
- Celebrating errors as they lead to solutions
- Giving praise generously
- Checking in on people as humans

Trust is the ultimate productivity hack.

Step 7 – Free up peoples futures (kindly and quickly)
If someone consistently violates your cultural values, even after coaching…

Let them go. Kindly, respectfully, without guilt and without delay.

Weak links damage culture and culture is what drives performance.

When you protect your culture, your culture protects your business.

So, let's give you a clear action checklist to actually make a positive change in your business. Do these 8 things this month:

1. **Define your cultural values and behaviours** (not just words).
2. **Hold a full-team workshop** to establish a mission and clear values as outlined above.
3. **Build a repeatable cultural onboarding process** for every new hire.
4. **Introduce a cultural agreement** and have the entire team sign it.
5. **Make culture visible in daily operations** (meetings, emails, feedback).
6. **Remove cultural mismatches** quickly and kindly. (Anyone who is not upholding your business values).
7. **Share your values digitally and verbally when onboarding new clients** so they are clear of expectations.
8. **Ask clients about their experience** to ensure your culture is felt externally.

When you intentionally design culture, strengthen relationships, and elevate the human experience, you no longer run "an accounting practice."

You build a business people are proud to work for, excited to refer to, and grateful to be part of.

CHAPTER 18

Burnout is a Business Problem – Not a Personal Failure

Amanda Gascoigne

Introduction

Why Burnout Is a Business Design Problem

Burnout has become so common in the accounting profession that many practice owners now see it as inevitable - an unfortunate but unavoidable consequence of responsibility, regulation, and growth.

Long hours are normalised. Constant availability is expected. Exhaustion is worn quietly, sometimes even proudly, as evidence of commitment and competence. Yet beneath this acceptance sits a more uncomfortable reality: burnout is not the price of success - it is a signal that something is wrong.

Burnout is not caused by a lack of resilience, motivation, or capability. Accounting practice owners are some of the most disciplined, conscientious, and hardworking professionals in business. They carry responsibility not just for clients, but for staff livelihoods, regulatory obligations, and their own financial futures.

Burnout is not a personal failure.

It is a business design problem.

The most successful practices I work with have learned this lesson the hard way - and redesigned before burnout forced their hand.

Practices rarely burn owners out overnight. Burnout develops gradually as small compromises accumulate. Boundaries soften. Scope expands. Clients dictate urgency. The owner fills gaps. Recovery is postponed. What begins as a temporary stretch becomes a permanent state of pressure.

From the outside, these practices often look successful. Revenue may be strong. Demand remains high. Yet internally, decision-making becomes reactive, margins tighten, energy drains, and the practice becomes increasingly dependent on the owner's endurance rather than its structure.

This has real commercial consequences.

Burnout erodes judgment. It narrows perspective. It leads to short-term decisions that prioritise relief over strategy. Over time, it undermines profitability, limits scalability, and reduces the long-term value of the practice. A business that relies on exhaustion to function is fragile - no matter how healthy the top-line numbers appear.

In an earlier chapter, we explored intentional practice design - aligning vision, clients, services, culture, and technology to create clarity and capacity. That alignment is essential. But without protection, it is fragile.

Even well-designed practices can lose alignment over time.

Pressure creeps back in. Old habits resurface. The owner steps forward again "just to get through this busy period". Without deliberate protection, the very structure that once created ease can slowly unravel.

This chapter focuses on what comes next.

It introduces a framework for protecting the practice you have designed - protecting your energy, your capacity, and your decision-making so that profit remains sustainable and the business continues to support, rather than consume, your life.

Sustainability is not a wellbeing initiative. It is a leadership discipline.

Practices that endure do not simply work harder or push through discomfort. They recognise that energy is a finite resource. They design boundaries that hold under pressure. They treat recovery, reflection, and restraint as essential inputs into performance - not indulgences to be earned later.

This chapter reframes sustainability as a commercial strategy.

By understanding where burnout truly comes from, and by addressing it at a structural level, practice owners can build businesses that perform consistently without relying on personal sacrifice. Profit improves not because more hours are worked, but because decisions are made from clarity rather than depletion.

The framework that follows does not promise ease without effort, nor does it suggest that practice ownership is without challenge. Instead, it offers a way to lead deliberately - protecting what you've built so it can continue to perform over the long term.

Burnout is not inevitable.

But sustainability must be intentional.

The Framework

Method – The R.E.S.T. Model for Sustainable Profit

Sustainable profitability does not come from pushing harder. It comes from protecting the conditions that allow good decisions, consistent delivery, and long-term performance.

In accounting practices, burnout is often treated as a personal issue - something to be managed through resilience, time management, or short-term relief. But when burnout is widespread and recurring, the problem is rarely the individual. It is the system they are operating within.

The R.E.S.T. Model is a practical framework for addressing burnout at its source - by redesigning how energy, capacity, and boundaries are protected inside the practice. It recognises that profit cannot be sustained if it relies on constant effort, emotional labour, or endurance from the owner.

Rest, in this context, does not mean disengagement. It means creating space for clarity, recovery, and leadership. It means ensuring the business works because of its structure - not in spite of it.

The R.E.S.T. Model focuses on four interconnected disciplines:

- Redefine Success
- Eliminate Energy Drains
- Systemise for Sanity
- Time for You

Together, they form a practical approach to building a practice that performs consistently without exhausting the people who run it.

R - Redefine Success

Burnout often begins with an unexamined definition of success.

Many practice owners measure success by external markers - revenue growth, client count, responsiveness, or reputation. While these indicators may signal progress, they rarely reflect sustainability. Over time, they can even become traps, encouraging growth without boundaries and effort without intention.

Redefining success is not about lowering standards. It is about choosing the right measures.

A sustainable definition of success considers questions such as:

- Does the practice support the life I want to live?
- Is profit improving without requiring more of me personally?
- Can the business operate effectively when I step back?
- Am I proud of how the practice runs, not just what it earns?

When success is defined narrowly, pressure increases. Owners continue to add clients, services, or responsibility without questioning whether those additions align with their desired future. Redefining success creates permission to prioritise sustainability alongside profit.

Importantly, this is not a one-off exercise. As practices evolve, success must be revisited. What worked at one stage of ownership may no longer be appropriate at another.

Redefining success provides the foundation for all other decisions. Without it, attempts to address burnout remain superficial.

E - Eliminate Energy Drains

Not all work drains energy equally.

In most practices, a small number of persistent issues consume a disproportionate amount of time, attention, and emotional bandwidth. These energy drains are often tolerated because they feel familiar or unavoidable.

Common examples include:

- Misaligned clients who demand urgency but resist boundaries
- Poorly defined services that invite scope creep
- Constant decision-making that should be delegated or systemised
- Owner involvement in tasks that no longer require their expertise

Left unaddressed, these drains create a constant state of low-level pressure. Over time, they erode enjoyment, clarity, and margin.

Eliminating energy drains does not require confrontation or dramatic change. It requires honest observation and deliberate choice. Identifying what consistently depletes energy - and why

- allows owners to intervene structurally rather than emotionally.

This may involve resetting expectations, redesigning services, clarifying roles, or making difficult but necessary client decisions. While these choices can feel uncomfortable in the short term, they are often the most effective way to restore capacity and protect profitability.

Burnout rarely comes from doing too much meaningful work. It comes from tolerating too much misaligned work.

S - Systemise for Sanity

In many practices, systems are introduced to improve efficiency. In sustainable practices, systems exist to protect people.

Systemising for sanity means creating structure that reduces reliance on memory, heroics, and constant availability. It shifts the practice away from reactive problem-solving and toward predictable delivery.

This does not require complex automation or a perfect tech stack. It requires clarity around:

- How work flows through the practice
- Who is responsible for decisions
- What "good" looks like at each stage of delivery

When systems are weak or inconsistently applied, owners step in to bridge gaps. Over time, this creates owner dependency and reinforces the belief that the business cannot function without constant oversight.

Systemising for sanity allows owners to step back without guilt. It enables the team to operate with confidence and consistency. Most importantly, it reduces the cognitive load that contributes to exhaustion.

Structure does not limit flexibility. It creates the stability that flexibility depends on.

T - Time for You

Time for recovery, reflection, and rest is often treated as something to be earned - a reward for surviving busy periods or meeting targets. In sustainable practices, it is treated as a non-negotiable input.

Rested leaders make better decisions. They communicate more clearly, think more strategically, and respond rather than react. Time away from the practice is not an absence of leadership - it is part of responsible leadership.

Time for you does not necessarily mean extended holidays or reduced ambition. It means building space into the business model so that the practice does not rely on constant availability to function.

This includes:

- Clear boundaries around working hours and accessibility
- Regular time for strategic thinking rather than operational firefighting
- Permission to step back without the practice stalling

When time for recovery is embedded into the design of the business, sustainability becomes achievable. Without it, burnout will eventually resurface - regardless of how well the practice is designed.

Sustainability Is the Strategy

The R.E.S.T. Model is not about doing less. It is about doing what matters - deliberately and sustainably.

Practices that apply these disciplines consistently do not just avoid burnout. They create environments where profit can grow without compromising wellbeing. Decisions improve. Energy stabilises. The business becomes resilient rather than fragile.

Burnout is not a weakness. It is feedback.

When practice owners listen to that feedback and respond structurally, they protect not only themselves, but the long-term performance and value of the practice they have worked so hard to build.

Case Study

From Burnout to Sustainable Performance

The practice featured in this case study was a well-established suburban accounting firm led by a sole principal with a team of five. From the outside, the business appeared successful. Revenue was stable, client demand was strong, and the firm had a solid reputation in its local market.

Internally, the picture was very different.

The principal was exhausted. Working long hours had become normalised, not just during peak periods, but year-round. Decisions piled up daily. Clients expected immediate responses. Staff relied heavily on the owner for reassurance and direction. Despite being busy, the practice felt fragile - one absence, one unexpected issue, and everything slowed down.

The principal initially believed the problem was capacity. More staff, better technology, or improved time management were all considered. But none addressed the underlying issue: the practice relied too heavily on the owner's constant availability to function.

Burnout was not the result of laziness or lack of skill. It was the product of a business model that demanded too much energy, too often, from one person.

Rather than attempting to "push through" another year, the principal took a step back and examined the practice through a sustainability lens. Using the R.E.S.T. framework, four core issues became clear.

First, success had never been clearly redefined. The practice had grown organically, but without revisiting what success actually meant at this stage of ownership. Revenue was acceptable, but the personal cost was high. The principal recognised that continuing on the same path would eventually lead to disengagement - or exit.

Second, several persistent energy drains were identified. A small group of long-standing clients created disproportionate stress through urgency, scope creep, and resistance to boundaries. These clients were tolerated out of loyalty rather than alignment. At the same time, the principal remained involved in too many day-to-day decisions that could have been handled elsewhere.

Third, while systems existed, they were inconsistently applied. Team members frequently escalated issues "just to be safe", reinforcing owner dependency. Processes were flexible, but at the cost of clarity and confidence.

Finally, time for recovery had slowly disappeared. Time off was taken reactively rather than intentionally, and strategic thinking was constantly postponed in favour of immediate demands.

Addressing these issues did not require radical change. Instead, the principal focused on deliberate, structural adjustments.

Success was redefined to prioritise sustainability alongside profit. Clear boundaries were reset with misaligned clients, and in some cases, relationships were transitioned respectfully. Decision-making authority was clarified, reducing unnecessary escalation. Systems were reinforced to support consistent delivery without constant oversight. Time for reflection and recovery was scheduled and protected.

Within twelve months, the practice felt fundamentally different. The principal worked fewer hours, yet decision-making improved. Team confidence increased. Client expectations stabilised. Profitability became more consistent, not because more work was done, but because the right work was done with greater clarity.

Most importantly, the practice no longer relied on exhaustion to operate.

Burnout had been addressed not through resilience, but through redesign - proving that sustainability is not a constraint on profit, but a prerequisite for it.

Implementation Guide

Embedding Sustainability into the Practice

Addressing burnout inside an accounting practice does not require dramatic change or a complete overhaul. In fact, the most effective shifts are often subtle, deliberate, and sustained over time.

Burnout develops when pressure is allowed to accumulate unchecked. Sustainability, by contrast, is built through intentional design choices that protect energy, capacity, and decision-making. The steps below provide a practical approach to embedding sustainability into the practice over the next twelve months - not as a one-off initiative, but as an ongoing leadership discipline.

Step 1: Recognise the Signals Early

The first step is awareness.

Burnout rarely announces itself clearly. Instead, it shows up as irritability, indecision, constant urgency, or a loss of enjoyment in work that once felt meaningful. Practice owners may feel permanently behind, even when working long hours. Strategic thinking is postponed. Recovery feels indulgent rather than necessary.

Rather than dismissing these signals as temporary or seasonal, treat them as information. Burnout is feedback from the business model. Ignoring it allows pressure to compound.

At this stage, the goal is not to fix anything. It is to observe honestly and acknowledge that sustainability requires attention.

Step 2: Identify the Structural Drivers of Pressure

Once the symptoms are recognised, the next step is to look beneath them.

Pressure is rarely caused by volume alone. It is driven by a small number of persistent structural issues that drain energy and attention. These may include misaligned clients, unclear service boundaries, excessive owner involvement, or decision-making bottlenecks.

Ask:

- Where does pressure consistently originate?
- What issues reappear despite effort?
- What work feels disproportionately heavy relative to its value?

This step requires objectivity. It is tempting to blame busy periods, staff shortages, or external change. While these factors contribute, sustainability is shaped by how the practice responds to them.

Identifying the true drivers of pressure allows intervention at the right level - the system, not the person.

Step 3: Reset Boundaries Deliberately

Boundaries are often discussed in terms of behaviour, but in sustainable practices, boundaries are structural.

Client expectations, response times, scope clarity, and decision authority should be defined by design - not negotiated repeatedly in moments of urgency.

When boundaries are unclear, owners absorb pressure by default.

Resetting boundaries does not require confrontation. It requires clarity.

This may involve:

- Clarifying what services include - and what they do not
- Re-establishing response expectations
- Reducing unnecessary availability
- Shifting decisions to where they belong

Boundaries protect energy and create consistency. When applied calmly and consistently, they stabilise the practice rather than disrupt it.

Step 4: Build Recovery Into the Business Model

One of the most common mistakes practice owners make is treating recovery as optional.

Time away from the business is often postponed until after deadlines, lodgements, or growth targets are met. In reality, without recovery, decision quality deteriorates and pressure increases.

Sustainable practices treat recovery as an input, not a reward.

This does not necessarily mean reducing ambition or output. It means designing the business so that the owner is not required to be constantly available for it to function. Strategic time, reflection, and rest should be protected just as deliberately as client commitments.

Embedding recovery into the business model reduces reliance on endurance and allows the owner to lead with clarity rather than depletion.

Step 5: Reinforce Sustainability Through Review

Sustainability is not achieved once and then forgotten. Like any strategic priority, it requires regular review.

Rather than waiting for pressure to return, sustainable practices review alignment and capacity proactively. This may involve quarterly reflection on workload, boundaries, decision-making, and energy.

Ask:

- What is working well?
- Where is pressure increasing?
- What needs to be adjusted before it becomes a problem?

These reviews should be calm and intentional, not reactive. They reinforce the idea that sustainability is part of how the business is run - not something addressed only when things feel overwhelming.

Step 6: Lead by Example

Finally, sustainability must be modelled.

Practice owners set the tone for what is acceptable, expected, and normal. When leaders consistently overwork, remain constantly available, or disregard their own boundaries, those behaviours become embedded in the culture.

Leading sustainably does not require perfection. It requires consistency.

By protecting their own energy and capacity, practice owners give their teams permission to do the same. This strengthens delivery, reduces reliance on heroics, and supports long-term performance.

Sustainability Is a Leadership Choice

Embedding sustainability into a practice is not about doing less or lowering standards. It is about designing a business that performs reliably without relying on personal sacrifice.

When burnout is addressed structurally, energy stabilises, decision-making improves, and profit becomes more predictable. Over time, the practice becomes more resilient, more enjoyable, and more valuable.

Sustainability is not an interruption to growth.

It is what allows growth to endure.

Action Checklist

Protecting Energy and Profit

The purpose of this checklist is not to add more to your workload. It is designed to help you identify where small, deliberate changes can protect energy, capacity, and decision-making - without disrupting the practice.

Use this as a practical starting point. Choose one or two actions to focus on over the next ninety days, rather than attempting to address everything at once.

1. **Redefine success for this stage of ownership**
   Write down what success looks like now - not when you first started the practice. Include sustainability, capacity, and quality of life alongside commercial outcomes.
2. **Identify one persistent energy drain**
   Consider a client, task, or responsibility that consistently creates pressure or frustration. Ask what structural change - not personal effort - would reduce its impact.
3. **Reset one boundary intentionally**
   Clarify an expectation around scope, response time, availability, or decision-making. Communicate it calmly and apply it consistently.
4. **Reduce one point of owner dependency**
   Identify a decision or process that currently relies on you but could be clarified, delegated, or systemised.
5. **Schedule recovery as a non-negotiable**
   Protect time for reflection, rest, or strategic thinking in your calendar. Treat it as an essential input into performance, not an optional extra.
6. **Burnout does not resolve through willpower.**
   It resolves through design. Small, consistent changes create the conditions for sustainable performance and long-term profit.

Closing Guide

Sustainability Is Not Optional

Burnout is not an inevitable part of practice ownership. It is a signal that the business is asking too much of the person leading it.

Sustainable, profitable practices are not built on endurance or sacrifice. They are built on clarity, boundaries, and deliberate design choices that protect energy and decision-making over time. When sustainability is treated as a leadership priority rather than a personal afterthought, the practice becomes more resilient, more enjoyable, and more valuable.

Protecting yourself is not a detour from success.

It is how success is sustained.

Practices that endure do so because their leaders choose to design for longevity - not just for growth.

Burnout does not resolve through willpower.

It resolves through design.

AFTERWORD

Darren Gleeson

After thirty years working in the accounting profession, one thing I know with certainty is that our industry cannot stand still. We must constantly improve, evolve and rethink how we run our firms.

Across Australia, there are thousands of accounting practices run by intelligent, capable professionals who work extremely hard for their clients. The partners care about their teams, the staff care about their clients, and the firms produce technically sound work. Yet many of those same partners are working far longer hours than they expected when they entered the profession, while earning far less than their businesses should be capable of producing. Tax seasons feel relentless, operational issues consume partner time, and the firm becomes heavier each year rather than easier to run.

The ATO, the Tax Practitioners Board, artificial intelligence or the economy does not cause this situation. Those factors certainly create pressure for accounting practices, but they are not the real problem.

The underlying issue is that most accounting firms were never deliberately designed to operate as profitable businesses.

Instead, they evolved slowly over time. Clients arrived one by one, staff were hired when the workload became overwhelming, and systems were developed informally as the firm grew. Fees were increased occasionally, often cautiously, and the partner remained at the centre of almost every decision — reviewing work, answering questions and solving problems.

Over time, the firm became bigger, but it did not necessarily become better.

Because the accounting profession rarely discusses business design, many accountants assume the problem must be with them. They believe they should work harder, become more efficient or push through another tax season.

In reality, the problem is the model.

The traditional compliance-driven accounting firm rewards busyness rather than efficiency and encourages partners to remain technicians rather than leaders. It trains clients to expect unlimited access while resisting meaningful price increases. Most importantly, it creates businesses that rely heavily on the partner's personal effort rather than on the system's strength.

Businesses built this way eventually reach a ceiling. As the firm grows, the partner becomes the bottleneck, and the workload becomes heavier each year.

Over the next decade, the accounting profession will experience one of the most significant shifts in its history. Artificial intelligence, automation and digital tax systems will dramatically reduce the amount of manual compliance work required to operate a practice. While some accountants view this change with concern, it will ultimately expose weak business models rather than destroy the profession itself.

Firms that rely almost entirely on compliance production will face increasing pressure on fees and margins as the work becomes faster and easier to complete. At the same time, firms that deliberately redesign themselves around advisory, insight and commercial guidance will become far more profitable.

The difference will not be intelligence or technical skill. It will be how the firm is structured and operated.

The eighteen chapters in this book were written with a clear objective: to provide practical ideas that accounting practices can implement to improve profitability materially. These ideas are not theoretical. They reflect the experience of professionals who have spent decades working within accounting practices and alongside them, providing advisory services, systems, training, and software to the profession.

Across hundreds of firms, the same pattern appears repeatedly. When the right clients are served, when services are structured intelligently, when pricing is disciplined and when systems allow work to flow efficiently through the firm, profitability improves quickly. In many cases, accounting practices have doubled their profits within twelve months simply by implementing the kinds of changes described throughout this book.

What happens next depends entirely on the reader.

Some accountants will read these chapters and begin applying the ideas immediately. Twelve months from now, their firms will look very different. The partners will have greater control over their time, their teams will operate with clearer systems, and the business will generate far stronger profits.

Other accountants will read the book, agree with many of the ideas and then continue running their firms exactly the way they always have.

The opportunity ahead for accountants has never been greater. Businesses need tax guidance, commercial insight and strategic advice more than ever before. However, the firms that capture that opportunity will not be the busiest. They will be the firms that are deliberately designed.

Once you understand that principle, one final truth becomes clear. Accounting firms rarely struggle because their owners lack intelligence, effort or technical skill. They struggle because the business itself was never deliberately designed to be profitable.

When the design changes, everything else changes with it.

About The Contributors

Kyelie Baxter is the Managing Director of IQ Accountants, a progressive accounting and advisory firm based on the Gold Coast, Australia. With more than 20 years' experience in public practice, Kyelie has built a reputation for a practical, grounded approach to accounting—one that prioritises clarity, commercial reality, and people over process for the sake of process.

Working closely with small and medium business owners, Kyelie helps clients move beyond compliance and into informed, confident decision-making. Her advisory work is centred on understanding what the numbers are really saying and using that insight to support sustainable growth, profitability, and long-term resilience. She is known for translating complex financial information into language that business owners can genuinely engage with and act on.

Kyelie is a strong advocate for the thoughtful use of technology, automation, and artificial intelligence in professional services. She believes digital transformation is not about replacing people, but about freeing them to do better work—creating space for deeper conversations, better outcomes, and more human relationships with clients. Her firm's technology-first approach has been widely recognised within the profession and serves as a practical example of how modern accounting practices can operate effectively and sustainably.

In addition to her work in practice, Kyelie is an active contributor to the accounting profession through speaking, mentoring, and governance roles. She currently serves on divisional council within CPA Australia and sits on several boards and committees across education and professional organisations. Guided by a service-first leadership mindset, Kyelie is committed to giving back to the profession, supporting future leaders, and helping shape a more relevant, respected, and human accounting industry.

Toni Eisenhut is a senior management consultant and operating advisor to professional-services firms, specialising in helping accounting and advisory practices move from partner-dependent execution to disciplined, scalable performance.

With a background as CEO of a large multidisciplinary professional services firm and experience across growth, integration, and operational redesign, Toni works with firm owners navigating the "growth squeeze" that emerges as complexity outpaces operating design. Her work focuses on execution ownership, leadership capacity, and embedding operating experiences that hold under pressure.

Toni is the founder of **Your Business Confidante**, where she partners closely with accounting firm owners to redesign how their businesses operate in practice, not just on paper. She is known for her calm, commercially grounded approach and her ability to translate strategic intent into lived operating reality.

Toni works exclusively with firm leaders who value clarity, discipline, and sustainable growth without heroic effort.

Richard Francis is the founder and CEO of Spotlight Reporting, a global business intelligence platform designed for accounting firms and CFOs. Founded in 2011, Spotlight now employs more than 40 staff across Australia, the UK, Canada, the US and New Zealand, and is used by over 2,000 accounting firms supporting 100,000+ businesses each month. The company is a multi-award-winning leader in management reporting and forecasting software.

Richard previously served as a General Manager at Xero (2012–2014), following the acquisition of his earlier software business in 2012.

Before founding Spotlight Reporting, Richard worked in practice as a Chartered Accountant. He began his career at a large firm before spending four years in the UK. After returning to New Zealand in 2001, Richard and his wife Julie established a boutique advisory practice specialising in Virtual CFO and strategic services.

spotlight
reporting

Amanda Gascoigne FCA, GAICD is a Chartered Accountant, business coach, speaker, and founder of Amanda Gascoigne Consulting and The Balanced Firm community. She works with small and solo accounting practice owners across Australia and New Zealand to help them build profitable, sustainable, and deeply aligned firms - without sacrificing their wellbeing, relationships, or sense of purpose.

With more than 30 years in the accounting profession and 18 years as the owner of her own chartered accounting practice, Amanda brings both lived experience and practical commercial insight to her work. She is known for helping practice owners clarify their vision, strengthen boundaries, refine client and service offerings, improve pricing confidence, streamline workflow, and create genuine capacity in their firms.

Amanda's work is grounded in a simple but powerful philosophy: better practice and better life go hand in hand. Through coaching, consulting, speaking, and community, she helps accountants design practices that are not only more profitable, but easier to run and more enjoyable to own.

Amanda also serves as a Member of the Tax Practitioners Board, having been appointed in March 2025, and as Co-Chair of the ATO's GST Stewardship Group. She is also the former Chair of CA ANZ's NSW Public Practice Panel and a member of the CA ANZ Trans-Tasman Public Practice Advisory Committee, reflecting her long-standing commitment to advocacy, leadership, and the future of small and solo practice.

AMANDA
GASCOIGNE

Darren Gleeson builds systems that help accounting firms double profits.

In 2003, he co-founded **Success Tax Professionals,** now Australia's third-largest tax franchise network, with 75+ franchisees lodging more than 50,000 returns annually. Scaling a national network exposed a hard truth: compliance is reliable — but it caps growth.

In 2016, Darren founded **TaxFitness** to remove that ceiling. Built for accountants, the software systemises structured tax planning, Top-20% benchmarking, and repeatable advisory workflows that convert everyday compliance meetings into high-value advisory revenue.

These aren't theory-driven models. They are commercial frameworks designed to lift partner profit, increase enterprise value, and create firms that scale beyond the owner.

Darren is the author of 11 books on tax strategy and advisory performance.

TaxFitness

www.taxfitness.com.au

His mission is simple: stop accountants relying on compliance and give them the software and systems to build more profitable, valuable firms.

Amy Holdsworth gained her training wheels in the accounting industry 15 years ago working for one of the first accounting practices in Australia to start the cloud software journey. Her role among other things at the time was to adopt Work-flowMax as it was known then, before Xero even acquired it to make it Xero Practice Manager, as a replacement for their server based PM system. “You almost have to try and break a piece of software and make it work the way you'd like it to, to work out what it will and won't do”.

Trying to mash old processes into software, doesn't work, so mindset changes to adopt were needed. Since that very first role, she has been part of the PSP channel for Xero implementing Xero Practice Manager, worked in firms as a Practice Manager, with the team at Ignition in their earlier days and worked with hundreds of firms implementing best of breed cloud accounting software.

She started Clarity Street after the realisation that none of the individual software providers in the ecosystem, had the time or the knowledge of how all of the cloud apps should be set up, to provide an efficient client lifecycle with clean dataflows between the apps. Clarity Street has been helping Accounting Practices get the most out their cloud app stack, reducing friction and increasing adoption for over 9 years now.

We're on a mission to help the industry understand how and what software connects to each other and what mindset, processes and procedures need to be changed, to achieve the success they are seeking both internally and externally with their team and clients.

Taryn Holman has spent more than 25 years in sales, partnerships and business development and she has seen firsthand what happens when businesses stop growing alone and start growing together.

Known for her ability to turn conversations into long-term commercial relationships, Taryn has helped scale businesses across professional services, finance and education by building strategic partnerships that don't just 'look good on paper' but drive real, measurable, and often explosive growth.

Her approach is anchored in a genuine dedication to serving the people in her network, building trust-driven relationships where care, integrity and long-term value sit at the centre of every partnership. She has learned that when you structure win-win collaborations, you are able to create momentum fast.

As the national sales manager at Seamless SMSF, Taryn has played a key role in building a nationally recognised outsourcing business supporting hundreds of accounting and financial planning firms.

Monique Parker is an award-winning marketer who helped to scale one of the accounting industry's first advisory networks to $40M within three years.

She has a successful track record in helping firms leverage AI and marketing strategies to maximise their impact, attract the clients they deserve, and grow their fee base.

Her latest business venture, AccountanXy, is a marketing platform for accounting firms with members across Australia and New Zealand. It is the first of its kind in the industry, empowering accountants to deploy effective marketing campaigns with ease and create big results with small budgets!

Known for her bold style, Monique is a passionate advocate for accountants owning their role as the "superheroes of the business world" and is a regular speaker and contributor to industry events and vendor partnerships.

Monique is based in Melbourne, but you'll find her riding her gravel bike across trails around the world and sampling good coffee and champagne along the way...

Her website includes free resources for accountants who want to fast-track their firm's growth journey.

Visit www.accountanXy.com

Melissa Voss is a Chartered Accountant, business leader, and co-founder of FuseWorks, a software company built by accountants, for accountants.

With a background in public practice, Melissa understands firsthand the pressures accountants face - tight deadlines, growing compliance demands, rising client expectations, and technology that too often promises efficiency but delivers frustration. Rather than accepting that tension as "just part of the job," Melissa has spent the past decade working to change it.

Over a decade ago, Melissa co-founded FuseWorks with a clear purpose: to help accounting firms free up time, improve consistency, and create better experiences for both clients and teams - without losing the human connection that makes the profession so trusted.

Today, FuseWorks supports more than 2,000 accounting firms globally with signature products FuseSign and FuseDocs, giving Melissa a front-row seat to the patterns that separate firms that scale well from those that struggle.

Melissa is deeply passionate about client experience, culture, and leadership. She believes that great firms are built intentionally - through clarity, transparency, and systems that protect relationships rather than replace them. Under her leadership, FuseWorks has been recognised as a Great Place to Work for consecutive years, reflecting her commitment to building engaged, accountable teams who understand the "why" behind their work.

Melissa works closely with accountants, partners, and teams across Australia and beyond and is a role model for people to rethink how they lead, how they serve clients, and how they build businesses that are both commercially successful and deeply human.

Connect with Melissa on LinkedIn at linkedin.com/in/melissajvoss and to find out more about FuseWorks head to www.fuse.work

www.ingramcontent.com/pod-product-compliance
Ingram Content Group UK Ltd.
Pitfield, Milton Keynes, MK11 3LW, UK
UKHW022026041026
15591UKWH00012B/522

9 781923 601383